Governing Diasporas in International Relations

This book analyzes how states extend their sovereignty beyond their territories through the language of diasporas.

An increasing number of states are interested in supporting, managing or controlling their populations abroad, something they define as their "diaspora." Yet what does it mean for governments to formulate claims of sovereignty over populations who reside outside the very borders that legitimate them? This book argues that "diaspora" should be understood as a performative discourse that enables transnational political practices that could otherwise not be justified in a normative structure of world politics, dominated by the imperatives of territorial sovereignty. The empirical analysis focuses on the former Yugoslavia and contemporary Croatia. The first part of the book examines the history of the relations between Croats abroad and their homeland, from the emergence of the question of emigration as a problem of government in the late nineteenth century until the years preceding the formation of the contemporary Croatian state. The second part explores how, in the 1990s, the merging of bureaucratic categories and state practices into the category of "diaspora" was instrumental in mobilizing Croats abroad during the 1991–1995 war; in reshuffling the balance between Serbs and Croats in the citizenry; and in the de facto annexation of parts of neighboring Bosnia-Herzegovina in the immediate aftermath of the war.

This book will be of much interest to students of critical security studies, international political sociology, diaspora studies, border studies, and International Relations in general.

Francesco Ragazzi is Lecturer in International Relations at Leiden University, The Netherlands, and associated scholar at the CERI/Sciences Po Paris and at the Centre d'Etude sur les Conflits, Liberté et Sécurité, France.

Routledge Studies in Liberty and Security
Series editors:
Didier Bigo, Elspeth Guild
and
R. B. J. Walker

This book series will establish connections between critical security studies and International Relations, surveillance studies, criminology, law and human rights, political sociology and political theory. To analyze the boundaries of the concepts of liberty and security, the practices which are enacted in their name (often the same practices) will be at the heart of the series. These investigations address contemporary questions informed by history, political theory and a sense of what constitutes the contemporary international order.

Exceptionalism and the Politics of Counter-Terrorism
Liberty, security and the War on Terror
Andrew W. Neal

Muslims in the West after 9/11
Religion, politics and law
Edited by Jocelyne Cesari

Mapping Transatlantic Security Relations
The EU, Canada and the War on Terror
Edited by Mark Salter

Conflict, Security and the Reshaping of Society
The civilisation of war
Edited by Alessandro Dal Lago and Salvatore Palidda

Security, Law and Borders
At the limits of liberties
Tugba Basaran

Justice and Security in the 21st Century
Risks, rights and the rule of law
Synnøve Ugelvik and Barbara Hudson

Transnational Power Elites
The new professionals of governance, law and security
Edited by Niilo Kauppi and Mikael Rask Madsen

Security and Defensive Democracy in Israel
A critical approach to political discourse
Sharon Weinblum

Managing State Fragility
Conflict, quantification, and power
Isabel Rocha de Siqueira

Governing Diasporas in International Relations
The Transnational Politics of Croatia and Former Yugoslavia
Francesco Ragazzi

Governing Diasporas in International Relations

The Transnational Politics of Croatia and Former Yugoslavia

Francesco Ragazzi

LONDON AND NEW YORK

First published 2017
by Routledge
2 Park Square, Milton Park, Abingdon, Oxon OX14 4RN

and by Routledge
711 Third Avenue, New York, NY 10017

Routledge is an imprint of the Taylor & Francis Group, an informa business

© 2017 Francesco Ragazzi

The right of Francesco Ragazzi to be identified as author of this work has been asserted by him in accordance with sections 77 and 78 of the Copyright, Designs and Patents Act 1988.

All rights reserved. No part of this book may be reprinted or reproduced or utilized in any form or by any electronic, mechanical, or other means, now known or hereafter invented, including photocopying and recording, or in any information storage or retrieval system, without permission in writing from the publishers.

Trademark notice: Product or corporate names may be trademarks or registered trademarks, and are used only for identification and explanation without intent to infringe.

British Library Cataloguing in Publication Data
A catalogue record for this book is available from the British Library

Library of Congress Cataloging in Publication Data
A catalog record for this book has been requested

ISBN: 978-1-138-73963-5 (hbk)
ISBN: 978-1-315-17713-7 (ebk)

Typeset in Times New Roman
by Wearset Ltd, Boldon, Tyne and Wear

Contents

	List of tables	vi
	Acknowledgments	vii
1	An international political sociology of diaspora politics	1
2	Seeing like an emigration state (1880–1991)	24
3	Croatian diaspora nationalism and the transnational political field (1945–1987)	59
4	Croatia, a diaspora forged in war (1987–1993)	82
5	Diaspora as a state category	111
6	Diasporic citizenship, territory, and the politics of belonging	134
7	Croatia and Bosnia-Herzegovina: diaspora, territory, annexation	157
8	Conclusion: theorizing the government of diasporas	177
	Index	200

Tables

1.1	Comparison of the populations of diasporas and states (2000)	5
2.1	Yugoslav migration flows (1968–1981)	41
2.2	National composition of emigrant workers and population (1971)	43

Acknowledgments

This is book is based on a PhD dissertation I wrote between Sciences Po Paris and Northwestern University. It would not exist without the help and support of people who were instrumental in my exhausting but ultimately rewarding journey from graduate student to the academic I am today. My journey starts in Café Basile, in front of Sciences Po when, at the end of my research Master's degree, I asked Didier Bigo if he would supervise my doctoral thesis. From the moment when he accepted until today, he has been an unfailing intellectual reference and supporter. Working with Didier has always meant working in a group. Philippe Bonditti, Stephan Davidshofer, Emmanuel-Pierre Guittet, Julien Jeandesboz, Christian Olsson, and Amandine Scherrer were all instrumental in my intellectual training. They have also extensively read and commented on parts of this work. In Paris, I am indebted to Riva Kastoryano and Stephane Dufoix, who took the time to discuss with me, guide me, and support me in my first years as a doctoral student. At Northwestern University, I was lucky to meet Michael Hanchard, who became my co-supervisor. I learned rigor, commitment, and academic generosity from him. I am equally grateful to Michael Loriaux, Will Reno, and Hendrik Spruyt for the intellectual exchanges and helping me navigate administrative complexities at Northwestern University. At the various conferences where I presented my early chapters, I learned a great deal from the kind attention and comments of Jef Huysmans, Vivienne Jabri, Peter Burgess, and Rob Walker. I owe a special intellectual debt toward Ole Wæver for inspiring the key theoretical argument upon which this book is organized.

Some key institutions made it possible for me to carry out this research: the first year of my thesis was supported by the Fondation Jean Monnet; my first visit to Chicago was initially supported by a Fulbright scholarship, and the following two years were made possible by a generous grant of the dual-PhD program between Sciences Po and Northwestern University. I would like to thank them warmly.

I visited Croatia in 2000, and it would not have been the same experience without Mirna Cieniewicz. Domagoj Cerovac, Vina Bravo, Damir Bencek, and Darko Ceglec were generous guides to the intricacies of the culture(s) of that part of the world. When I came back to Croatia in 2003, Dijana Jakšić, as well as Vanja, Olga, and Radovan Jakšić all made me feel at home and part of their family, and I fondly recall our discussions. In Chicago, I discovered the world of US academia with the help of Gabi Abend, Umud Dalgıç, and Magnus Briem. Along with Igor Štiks, as true emigrants, we spent long evenings longing for "the old country." His views on citizenship in the former Yugoslavia were key to my own understanding. Thanks to Igor, I later got to know the Edinburgh group of post-Yugoslavia citizenship, led by Jo Shaw. I thank them for letting me present my first dissertation drafts. In London, Fiona Adamson allowed me to continue writing my thesis while working as a research fellow at the School of Oriental and African Studies (SOAS). I learned a lot with her. My journey ends in Leiden, where I have found an academic home for the past seven years. I am grateful to Tanja Aalberts, Ingrid van Biezen, Jan Erk, Petr Kopecky, Maria Spirova, Niels van Willigen, and Frank de Zwart for their support and for making it possible to finish this book. Finally, Ognjenka Manojlovic's knowledge, patience, and attention were indispensable in editing the last drafts of the manuscript.

The first book one writes as an academic is a journey taken not only by oneself, but also by everyone around them; it is made of great hope, intellectual excitement, frustration, desperation, and a large portion of guilt for not being finished already. I would like to thank Magdalena Szymków for having been there through all these steps.

1 An international political sociology of diaspora politics

This statement by Croatian president Franjo Tuđman prefaced a handbook for returning Croatian migrants published by the Croatian Ministry for Return and Immigration in 1997.

> Dear Croats,
> When we started to create the independent state of Croatia in 1990, the main thought and moving force was the union between Homeland and Emigrant Croatia.... In the past seven years, Croatia has made progress which has taken other countries decades, from the hardest days of Yugo-communism and the Great-Serbian aggression, when the world even questioned our survival, to today, when Croatia is a key factor in the peace and stability of this region and is respected by the most important international actors. All of this would have been impossible if the historical moment had not been grasped from the very beginning by Croats both within the homeland and within the million-strong Croatian emigration spread around the world.
> (1997)[1]

Although formulated in straightforward nationalist rhetoric, the Croatian president's acknowledgment of a "Croatia abroad" echoed Yugoslavian discourses of the 1930s and 1970s, glorifying an extraterritorial "tenth banovina" (Antić 1990: 233) and a "seventh republic" (Zimmerman 1987: 83).[2] This short passage, both as a manifestation of the political project of Tuđman's *Hrvatska Demokratska Zajednica* (HDZ) and as an indication of the political atmosphere in post-Yugoslavia, challenges common assumptions of the discipline of international relations. How can a nation be conceived as encompassing people living both inside and outside their homeland, yet form a single political constituency? What does it mean when a head of state such as Franjo Tuđman, a leading figure of the horrifying war in former Yugoslavia, insists that the "main thought and moving force" of his newly independent nation was the union between the homeland and emigrant Croatia? How can theories of international relations, based on the principle of territorially bound sovereign states, account for this assertion and its underlying assumptions?

2 *International political sociology of diaspora*

Questioning the Westphalian definition of the state

In 2000, when I was working as an intern with the United Nations High Commissioner for Refugees (UNHCR) in former Yugoslavia, I spent several months in Sisak, a former industrial center located an hour's drive from the Croatian capital, Zagreb. The office had been established there because it was the closest important town to the former front line between the Croatian forces and the Serbian-ruled breakaway territory *Republika Srpska Krajna*. In addition to contemplating ruined houses that had been heavily shelled during the war and conversing with Croatian Serb[3] grandmothers returning to empty villages surrounded by minefields, I made tiring trips to local NGO offices where I spoke for hours with the local staff of the UNHCR. As was often the case during and after the war in former Yugoslavia, the highly paid United Nations (UN) international staff worked with local staff who had a better education and a better understanding of the causes of the war. Local staff members told me a side of the story of the war in former Yugoslavia that outsiders largely ignored.

Before coming to the region I had done extensive research on the subject, yet my everyday conversations in Croatia revealed one element that had been missing from all those sources: the Croatian diaspora. The position of Croats living abroad was one of the most important topics in the public debates conducted in Croatia during the 1990s. The diaspora had helped to elect Tuđman's HDZ in the first democratic elections; the diaspora had sent humanitarian aid during the war; the diaspora had sent weapons for the defense of the country; the diaspora was bringing new investments home; the diaspora was dominating the government. Yet in the majority of journalistic bestsellers published in English, as well as in academic books and articles describing the dynamics of the war, the diaspora was at most a footnote.

Croatian and Yugoslav diasporic institutions, individual political émigrés, *gastarbeiter* (guest workers) and other Croats living abroad played central roles in the drive to establish an independent Croatia. The contribution of external funds to the HDZ's nationalist campaign in 1990 was crucial to its success. Three émigré figures—Gojko Šušak, Ante Beljo, and Marin Sopta—were key to establishing an annexationist lobby within and outside the Croatian government throughout the 1990s. More than half of the Croatian arsenal during the initial period of the war is estimated to have been directly obtained from or financed by supporters in the diaspora. These three crucial elements of the war in former Yugoslavia between 1991 and 1995—the increase in Croatian nationalism, the rise of Croatian expansionism and the militarization of the country—cannot be understood without first understanding the diaspora and its relationship with the government. Scholars largely ignore these facts, despite what local newspapers reported and still discuss, what appeared on public television and what everyone in Croatia knows.

Why this academic blind spot? At the time when I started my research in 2004, only two journalists, one Croatian (Hudelist 1999, 2004) and one foreign (Hockenos 2003), had carried out in-depth investigations of the importance of the diaspora during the war.[4] It seems that this omission is the result of what Andreas Wimmer and Nina Glick Schiller have called methodological nationalism. They remark that, with the exception of some Marxian approaches, "the epistemic structures and programs of mainstream social sciences have been closely attached to, and shaped by, the experience of modern nation-state formation" (Wimmer and Schiller 2002: 303). International relations (IR), for example, established itself as a discipline distinct from political science precisely on the assumption that the type of politics that takes place inside sovereign states is different from that which takes place at the international level. The treaties of Westphalia (1648) have served as the founding myth of the discipline, marking the moment at which the modern nation-state established a distinction between a domestic and an international sphere of politics. The "Westphalian state" came therefore to be understood as the basic political unit of IR, a sovereign unit which has absolute power within its territorial marked borders, but is in an anarchic conflict with other states outside (Osiander 2001).

Diaspora policies and diaspora politics question these established distinctions and therefore lie outside our theoretical habits as social scientists. If we focus on the practices and not the principles, however, we realize "how transnational the modern world has always been, even in the high days when the nation-state bounded and bundled most social processes" (Wimmer and Schiller 2002: 302). Political scientist Aristide Zolberg called attention to this problem in 1981:

> International migration constitutes a deviance from the prevailing norm of social organization at the world level. That norm is reflected not only in the popular conception of a world consisting of reified countries considered as nearly natural entities, but also in the conceptual apparatus common to all the social sciences, predicated on a model of society as a territorially-based, self-reproducing cultural and social system, whose human population is assumed, tacitly or explicitly, to renew itself endogenously over an indefinite period.
>
> (1981: 6)

The neglect of international migration may also stem from academic Eurocentrism. With the exception of demographers, European and American social scientists who study migration have been concerned primarily with immigration rather than emigration. Sociologist Abdelmalek Sayad pointed out that migration must be studied transnationally.

> As an object that has been divided between political powers rather than disciplines, and between divergent social and political interests on continents that have been separated by a frontier that divides emigration and immigration, the migratory phenomenon cannot be fully understood unless science mends the broken threads and puts together the shattered fragments.
>
> (2004: 1)

4 *International political sociology of diaspora*

Our deeply embedded theoretical habit of seeing the world as a juxtaposition of populations living in bounded territories and approaching international processes through the prism of a territorial Western state—a bias elevated to a paradigm in realist and neorealist approaches to international relations—prevents us from fully understanding the complex processes involved in the wars in former Yugoslavia.

Assessing the importance of diasporas in international relations

Diasporas are key to understanding the dynamics of contemporary wars, for emigration is part of the political economy of development of countries that are subordinated within the international capitalist system, which together form what is called the global South.[5] Diasporas often play an important or even central role in conflicts and post-conflict processes (Shain 1999, 2002). Since the end of the Cold War, most international and intranational conflicts have taken place in countries historically poorer, and these countries have usually experienced major flows of emigration.

Diasporas have been active in many of these conflicts, starting with Northern Ireland (late 1960s–1998) and within former Yugoslavia: Slovenia-Croatia (1991–1995), Bosnia (1992–1995), Kosovo (1996–1999) and Macedonia (2001). Similar patterns occurred in the Caucasus and Central Asia: Ossetia-Ingushetia (1991–1992), Chechnya (1994–1996, 1997–), Tajikistan (1992–1997), and Afghanistan (1992–1996, 2002–); in the Middle East: Israel–Palestine (Al Aqsa intifada 2000–2006) and Kurdistan (in Turkey 1985–2000, in Iraq 2003); in Africa: Sierra Leone (1991–2002) and Congo (1996–1997, 1998–2003); in Asia: Timor-Leste (1976–1999) and Sri Lanka (1983–2009). Diaspora populations played a major part in all these conflicts, in forms ranging from humanitarian aid, weapons, support from exiled governments and associations, and participation in guerrilla movements or liberation armies to lobbying and raising international awareness. In the case of Iraq, for example, exile groups were crucial in misinforming Washington about the situation and actions of Saddam Hussein's regime, recommending military intervention, shaping policy and providing candidates to exercise power after regime change who were chosen by the George W. Bush administration. Kurdish organizations were also influential, relaying communications between Washington and organizations in northern Iraq. Iraqis living elsewhere were included in the "out-of-country vote" program of the International Organization for Migration (IOM) and called upon to aid in reconstruction. Thus, Iraqis abroad have fundamentally affected the war politically and economically.

The relationship between the diaspora and the homeland is crucial in peacetime as well. Increasingly, countries of the global South are proactively including their diasporas in national development plans. The flow of remittances makes a substantial difference in national economies. In 2008, for Tajikistan remittances represented 49.6 percent of GDP, for Moldova 31.4 percent and for Lebanon 25.1 percent (IOM 2010: 118). According to IOM estimates, in the year 2009 alone India received US$49 million worth of remittances, China US$47 million and Mexico US$22 million (IOM 2010). Significantly, Tajikistan, Moldova, Lebanon, Mexico, China, and India have all developed active policies aimed at establishing strong links with their populations abroad.[6] States that occupy subordinate positions in the international capitalist system are deeply engaged with their diasporas, in most cases economically and in some cases politically.

For many countries, paraphrasing R. B. J. Walker, it can be said that the national population is "not where it is supposed to be" (Walker 2000). The territorial borders of the state do not contain what it regards as its population, a situation that can have economic, social, intellectual, and even military dimensions. According to the IOM, in 2002, one in 35 inhabitants of the planet was an international migrant. These 175 million migrants exceed the populations of Mexico or Germany and equal those of Pakistan, Brazil, or Russia (IOM 2003: 4–5). In addition to their sheer numbers, these groups' skills, wealth, and political organization make them crucial political actors. Yet the inclusion of a substantial number of people living abroad in the national population matters to the definition of the legitimate geography of the nation. This phenomenon affects some of the most important emerging economies, as can be seen from the following table.

Table 1.1 Comparison of the populations of diasporas and states for selected countries (2000)[1]

State	Official resident population[2]	Claimed diaspora[3]	Proportion of diaspora to resident population (%)
Armenia	3,002,000	5,500,000	183.2
Israel	7,208,520	8,000,000	110.9
Hungary	10,053,000	4,500,000	44.7
Mexico	106,535,000	20,000,000	18.7
Italy	59,206,382	8,000,000	13.5
Poland	38,125,479	4,500,000	11.8
China	1,321,000,000	35,000,000	2.6
Philippines	88,706,300	2,000,000	2.2
Haiti	9,598,000	750,000	7.8
India	1,169,016,000	9,000,000	0.7

Notes
1 It is difficult to count diasporas, since the very definition of who belongs to the nation and who does not is blurry and subjective. It is useful, however, to have a general quantitative view of the phenomenon based on competing claims by governments or diaspora associations. Gabriel Sheffer has attempted to quantify diasporas. His estimates show that countries such as Armenia and Israel have larger diasporas than their resident populations. For other countries, such as China, Poland, Mexico, and Haiti, the diaspora includes populations equivalent to those of a province or region.
2 Source: (United Nations 2007).
3 Estimation according to Sheffer (2003: 104–105). Sheffer's sources comprise data collected from 1984 until 1999.

The importance of diaspora populations in three fundamental aspects of the existence and survival of these states—war and security, economy and development, and the geography of the nation—has deeply reconfigured the classical Westphalian assumptions about the bundling of identities, borders, and order. Contrary to a general movement toward the fixation of populations in the model of the national, territorial state, a trend which probably lasted until a few decades after World War II and is epitomized by Zionism and the creation of Israel (Tölölyan 1991; Schnapper 2001), today we are witnessing the unbundling of government, populations, and territories (Albert *et al.* 2001). Dual citizenship is on the rise and is increasingly recognized as a right (Faist 2001). Voting by citizens residing outside the country is gaining legitimacy. More and more diasporas are granted representation in their homeland parliaments. New measures are taken to encourage diasporas to invest in their home countries. In Croatia, India, Ireland, Lebanon, the Philippines, and Sierra Leone, for example, governments have instituted diaspora commemoration days, built monuments to their emigrants, opened museums of the diaspora, and rewritten history books to include those who left. More and more, diasporas are symbolically, materially, and politically included in their homelands. In return, these populations are expected to engage in political lobbying and citizen diplomacy, particularly if the host country is an influential state. It is also increasingly taken for granted that nationals living abroad contribute to the economy of their homelands (Smith 2003a, 2003b). This new situation poses two related puzzles for scholars of international relations.

A first set of questions penetrates the heart of the fields of international relations and political science. The practices of diaspora require us to re-examine traditional assumptions regarding the territoriality of power in the principle of sovereignty. How are we to understand practices of sovereignty that disregard the territorial limits on which the state's legitimacy is based? What is then the object and locale of sovereignty? These questions force us to turn away from essentialized and taken-for-granted assumptions about the entanglement of territory, populations, and power in the conventional model of the nation-state. Furthermore, they raise the question of the modality of power that is deployed in reaching out to encompass diaspora populations. Are these practices part of foreign policy and diplomacy, which are legitimate extraterritorial state practices, or are they inscribed in a broader picture of the domestic government of populations who live abroad? If they are part of a state's internal politics, what are the characteristics of this form of government, and how does it intersect with prevailing ideas about population and depopulation, which are enmeshed with hegemonic beliefs concerning political economy? What is at stake in these processes for the rationalities and practices of government?

Second, what and where are nations and diasporas as political communities? What are the geographies of contemporary nations? What are the possible politics of belonging when the common criteria for membership are increasingly and deliberately not based on a common existence on a territory but are instead dictated by assumptions of common blood, culture, religion, or origin as the sole markers of belonging? This set of questions inevitably drives us to interrogate prevailing assumptions regarding citizenship and rights, and how these are negotiated and redistributed along the lines of deterritorialized belonging.

Diasporas in political discourse

If the central premise of this book could be summarized in a blunt statement, I would say that there is no such "thing" as diaspora. Diasporas are not clearly bounded, nor are they mobile and transnational communities; such a formulation implies the existence of a distinct group to which the adjective diasporic can be attributed. Rather, "to be a diaspora" and "to represent a diaspora" are claims made by particular social actors in specific social-historical contexts and are designed to have distinct political effects. Indeed, speech acts constitute diasporas. The fact that these claims may be appropriated by others and even backfire on those who articulate them does not mean that they are not informed by clear rationalities and directed toward specific ends. The power of diaspora resides in its ability to mobilize material and symbolic resources transnationally and stake a claim to the legitimacy enjoyed by states even as it exists outside their boundaries. As such, diaspora is an identity and political program that produces truth effects. But not everyone can claim to "be" or "represent" a diaspora with the same success; some voices are more authoritative than others. The study of diaspora politics is therefore a sociology of the social agents, institutions, organizations, and bureaucracies—in sum, the spokespersons—who produce, reproduce, and are in competition over the authorized definition of what the diaspora is, and what it ought to do politically.

The study of diasporas developed concurrently with the study of transnationalism and has brought together scholars from various disciplines for almost two decades. The emergence of the field was marked by seminal essays by political scientist William Safran (1991), anthropologist James Clifford (1994), cultural studies scholar Paul Gilroy (1994), and sociologist Robin Cohen (1996). *Diaspora: A Journal of Transnational Studies* was founded by Khchachig Tölölyan in 1991, and transnational ties were debated in the *International Migration Review*, *Ethnic and Racial Studies*, and the *Journal of Ethnic and Migration Studies*. Research initiatives included the program in "Transnational Communities" at Oxford University between 1997 and 2003. Major works such as Gabriel Sheffer's *Modern Diasporas in International Politics* (Sheffer 1986), Yossi Shain's *The Frontier of Loyalty: Political Exiles in the Age of the Nation-State* (1990), Avtar Brah's *Cartographies of Diaspora* (1996), and Robin Cohen's *Global Diasporas* (1997) helped to make diasporas a legitimate object of study.[7]

As the concept was broadened from Jewish history to the histories of other groups, Safran, Sheffer, and Cohen proposed definitions that applied to several cases. A typological definition of diaspora opened up the intellectual space for comparative analyses, as the publication of the *Global Diasporas* series indicated. In adopting this stance, however, the three authors moulded a concept with fixed analytical boundaries.[8] Their typological approach does not provide a theoretical basis for considering how group boundaries are constituted and contested. Instead, it presupposes a social reality that corresponds to the term and an objective, scientific language that is not affected by social or political processes.

Approaching the problem with greater attentiveness to the term's changing significance in contemporary politics, Stuart Hall (1990), James Clifford (1994) and Paul Gilroy (1994) treated diaspora as a signifier of hybridization, of symbolic struggles, and of self-preservation strategies for dispersed populations. They saw the concept of diaspora as a way to assert the impossibility of fixing identities and to counter a discourse of racism and state categorization. Yet along the way they, too, failed to capture the performative nature of the term and attributed to it a normatively positive connotation. With diaspora comes the idea of a dynamic interaction with others in the host society and a process of continuous change, which serves as an antidote to the narrow vision of identity as national and territorial. Yet discourses of diaspora can be exclusionary, as the case of Croatia demonstrates. What is lost to both the more positivist and the more cultural approaches is that academic definitions of the term are inextricably enmeshed in the debate among social actors about what a diaspora is and who belongs to it.

Taking up the issues raised by these discussions, I question the analytical validity of the term diaspora in the face of its political currency. My approach resonates with the way in which Brubaker posed the question of nationalism fifteen years ago: "We should not ask what is a nation but rather: how is nationhood as a political and cultural form institutionalized within and among states? How does nation work as a practical category, as classificatory scheme, as cognitive frame?" (1996: 15).[9] Accordingly, this book asks: What does the use of the word diaspora do? What is at stake, symbolically and practically?

Diaspora as a speech act

I contend that diaspora is proliferating as a signifier to designate populations in dispersion because it is an efficient political discourse. Diaspora is not only a label but also a symbolically charged signifier, a speech act that enforces the narrative of a homogeneous community legitimately linked to a distant land.[10]

Philosopher of language John Austin argues that sometimes the only possible way to act is to use words. A promise is made by saying "I promise." But these are not just words; after a promise is made, breaking it can have severe consequences. Similarly, in a court of law a defendant is generally considered innocent until the judge pronounces the verdict. If found guilty, the person is immediately reclassified as a criminal and can legitimately be fined or incarcerated. I argue in a similar vein that diaspora is a label that constitutes a population as a particular type of group that is entitled to do certain things, or in the name of which certain things can be done.

Not every speech act is successful; its success has much to do with who utters it. If the defendant herself, her family, or a support group declares the defendant innocent, that does not override the verdict of the jury and the judge. Austin's theory relied mainly on the linguistic level and on the intrinsic force of the proposition, which he called the "illocutionary force." Sociologist Pierre Bourdieu has contended that the success of a speech act lies elsewhere, namely in the speaker's social position of authority.

In a courtroom, for example, the defendant is found guilty because the judge is considered a legitimate spokesperson for the state or society. As Bourdieu puts it, "the spokesperson endowed with full power to speak and act in the name of the group" and acts as "the substitute for the group"; by personifying the group he lifts it "out of the state of a simple aggregate of separate individuals, enabling them to act and speak, through him, 'like a single person'" (Bourdieu and Thompson 1991: 106). In many aspects of social life, speech acts are uttered by people who hold an institutionalized position of authority: a judge, a professor, a prime minister. But in the case of diaspora politics, who is a legitimate, authoritative spokesperson?

At least four significant categories of speakers can be identified: those who represent institutions that claim to represent the diaspora; those in the hostland who identify an immigrant population as a diaspora; those in the homeland who use diaspora to designate populations living abroad; and, not to be forgotten, those in academia whose assertions about diaspora may be relied upon by others to buttress their claims. The views of each set of spokespersons are connected to their position.

First, the institutions that claim to represent a diaspora play a crucial role in constituting the group they represent. Various political and cultural associations, churches, and newspapers compete to define the group symbolically and practically and to be recognized by others as its legitimate representative. They all articulate a narrative of authenticity, homogeneity, and legitimate relationship to a distant land. For example, what used to be known and define itself as "the" Sudanese diaspora had unitary organizations in numerous cities and countries that claimed to include and represent Sudanese from all regions. The organizations achieved some degree of unity between northerners and southerners during the civil war by a shared opposition to the Bashir government. They rejected its imposition of cultural uniformity by military means and referred instead to a common, albeit distant, affiliation with Garang's program for a multicultural, religiously pluralistic, and socialist-style government that would favor economic development that served the poor. Then came the conflict in Darfur, which undid the bridges so carefully built by previous waves of migrants among Darfurians who had been displaced by famine and blamed the central government, southern Sudanese who resented the fact that many Darfurians served in the north's armies during the civil war, and political exiles from the north. The indictment of Bashir by the International Criminal Court was followed by opposing demonstrations in several cities in the US and Canada. Recently, as South Sudan has seceded and the conflict between north and south has heated up again, those organizations are in such disarray that there is no "Sudanese diaspora" in the singular (Abusharaf 2010). Successive waves of emigration, coupled with shifting conflicts in the homeland, can prevent diasporic organizations from maintaining whatever fragile unity they managed to achieve.

On the other hand, these different waves can reinforce homeland culture and dissident politics. The first wave of Ukrainians in upstate New York were dead or aging and Ukrainian organizations were controlled by the second generation, who tended to be secular and to reduce their ethnic identity to food and holidays rather than politics, though they had a residual anti-communism that was regarded as mainstream in the US. Then they were joined by a new wave of migrants who were fervently anti-socialist and much more nationalistic and religiously committed than the working-class Ukrainian Americans they met. These new migrants, who were young and energetic, revitalized the institutions they found, even constructing replicas of the wooden churches that had largely been destroyed in the USSR, and directed the organizations toward assisting agents of transformation in Ukraine during the break-up of the Soviet Union. Some of these migrants went back, and they took with them some third-generation Ukrainian Americans who had never dreamed of such a future before they met the new arrivals. Unity was therefore not a sociological fact, but constituted through the discourses and practices of representatives of the latest wave of migrants who managed to mobilize the others and establish themselves as the legitimate spokespersons of the group (Kuropas 1991).[11]

Second, in the host country, diaspora can be produced by administrative or governmental labeling of immigrants and their descendants. The term is often used in a more diffuse or negative way by dominant social groups to designate a population that is not integrated, or should not be integrated, into the local, regional, and national identity. In the United States, for example, some condemn Mexican immigrants for what they interpret as stubbornly retaining their native language and refusing to assimilate to the dominant culture, threatening the country's "Anglo" identity (Huntington 2005). Some US citizens (including a few who are of Mexican origin) seek to have non-citizens repatriated to Mexico and have persuaded both the federal and state governments to have undocumented immigrants detained and ejected, as well as to militarize the international border (Doty 2007). Employers in search of low-wage, transient, and disempowered workers, however, continue to resist those initiatives. As the bureaucratic system of the host country seeks to control who comes and who cannot and tries to count who is actually there, it generates the categories of "illegal" immigrants who have no rights and "resident aliens" who are potential citizens (Coleman 2005).

Even in France, which has an official policy of assimilating immigrants, African migrants and their descendants are regarded by some French politicians and parties as unassimilated or unassimilable because of their cultural and religious practices, which disqualify them from belonging to the secular body of French citizens (Noiriel 2007). Their physical isolation and un- or underemployment, which result from discrimination coupled with recent contractions and structural shifts in the labor market, reinforce that ascription (Le Goaziou and Mucchielli 2006). These migrants generally come from countries that are in no position to defend them, much less welcome them home (Gueye 2006). Interestingly, whereas in the US Mexican immigration seems an issue to be discussed with the homeland, Mexico, in France the dominant discourse frames it in the language of social or urban troubles that concern only the French. Language from Sarkozy about "cleansing" the *banlieues* that would cause an international incident if it were applied to Mexicans in the US or to anyone in former Yugoslavia is regarded as acceptable or deplored as unenlightened by the French but does not arouse protests from African states.

Third, in spite of the fact that no discursive practice can originate directly from the mythical homeland that is posited by some rhetoric of diaspora, discourses and practices can and do come from spokespersons of the governments that control the land to which the myth refers, as well as of states whose territories emigrants left more recently. For many years, emigrants were considered a shameful sign of the failure of the sending state. In communist countries, emigrants were (and still are) considered not merely as suspicious but as traitors to the political cause to be controlled, repressed, and even killed. The Litvinenko affair, in which a political opponent of the Russian regime was poisoned in London in 2008, echoes other instances, such as the Soviet-planned "Bulgarian umbrella" affair in which Bulgarian secret police killed several opponents in Europe (Goldfarb and Litvinenko 2008; Kostov 1988). In postcolonial countries which in the 1960s and 1970s adopted economic strategies based on self-reliance and independent development, emigration was considered an economic form of defection. India, for example, long considered its emigrants as "lost" populations that were deserting the nation as it undertook reconstruction after independence. This situation changed dramatically in the early 1990s. Pravasi Bharatiya Divas, annual celebrations commemorating the successes of non-resident Indians, are part of a revalorization of Indians abroad, now recast as part of the "global Indian nation" (Varadarajan 2010: 15). Similarly, in 1995 the president of the Republic of Ireland gave a speech entitled "Cherishing the Irish Diaspora," in which she argued that the "great narrative of dispossession and belonging, which so often had its origins in sorrow and leave-taking, has become—with a certain amount of historic irony—one of the treasures of our society" (Robinson 1995, quoted in Dufoix 2008: 87).

In practice, governments may facilitate return by offering the privileges of citizenship or by integrating the diaspora into the nation-state at the political level. The ultimate form of integration into political life of the homeland is the election of members of the diaspora to the parliament, as is now the case in Haiti, Armenia, Macedonia, and even Italy and France. Members of the diaspora not only can vote in presidential and legislative elections, but they have a dedicated voting unit and a reserved quota of seats in the lower chamber. Increasingly, national governments and international bodies seek to delimit what is or is not a diaspora, putting into gear all the administrative and bureaucratic force that can be deployed to define what is inside versus what is outside the state. The Mexican government, for example, developed a document for its emigrants called the "Matricula Consular," a consular identification document. Although the document was conferred by the Mexican authorities, it allowed undocumented workers in the US to open a US bank account, and in some states for a short time it allowed them to obtain a driver's license (Lomeli-Azoubel 2002; Pérez Juárez 2003). Likewise, India has introduced cards for Non Resident Indians (NRI, for citizens) and Persons of Indian Origin (PIO, for non-citizens) to lift several taxation and immigration restrictions for members of the official diaspora. A similar provision was passed in Turkey in 1995, introducing the status of privileged non-citizens to members of its diaspora through a document called the "pink card" (Kadirbeyoğlu 2010).

Finally, we must acknowledge that academics represent a fourth set of actors who take part in symbolic struggles over the definition of diaspora, delineating criteria and typologies which are then reintroduced into other social actors' language after being invested with the weight of academic authority (Schnapper 2001: 33). Scholars' criteria for defining diaspora may be used by groups and governments seeking recognition as a diaspora.[12] Since those who take an interest in diasporas are by and large connected to a diaspora, Barbara Kirshenblatt-Gimbett's question is apropos: "Can (or should) the discursive field of 'diaspora' ... remain exempt from the risk of practicing the discourse that is being analyzed?" (1994).

Diaspora and governmentality

Outlining the social actors that might have a stake in defining the boundaries of diaspora does not answer one of the key questions of diaspora politics. Why does the term diaspora now figure so centrally in political discourse? What effects does this speech act have?

I contend that the discourse of diaspora is used because it fits with changes in the objects and the modalities of contemporary forms of power, which are progressively less over territory and more over populations. In a world still ordered by principles of territorial sovereignty but permeated by migration flows, the discourse of diaspora resolves the tension between the increasingly transnational character of governmental objectives and practices and the principle of respect for territorial sovereignty. Some theorists of globalization, such as Arjun Appadurai (1996), have announced the withering away of the state. Zygmunt Bauman proclaimed that "the territorial constraint has been overcome, and state sovereignty means less and less sense" (1998: 56).

But states are neither resisting nor overwhelmed by the globalization of migration; rather, they are adapting to it. Immanuel Wallerstein's world-system theory has inspired scholars to emphasize inequalities of development between migration flows (Sassen 1988; Wallerstein 1989).[13] In international relations, where relations of economic power are often overlooked, these studies remind us of the material structuration of the world economy that provides the conditions of possibility for the politics of emigration. From this perspective, states are not the primordial containers of societies but institutions that have been characterized by attempts to reduce transnational flows of people and capital to limited territorial geographies. The heyday of the territorialization of citizens and laborers is over, but it does not mean that state power is declining.

Instead, I argue, states are increasingly adapting to the transnationalization of their populations, and state practices are currently being redeployed in order to follow them on their transnational routes. Far from actualizing a cosmopolitan ideal that accepts diversity, this deterritorialized redeployment of governmental power redefines the borders of populations to be governed less as territorial societies defined by a universal relationship of citizens to the state and increasingly as communities defined by ancestry, ethnicity, or culture. Therefore, contrary to common assumptions, diasporas do not escape or defy the logic of sovereign power but are instead defined, channeled, and constrained by it.

These questions lead me to reconceptualize the state in terms of localized, networked, and contradictory practices of power, which Michel Foucault called governmentality. Studies based on the concept of governmentality, like studies of transnationalism, have generated interdisciplinary dialogue involving sociology, political science, and international relations.[14] Despite its critical edge, this scholarship has focused largely on aspects of governmentality in Western, liberal regimes and neglected states in the process of transition and those outside of Europe, a shortcoming that others have pointed out (Hindess 2001). This book extends the discussion of governmentality by exploring the rationalities and modalities of government in an authoritarian state as it shifted from a communist to a nationalist form. How does a Foucauldian analysis apply to these non-Western, non-liberal contexts? It also explores governmentality in relation to issues that, for reasons linked to the international division of labor, arise in poor rather than rich countries, particularly emigration rather than immigration and the management of its own population abroad instead of "the other" on its territory.

Taking Foucault's methodology seriously requires a constant back and forth between theoretical considerations and detailed empirical, archival work, for the rationalizations and ends of power are found in what social actors do, including their speech acts. This marriage of the theoretical and the empirical is contrary to some of the uses of Foucault in Britain and the United States, where the disciplinary divisions between political theory, comparative politics, and international relations dramatically separate theoretical discussions from empirical work. The theoretical questions that follow from the framework adopted here, especially the efficacy of political discourse, the nature of contemporary forms of belonging, and the locale of sovereignty and governmental power, cannot be answered a priori. I address these questions through a detailed analysis of diaspora politics in Croatia during and after the war in former Yugoslavia (1991–1995).

Transnational social fields

Refusing to treat diaspora as an analytical concept and instead considering diaspora politics as articulated by spokespersons who compete to be accepted as legitimate and to have their viewpoint prevail raises another question about the object of analysis. How should we delimit and apprehend what we study?

Perhaps the most widely accepted concept is that of transnational communities, which sociologists of migration use to describe the "working-class response to the globalization of capitalist production." According to Alejandro Portes, migrants have created "communities that sit astride political borders and that, in a very real sense, are 'neither here nor there' but in both places simultaneously" (1998: 3).[15] Yet, as Martin Sökefeld and Susanne Schwalgin have noted, the term "community" always runs the risk of assuming the existence of a unified, homogeneous, and clearly bounded group, precisely the trap we are trying to avoid (2000: 3).

I conceptualize social actors as both structuring and being structured by a variety of political, economic, intellectual, or cultural transnational social fields that together constitute transnational social space.[16] In contrast to the term community, the concept of social fields presupposes conflict and competition rather than unity and identity. It offers a conceptual frame for the production of discourses and practices by social actors in transnational settings that acknowledges the structures of home societies, host societies, and migrants themselves. Bourdieu defines a field as "a network, or a configuration, of objective relations between positions" that are "the site of a logic and a necessity that are specific and irreducible to those that regulate other fields" (Bourdieu and Wacquant 1992: 97). Social fields are conceived as both "magnetic fields," attracting social actors around particular stakes, and "battlefields," providing the grounds for symbolic and material struggles within social spaces. In this dynamic conceptualization, the borders of the field itself are at stake, but can be located wherever the magnetic effects of the field end (Bourdieu 1977).

The structuration of a transnational social space by different interacting and overlapping social fields is both the result of and the conditions of possibility for diasporic identification and mobilization. This conceptualization allows us to treat specific fields, such as the bureaucracies of home and host states, diasporic institutions in different countries, and the transnational political, artistic, and economic fields that constitute the diaspora as neither reducible to another nor connected in any determinate manner.

Importantly, this distinction allows us to avoid attributing agency or determinative force to structural conditions. This fallacy troubles some analyses of diasporic politics; for example, Benedict Anderson attributes extremist positions to the mere fact of living in a diasporic setting (1998: 62). This understanding also allows us to avoid making unwarranted assumptions about the hegemonic nationalizing projects of states in which transmigrants are supposedly caught (Basch *et al.* 1995: 36). The territorial nation-state is sometimes, but not always, committed to a hegemonic governmental project. Conversely, diasporic practices should not be glorified as acts of resistance to state practices or instances of liberatory politics. Neither the nationalist nor the emancipatory character of diasporic social actors can be derived from their diasporic condition (Guarnizo and Smith 1998a: 5). In itself, transnational social space does not explain the behavior of social actors.

Croatian nationalism and diasporic politics

I address these questions through a detailed analysis of diaspora politics in Croatia during and after the war in former Yugoslavia (1991–1995). In carrying out this study, I spent a year conducting field research in Zagreb (2004–2005) and three years at Northwestern University in Chicago (2005–2008). I used secondary sources in the language of former Yugoslavia and Croatia,[17] English, French, and Italian, and numerous primary sources, including Croatian diaspora newspapers and magazines, Yugoslav and Croatian newspapers and magazines, and laws, ministerial bulletins, and other official documents. I interviewed Croatian government officials, United States government officials, and representatives of the Croatian diaspora. These sources allowed me to reconstruct the discourse of diaspora over time and analyze the dynamics of diaspora politics as it was practiced during and after the dissolution of former Yugoslavia.

The war in former Yugoslavia, which was the first nationalist war in Europe since World War II and the paradigmatic war of the ethnic conflicts that erupted around the globe during the 1990s, cannot be fully explained without considering diasporic politics. The history of Croatia and its diaspora clearly shows how diaspora is constructed as a political discourse that fits new modalities of governmentality that simultaneously include populations beyond the borders of the state and exclude populations deemed not to belong to the nation. Croatia is an interesting example of a wider phenomenon linked to the international redefinition of the politics of belonging.

The first part of the book traces how Yugoslav governmental practices constituted three successive separate categories of populations abroad. The "old emigration" designated all of those who had emigrated between the early 1870s up until World War II. These populations were of peripheral economic interest to the Yugoslav state in the interwar period. After World War II, they were dealt with mostly through the promotion of folklore. The government's goal in maintaining a Yugoslav identity abroad was to attract capital and remittances, as well as to weaken the appeal of political opposition to the regime. A second category of the population abroad was designated the "enemy emigration": comprising those who left after World War II, it included political exiles, most of whom were right wing, and individuals perceived as carrying out anti-Yugoslav activities. These emigrants were closely monitored, controlled, and occasionally executed by the Yugoslav secret police. The third category, "workers temporarily employed abroad," embraced those enrolled in guest worker programs from the 1960s onwards. These populations were managed as part of Yugoslavia's broader economic development plan. Their loyalty to the state was assured through social and economic provisions such as pensions, healthcare, and unemployment benefits and, most importantly, by the threat to withdraw a passport, a crucial document for most families who depended on the income of Yugoslav workers abroad. While the main modality of exclusion from the polity remained territorial, these policies created several institutional precedents for the management of extraterritorial populations. As the Yugoslav government was dealing

16 *International political sociology of diaspora*

with its population abroad through these differentiated policies and institutions, an active, though heterogeneous, political field was gradually organized among exiles.

As Yugoslavia's communist system started crumbling from within, multiparty elections were organized. Franjo Tuđman, a disillusioned former general, became the leader of a small faction of hardline communists turned nationalists. During the late 1980s, he toured the Croatian populations abroad and rallied supporters through a new language of post-territorial nationalism, defining the Croatian nation as constituted by "Croatia at home" and "Croatia abroad." This was the birth of the idea of the Croatian diaspora. With massive support from Croats abroad for this new pro-independence platform, the HDZ took office in 1990. Interethnic tensions between the Serbian and Croatian republics, which translated within Croatia into conflict between the Croatian nationalist government and a rebellious Serbian minority, culminated in the war that erupted in April 1991. Croatia declared its independence two months later.

In the second part of the book, I show that this form of nationalism, elaborated both at home within sections of the Croatian communist party and abroad by diasporic political organizations, merged with elements of the institutional memory of socialist management of populations abroad to shape a new, official Croatian diaspora policy. The state practices that followed were based on the legitimate rights of a state to define its criteria for citizenship and to protect its co-ethnics abroad and were justified as repaying the diaspora for its crucial role in supporting independence and providing aid during the war. Yet, paradoxically, the state practices that followed had little to do with the diaspora itself. While institutions were erected and symbolic policies enacted, the language of diaspora served to justify two main practices. The ethnicity of the Croatian citizenry was reshuffled by including ethnic Croats abroad while excluding non-Croats at home in the main citizenship law as well as other legal and administrative provisions. The primary effect of these policies was to redefine the boundaries of the nation in a non-territorial manner. At the same time, it restricted the access of non-Croats in the territory to citizenship. People who had lived in Croatia all their lives were denied the right to vote, entitlements to land and real estate ownership, and post-war welfare benefits.

The second broad set of practices that the official diaspora discourse justified is the post-territorial annexation of certain regions of Bosnia-Herzegovina (BiH). Herceg-Bosna (1991–1994) was a short-lived entity in the south of BiH at the border with Croatia. Nationalists have always considered these territories part of the Croatian homeland. During the 1991–1995 war in Bosnia, the Croatian Republic of Herceg-Bosna declared its independence. This move was part of a broader agreement between Tuđman and Serbia's Slobodan Milošević to divide BiH in two and annex it to their respective republics. The Dayton peace agreements of 1995 sealed the failure of the plan of division. However, most Croats from BiH had acquired Croatian citizenship through the law of 1991. Indeed, 90 percent of the Croatian "diaspora" was constituted by Croats living in neighboring BiH. Contrary to the Dayton agreements that recognized BiH as an independent state, Croatia developed a special relationship with the former Herceg-Bosna territories. It financed and controlled the military, healthcare system, and the schools and universities, as well as the cultural sector. The Croatian flag and Croatian currency were officially used, and the local political party was a branch of Croatia's HDZ. In sum, this was a de facto annexation without *de jure* recognition done under the cover of diaspora policies.

The concluding chapter presents the theoretical implications of the study of Yugoslavia and proposes tentative generalizations by comparing the Croatian case with other historical examples. While governmental practices toward co-ethnic populations abroad can be contradictory and confused, they can be made more intelligible through an understanding of the broader material, intellectual, and political contexts in which they emerge and in particular the governmental rationality that underpins them. By moving away from juridical-legal conceptions of sovereignty, we can better understand the transnationalization of governmental practices.

Notes

1 Unless otherwise indicated in the reference, all translations from the Croatian are by the author.
2 A banovina was an administrative unit in the first Yugoslavia (1929–1941). The Socialist Federal Republic of Yugoslavia (SFRY) comprised six republics (1945–1992). For the original text in Croatian, see Appendix.
3 Citizens of former Yugoslavia all had a double "affiliation." They were citizens of a Republic (Bosnia-Herzegovina, Croatia, Macedonia, Montenegro, Serbia, Slovenia), but in parallel they self-identified or were identified with an ethnic group (Albanian, Croatian, Hungarian, Macedonian, Montenegran, Muslim, etc.). Only a small portion of Yugoslav citizens declared their ethnicity to be "Yugoslav." This complex institutional setup is explained in Chapter 6. I adopt the general convention of mentioning the republic of citizenship first and ethnic group identification second. Hence a person I call a Croatian Serb holds Croatian citizenship and identifies or is identified with Serbian ethnicity.
4 Scholarship has not really caught up since. For exceptions, see Winland (2009); Radeljić (2012).
5 Global South is used here not in a geographical sense, but in a political and economic sense.
6 For Morocco, see van Dalen *et al.* (2005); for Mexico, see Fitzgerald (2006) and Smith (2003a, 1995); for China, see Biao (2003) and Zhang (2001); for India, see Therwath (2003), Hansen and Jaffrelot (1999) and Jaffrelot and Therwath (2007); for Moldova, see Pantiru *et al.* (2007); for Tajikistan, see Newland and Patrick (2004); for Lebanon, see Brand (2007).
7 On the emergence of the field of diaspora studies, see Tölölyan (1996), Vertovec (1997), and Butler (2001); for a more recent review of the literature, see Kafle (2012). Braziel and Mannur (2003) have edited a reader which contains the most influential texts. For a review of the literature on transnationalism, see Faist (2004, 2010).
8 Cohen lists nine defining features of diasporas: (1) Dispersal from an original homeland, often traumatically, to two or more foreign regions; (2) alternatively, the expansion from a homeland in search of work, in pursuit of trade, or to further colonial ambitions; (3) a collective memory and myth about the homeland, including its location, history, and achievements; (4) an idealization of the putative ancestral home and

a collective commitment to its maintenance, restoration, safety, and prosperity, or even to its creation; (5) the development of a return movement that gains collective approbation; (6) a strong ethnic group consciousness sustained over a long time and based on a sense of distinctiveness, a common history, and the belief in a common fate; (7) a troubled relationship with host societies, suggesting a lack of acceptance at least or the possibility that another calamity might befall the group; (8) a sense of empathy and solidarity with co-ethnic members in other countries of settlement; and (9) the possibility of a distinctive creative, enriching life in host countries with a tolerance for pluralism (Cohen 1997: 29).
9 Brubaker also directly addressed the concept of diaspora; see Brubaker (2005).
10 Dufoix was the first to propose to approach diaspora as a performative utterance, but never fully developed the idea; here I build on his early work (Dufoix 2002). Scholars of security studies will be familiar with a similar move that was made earlier by Ole Wæver and Barry Buzan concerning the notion of security (Wæver *et al.* 1998; Wæver 1995).
11 For an account of this process from the largest association in the US, see the website of the Ukrainian Congress Committee of America, www.ucca.org/about-us/history (accessed 5 March 2012).
12 The *High Level Committee Report on the Indian Diaspora*, for example, uses Robin Cohen's criteria to define the Indian diaspora.
13 Criticizing migration theories inspired by neoclassical economics, they rejected models based on push-pull or cost-benefit calculations by underlining the structuration of a labor market at the international level and neo-imperial forms of capitalist penetration that provoke the forced mobility of developing countries' populations as well as the formation of transnational communities (Portes and Walton 1981; Portes 1999; Sassen 1988) or networks (Massey 1987).
14 For a review of this literature, see Rose *et al.* (2006). For uses of governmentality in international relations, see, among many others, Bigo (2002), Dillon and Neal (2008), Neumann and Sending (2007).
15 This concept is often associated with "transnationalism from below," a form of transnational activity that is distinguished from the transnational practices of corporations and governments (Guarnizo and Smith 1998b).
16 Nina Glick Schiller defines a transnational social field as "an unbounded terrain of interlocking ... networks." This concept "allows us a conceptual and methodological entry point into the investigation of broader social, economic and political processes through which migrating populations are embedded in more than one society and to which they react." I draw from this analysis the idea that spaces of social interaction are not bounded by state borders but are transnational and overlapping (Glick Schiller and Fouron 1999: 344). Others have developed similar concepts of "transnational social space" (Pries 2001; Faist 2004, 2010).
17 The official language of the Republic of Croatia is Croatian. It is very close to the official language of Bosnia-Herzegovina (Bosnian) and Serbia (Serbian). During the Yugoslav period it was considered only one language, Croato-Serbian (*Hrvatskosrpski*) or Serbo-Croatian (*Srpskohrvatski*).

References

Abusharaf, R. M. (2010) "Debating Darfur in the World," *Annals of the American Academy of Political and Social Science*, 632(1), pp. 67–85.

Albert, M., Jacobson, D., and Lapid, Y. (2001) *Identities, Borders, Orders: Rethinking International Relations Theory* (Borderlines; vol. 18), Minneapolis, MN; London: University of Minnesota Press.

Anderson, B. (1998) "Long Distance Nationalism" in *The Spectre of Comparisons: Nationalism, Southeast Asia and the World* (p. 374), London: Verso.
Antić, L. (1990) "Iseljenička politika stare Jugoslavenske Države" in Sehic, N., ed., *Migracije i Bosna i Hercegovina* (pp. 229–235), Sarajevo: Institut za istoriju u Sarajevo—Institut za proučavanje nacionalnih odnosa.
Appadurai, A. (1996) *Modernity at Large: Cultural Dimensions of Globalization* (Public Worlds; vol. 1), Minneapolis; London: University of Minnesota Press.
Basch, L. G., Glick Schiller, N., and Szanton Blanc, C. (1995) *Nations Unbound: Transnational Projects, Postcolonial Predicaments, and Deterritorialized Nation-States*, Basel; UK: Gordon and Breach.
Bauman, Z. (1998) *Globalization: The Human Consequences*, Cambridge: Polity.
Biao, X. (2003) "Emigration from China: A Sending Country Perspective," *International Migration*, 41(3), pp. 21–48.
Bigo, D. (2002) "Security and Immigration: Toward a Critique of the Governmentality of Unease," *Alternatives: Global, Local, Political*, 27(1), pp. 63–92.
Bourdieu, P. (1977) *Outline of a Theory Of Practice, Cambridge Studies in Social Anthropology 16*, Cambridge, UK; New York: Cambridge University Press.
Bourdieu, P. and Thompson, J. B. (1991) *Language and Symbolic Power*, Cambridge, MA: Harvard University Press.
Bourdieu, P. and Wacquant, L. J. D. (1992) *An Invitation to Reflexive Sociology*, Chicago: University of Chicago Press.
Brah, A. (1996) *Cartographies of Diaspora: Contesting Identities*, London; New York: Routledge [electronic resource].
Brand, L. A. (2007) *State, Citizenship, and Diaspora: the Cases of Jordan and Lebanon*, San Diego, CA: University of California Center for Comparative Immigration Studies.
Braziel, J. E. and Mannur, A. (2003) *Theorizing Diaspora: A Reader* (KeyWorks in Cultural Studies 6), Malden, MA: Blackwell.
Brubaker, R. (1996) *Nationalism Reframed: Nationhood and the National Question in the New Europe*, Cambridge, UK; New York: Cambridge University Press.
Brubaker, R. (2005) "The 'Diaspora' Diaspora," *Ethnic and Racial Studies*, 28(1), pp. 1–19.
Butler, K. D. (2001) "Defining Diaspora, Refining a Discourse," *Diaspora*, 10(2), pp. 189–219.
Clifford, J. (1994) "Diasporas," *Cultural Anthropology*, 9(3), pp. 302–338.
Cohen, R. (1996) "Diasporas and the Nation-State: From Victims to Challengers," *International Affairs*, 72(3), pp. 507–520.
Cohen, R. (1997) *Global Diasporas: An Introduction*, Seattle: University of Washington Press.
Coleman, M. (2005) "US Statecraft and the US–Mexico Border as Security/Economy Nexus," *Political Geography*, 24(2), pp. 185–209.
Dillon, M. and Neal, A. W. (2008) *Foucault on Politics, Security and War*, Basingstoke, UK; New York: Palgrave Macmillan.
Doty, R. L. (2007) "States of Exception on the Mexico–US Border: Security, 'Decisions,' and Civilian Border Patrols," *International Political Sociology*, 1(2), pp. 113–137.
Dufoix, S. (2002) *Notion, concept ou slogan: qu'y a-t-il sous le terme de "diaspora"?*, paper delivered at the conference "2000 ans de diaspora," Poitiers, France.
Dufoix, S. (2008) *Diasporas*, translated by William Rodamor, Berkeley, CA: University of California Press.
Faist, T. (2001) "Dual Citizenship as Overlapping Membership," *Willy Brandt Series of Working Papers in International Migration and Ethnic Relations*, 3(1).

Faist, T. (2004) "Towards a Political Sociology of Transnationalization: The State of the Art in Migration Research," *European Journal of Sociology*, 45(3), p. 36.

Faist, T. (2010) "Towards Transnational Studies: World Theories, Transnationalisation and Changing Institutions," *Journal of Ethnic and Migration Studies*, 36(10), pp. 1665–1687.

Fitzgerald, D. (2006) "Inside the Sending State: the Politics of Mexican Emigration Control," *International Migration Review*, 40(2).

Gilroy, P. (1994) "Diaspora," *Paragraph*, 17(1), pp. 207–212.

Glick Schiller, N. and Fouron, G. (1999) "Terrains of Blood and Nation: Haitian Transnational Social Fields," *Ethnic and Racial Studies*, 22(2), pp. 340–366.

Goldfarb, A. and Litvinenko, M. (2008) *Death of a Dissident: The Poisoning of Alexander Litvinenko and the Return of the KGB*, London: Pocket.

Guarnizo, L. and Smith, M. P. (1998a) "The Locations of Transnationalism" in Smith, M. P. and Guarnizo, L., eds., *Transnationalism from Below* (pp. 3–34) [electronic resource], New Brunswick, NJ: Transaction Publishers.

Guarnizo, L. and Smith, M. P., eds. (1998b) *Transnationalism from Below*, New Brunswick, NJ: Transaction Publishers.

Gueye, A. (2006) "De la diaspora noire: enseignements du contexte français," *Revue Européenne des Migrations Internationales*, 22(1), pp. 11–33.

Hall, S. (1990) "Cultural Identity and Diaspora" in Rutherford, J., ed., *Identity. Community, Culture, Difference* (pp. 222–237), London: Lawrence & Wishart.

Hansen, T. B. and Jaffrelot, C. (1999) *The BJP and the Compulsions of Politics in India* (Oxford India paperbacks), New Delhi; New York: Oxford University Press.

Hindess, B. (2001) "The Liberal Government of Unfreedom," *Alternatives*, 26(2), p. 20.

Hockenos, P. (2003) *Homeland Calling, Exile Patriotism and the Balkan wars*, Ithaca and London: Cornell University Press.

Hudelist, D. (1999) *Banket u Hrvatskoj* (Drugo izdanje) ed., Zagreb: Globus International.

Hudelist, D. (2004) *Tuđman, biografija*, Zagreb: Profil international.

Huntington, S. (2005) *Who Are We?: The Challenges to America's National Identity*, 1st paperback ed., New York: Simon & Schuster.

IOM (2003) *World Migration 2003: Managing Migration Challenges and Responses for People on the Move, IOM World Migration Report Series*, Geneva: IOM.

IOM (2010) *World Migration 2010. Managing Labour Mobility in the Evolving Global Economy*, Geneva: IOM.

Jaffrelot, C. and Therwath, I. (2007) "The Sangh Parivar and the Hindu Diaspora in the West: What Kind of 'Long-Distance Nationalism'?" *International Political Sociology*, 1(3), pp. 278–295.

Kadirbeyoğlu, Z. (2010) "Country Report: Turkey," Fiesole: EUDO Citizenship Observatory.

Kafle, H. R. (2012) "Diaspora Studies: Roots and Critical Dimensions," *Bodhi: An Interdisciplinary Journal*, 4(1), pp. 136–149.

Kirschenblatt-Gimbett, B. (1994) "Spaces of Dispersal," *Cultural Anthropology*, 9(3), pp. 339–344.

Kostov, V. (1988) *The Bulgarian Umbrella: The Soviet Direction and Operations of the Bulgarian Secret Service in Europe*, Hemel Hempstead, UK; New York: Harvester Press; St. Martin's Press.

Kuropas, M. B. (1991) *The Ukrainian Americans: Roots and Aspirations, 1884–1954*, Toronto; Buffalo: University of Toronto Press.

Le Goaziou, V. and Mucchielli, L. (2006) *Quand les banlieues brûlent ...: retour sur les émeutes de novembre 2005, Sur le vif*, Paris: La Découverte.
Lomeli-Azoubel, R. P. (2002) *La matrícula consular y los servicios bancarios*, Los Angeles, CA: Cónsul General de México.
Massey, D. S. (1987) *Return to Aztlan: The Social Process of International Migration from Western Mexico* (Studies in Demography), Berkeley, CA: University of California Press.
Neumann, I. and Sending, O. (2007) "'The International' as Governmentality," *Millennium: Journal of International Studies*, 35(3), pp. 677–701.
Newland, K. and Patrick, E. (2004) *Beyond Remittances: the Role of Diaspora in Poverty Reduction in their Countries of Origin*, Washington, DC: Migration Policy Institute.
Noiriel, G. (2007) *Immigration, antisémitisme et racisme en France, XIXe–XXe siècle: discours publics, humiliations privées*, Paris: Fayard.
Osiander, A. (2001) "Sovereignty, International Relations and the Westphalian Myth," *International Organization*, 55(2), pp. 251–287.
Pantiru, M. C., Black, R., and Sabates-Wheeler, R. (2007) *Migration and Poverty Reduction in Moldova*, Brighton, UK: Sussex Centre for Migration Research, Institute for Development Studies.
Pérez Juárez, G. I. (2003) *Matrícula consular, instrumento de identificación para inmigrantes indocumentados mexicanos en Estados Unidos*, San Pedro Garza García, Mexico: Tesis (Lic. en Estudios Internacionales)–UDEM.
Portes, A. (1998) "Globalization from Below: The Rise of Transnational Communities WPTC-98-01," *Transnational Communities Working Papers*, University of Oxford.
Portes, A. (1999) "Conclusion: Towards a New World—The Origins and Effects of Transnational Activities," *Ethnic and Racial Studies*, 22(2), pp. 463–477.
Portes, A. and Walton, J. (1981) *Labor, Class, and the International System: Studies in Social Discontinuity*, New York: Academic Press.
Pries, L. (2001) "The Disruption of Social and Geographic Space: Mexican–US Migration and the Emergence of Transnational Social Spaces," *International Sociology*, 16(1), pp. 55–74.
Radeljić, B. (2012) *Europe and the Collapse of Yugoslavia: The Role of Non-State Actors and European Diplomacy*, London/New York: I. B. Tauris.
Rose, N., O'Malley, P., and Valverde, M. (2006) "Governmentality," *Annual Review of Law and Social Science*, 2(1), pp. 83–104.
Safran, W. (1991) "Diasporas in Modern Societies: Myths of Homeland and Return," *Diaspora: A Journal of Transnational Studies*, 1(1), pp. 83–99.
Sassen, S. (1988) *The Mobility of Labor and Capital: A Study in International Investment and Labor Flow*, Cambridge, UK; New York: Cambridge University Press.
Sayad, A. (2004) *The Suffering of the Immigrant*, Cambridge, UK; Malden, MA: Polity.
Schnapper, D. (2001) "De l'Etat-nation au monde transnational (Du sens et de l'utilité du concept de diaspora)," *Revue Européenne des Migrations Internationales*, 2(17), pp. 9–36.
Shain, Y. (1990) *The Frontier of Loyalty: Political Exiles in the Age of the Nation-State*, Middletown, CT: Wesleyan University Press.
Shain, Y. (1999) *Marketing the American Creed Abroad*, Cambridge, UK: Cambridge University Press.
Shain, Y. (2002) "The Role of Diasporas in Conflict Perpetuation and Resolution," *SAIS Review*, XXII(2), pp. 115–144.
Sheffer, G. (1986) *Modern Diasporas in International Politics*, London: Croom Helm.

Sheffer, G. (2003) *Diaspora Politics: At Home Abroad*, Cambridge, UK; New York: Cambridge University Press.
Smith, R. C. (1995) "Transnational Localities: Community, Technology, and the Politics of Membership within the Context of Mexico–US Migration" in Smith, M. P. and Guarnizo, L., eds., *Transnationalism from Below* (pp. 3–34), New Brunswick, NJ: Transaction Publishers.
Smith, R. C. (2003a) "Diasporic Memberships in Historical Perspective: Comparative Insights from the Mexican, Italian and Polish Cases," *The International Migration Review: IMR*, 37(3), p. 36.
Smith, R. C. (2003b) "Migrant Membership as an Instituted Process: Transnationalization, the State and the Extra-Territorial Conduct of Mexican Politics," *The International Migration Review: IMR*, 37(2), p. 47.
Sökefeld, M. and Schwalgin, S. (2000) "Institutions and their Agents in Diaspora: A comparison of Armenians in Athens and Alevis in Germany," Working Paper on Transnational Communities, University of Hamburg.
Therwath, I. (2003) *L'Etat face à la diaspora. Stratégies et trajectoires indiennes*, unpublished thesis (Mémoire de DEA), Institut d'Etudes Politiques.
Tölölyan, K. (1991) "The Nation-State and its Others: In Lieu of a Preface" in Eleyand, G. and Grigor Suny, R., eds., *Becoming National: A Reader*, Oxford: Oxford University Press.
Tölölyan, K. (1996) "Rethinking Diaspora(s): Stateless Power in the Transnational Moment," *Diaspora*, 5(1), pp. 3–36.
Tuđman, F. (1997) "Poruka Predsjednika Republike Dr. Franje Tuđmana Hrvatskim Iseljenicima" in Ministarstvo povratka i useljeništva, ed., *Vodic za povratnike u Hrvatsku* (pp. 7–8), Zagreb: Ministarstvo povratka i useljeništva.
United Nations (2007) *World Population Prospects, The 2006 Revision*. New York: United Nations.
Van Dalen, H., Groenewold, G., and Fokkema, T. (2005) "The Effect of Remittances on Emigration Intentions in Egypt, Morocco, and Turkey," *Population Studies*, 59(3), p. 18.
Varadarajan, L. (2010) *The Domestic Abroad: Diasporas in International Relations*, Oxford: Oxford University Press.
Vertovec, S. (1997) "Three Meanings of 'Diaspora' Exemplified Among South Asian Religions," *Diaspora*, 6(3), pp. 227–299.
Wæver, O. (1995) "Securitization and Desecuritization" in Lipschutz, Ronnie D., ed., *On Security*, New York, Chichester: Columbia University Press.
Wæver, O., de Wilde, J., and Buzan, B. (1998) *Security: A New Framework for Analysis*, Boulder, CO: Lynne Rienner.
Walker, R. B. J. (2000) "Europe is Not Where it is Supposed to Be" in Kelstrup, M. and Williams, M., eds., *International Relations and the Politics of European Integration*, London: Routledge.
Wallerstein, I. M. (1989) *The Modern World-System 1730–1840s: Studies in Social Discontinuity*, San Diego, CA; New York: Academic Press.
Wimmer, A. and Schiller, N. G. (2002) "Methodological Nationalism and Beyond: Nation-State Building, Migration, and the Social Sciences," *Global Networks*, 2(4), pp. 301–334.
Winland, D. (2009) "Between Two Wars: Generational Responses of Toronto Croats to Homeland Independence," *Diaspora*, 18(1/2), pp. 117–137.
Zhang, L. (2001) "Migration and Privatization of Space And Power in Late Socialist China," *American Ethnologist*, 28(1), pp. 179–205.

Zimmerman, W. (1987) *Open Borders, Nonalignment, and the Political Evolution of Yugoslavia*, Princeton, NJ: Princeton University Press.

Zolberg, A. (1981) "International Migrations in Political Perspective" in Kritz, M. M., Keely, C. B., and Tomasi, S. M., eds., *Global Trends in Migration: Theory and Research on International Population Movements*, 1st ed. (pp. xxxi, 433), Staten Island, NY: Center for Migration Studies.

2 Seeing like an emigration state (1880–1991)

In the 1990s the nationalist party of Franjo Tuđman, the HDZ, defined the Croats as a nation whose borders lay outside of the territorial limits of the state and justified its extraterritorial practices under the label diaspora policies. How is it that the Croatian nationalist project, unlike the nationalist projects of the past century that focused on the necessary adequacy of nation and territory, was transformed into a state-sponsored diasporic nationalism?

Explaining this shift requires us to examine the policies and practices of the homeland toward its population abroad before we focus on diasporic institutions and the state's responses to them. The seemingly state-free or stateless condition of what are commonly called transnational communities is actually dependent upon state practices. For instance, the sending state's categorizations of emigrants through official documents such as passports and social security cards, as well as its bureaucratic practices encouraging remittances, policing opposition to the regime, or promoting folk culture abroad, have concrete social and political effects. Analyzing governmental practices toward the Croats who left in large numbers throughout the twentieth century, starting from the period when the region was under Austro-Hungarian rule spanning the emergence and dissolution of Yugoslavia, helps us contextualize the causes and effects of the "invention"[1] of the Croatian diaspora by the Croatian government in the 1990s.

How do we make sense of policies and practices that turn on their head the fundamental assumptions of the Westphalian state, particularly the territorial limits of sovereignty? The Croatian state extended its de facto sovereignty outside the borders within which its practices would be regarded as legitimate by other states. In situating the politics of emigration within a broader concept of the state, conceptual frameworks offered by James C. Scott and Aristide Zolberg are particularly helpful.

In his book *Seeing Like a State* (1998), which inspires the title of this chapter, Scott shows that state policies are necessarily determined by the way in which existing knowledge renders an issue *legible* as a political problem that can or should be acted upon. In Scott's words:

> Certain forms of knowledge and control require a narrowing of vision. The great advantage of such tunnel vision is that it brings into sharp focus certain

limited aspects of an otherwise far more complex and unwieldy reality. This very simplification, in turn, makes the phenomenon at the centre of the field of vision more legible and hence more susceptible to careful measurement and calculation. Combined with similar observations, an overall, aggregate, synoptic view of a selective reality is achieved, making possible a high degree of schematic knowledge, control and manipulation.

(1998: 11)

Zolberg has adopted a similar starting point in much of his work on the politics of migration, exploring the way in which the movement of people is captured, conceptualized, and ruled in relation to the broader modalities of government in which it takes place (1978, 1981, 2007: 34).[2]

I draw on Scott's and Zolberg's approaches to analyze the ways in which the government of populations abroad has emerged out of a series of "narrowings of vision" that made the phenomenon of emigration legible, calculable, and therefore governable. I use five entry points to analyze diaspora policies. First, what we might call episteme. What are the broader material conditions, such as economic crisis or war, and intellectual frameworks, such as nationalism or liberalism, within which an issue of emigration or citizens abroad arises? What specific problems is policy designed to address, such as depopulation, overpopulation, or economic decline? What taken-for-granted assumptions underpin, channel, and define emigration and populations abroad as helpful or dangerous? Second, knowledge. Which techniques of knowledge render this phenomenon visible and manageable? What are the knowledge tools, such as maps, censuses, and statistics, through which populations are classified in discrete, governable entities? Third, categorization. What categories are created—émigré, guest worker, political exile, diaspora—and what specific governmental rationality is attached to each? What function is attributed to each group? Which are seen as assets, potentially generating wealth or lobbying other governments, and which are regarded as posing a threat? Fourth, the positions of the social actors who engage in discourses of diaspora. What social actors struggle materially and symbolically for the imposition of their visions, categorizations, and functions? Are there competing framings of the problem, such as emigration as a shame and emigrants as a resource? How are these competing visions linked to specific groups within the bureaucratic or political field? What are the modalities through which populations resist or redefine the categorizations or functions imposed on them? Finally, techne. What are the techniques and technologies through which these categories of population are governed, and what are their effects?

The transnational practices of the Croatian state began long before the 1990s. Since the late nineteenth century, authorities in Zagreb and Belgrade have problematized, organized, and planned ways to reach out to their populations abroad. In addition to the material practices they instituted or considered, they struggled to affix an official meaning to the various forms of the atypical relationship between citizens at home and abroad. In the 1990s, both the nationalist parties within Croatia and right-wing organizations abroad drew selectively on this

26 Seeing like an emigration state (1880–1991)

repertoire of discursive and material practices to accomplish and justify the inclusion of non-resident Croats in the polity and the exclusion of resident non-Croats from citizenship. These rather startling policies were of long gestation, as analysis of the history of state practices with respect to emigration and populations abroad makes clear.

In this chapter, I trace these developments through a century in which the position of Croatia as a state shifted repeatedly, yet state policies and practices toward Croats abroad exhibited substantial continuity. Equally important, they exhibited clear connections with those which were espoused by the nationalist parties, supported by spokespersons for the diaspora, and institutionalized by the newly independent state in the 1990s.

We begin with the Austro-Hungarian Empire (1867–1914), when Croatia (together with Slavonia) was governed by the kingdom of Hungary. The late nineteenth and early twentieth centuries were marked by the massive emigration of Croats to North and South America. The ruling state tended to see emigration as a solution to the problems of poverty and tensions fuelled by ethnic difference, rather than as an issue which was to be addressed.

The situation shifted significantly with World War I, which ended in the formation of the Kingdom of Serbs, Croats, and Slovenes (SHS, 1919–1930) out of the ruins of the empire. Concerns about emigration were being voiced even before the war, as Croatian civil society organizations worried that the massive loss of population was depleting the nation and sought to extend benefits to Croats living abroad. Croatian émigrés were at the table when the agreement creating the SHS was signed. Economic conditions continued to spur emigration through the interwar period, although some of the flow was redirected toward Europe. The state sought to manage this movement, creating agencies to count and protect migrants. At the same time, non-governmental associations advocated for and provided services to Croats abroad.

The Kingdom of Yugoslavia (1929–1941), which was inaugurated by the abolition of parliament and the consolidation of the monarchy, was forced to shift state policies toward emigrants by the depression that engulfed Europe and the Americas during this decade. The question of return migration came to the forefront, and the notion of temporary labor migration was articulated for the first time. Concurrently, organizations of Croats abroad began to speak of the diaspora as the "tenth bovina," an integral, though extraterritorial, part of the nation and, ideally, of the polity. The material and political conditions that would have enabled the state to translate these discourses into practice, however, did not exist.

The formation of communist Yugoslavia (1946–1990),[3] under the leadership of the pan-Yugoslav Partisans who fought against the Axis powers and their allies, created a multi-ethnic, socialist state with six constituent republics, including Croatia. The government faced serious opposition at home and abroad. The policies the state adopted toward emigrants were highly politicized, as were the new organizations formed abroad. Security concerns largely trumped economic ones until the 1960s, when Yugoslavia began allowing and, indeed, encouraging its citizens to work temporarily abroad. Debates over state policies and emigrants' ties to the homeland led to the articulation of policies that extended Yugoslav governance over those living outside its territory. While the economic, social, and political collapse of Yugoslavia meant that this program was not systematically implemented, it laid the basis for the transnational policies and practices that were taken up by Croatian nationalists in the 1990s.

Emigration under the Austro-Hungarian Empire, 1867–1914

Between 1867 and 1914, when the Austro-Hungarian Empire dissolved, Croatia was not a distinct territorial entity; ethnic Croats were spread through the region and came under several governments. The largest number lived in Croatia-Slavonia, which belonged to the kingdom of Hungary.[4] The rest were in Istria, Dalmatia, and Herzegovina, which were ruled by the Austrian monarchy.

This division was part of the 1867 compromise in which the Austrian monarchy re-established the sovereignty of the kingdom of Hungary, forming the dual monarchy of Austria-Hungary. As the Austro-Hungarian Empire had been defeated in the 1866 war with Prussia, the Austrians sought to accommodate Hungarian nationalist forces rather than provoking a conflict which might have led to a questionable future for the dual monarchy. Contrary to sympathetic contemporary readings of Austria-Hungary's past as a multinational experiment, the Hungarian government did not conceive its state as multinational. Since Hungarian leaders understood the 1867 compromise as the division of the kingdom along national lines, they engaged in several waves of coerced nationalization of the Croatian, Slovakian, and Romanian minorities, a process known as "magyarization" (Kann 1950: 131–141). National minorities in the Austrian territories were less oppressed, in part due to article 19 of the constitution which recognized the right of each group to the "preservation and cultivation of its nationality and language in education, administration and public life" (Wank 1993: 11). The actual application of article 19 was limited, however, and failed to fulfil the expectations of nationalist parties (Wank 1993: 12).

It is in this political context of rising but frustrated nationalism that a substantial Croatian emigration from territories governed by Austria and Hungary took place between 1870 and 1914. The flow is difficult to quantify because many immigrants were recorded under different labels by the receiving countries; statistical information is incomplete and unreliable (Holjevac 1968; Antić 1985; Čizmić 1974–1975).[5] Since the majority of emigrants went to the United States (although significant numbers went to South America), data compiled by the US Senate Immigration Commission suggests the magnitude of this movement. Between 1899 and 1910, 362,201 immigrants from Croatia, Slovenia, Dalmatia, Bosnia, and Herzegovina arrived in the US, comprising 15.5 percent of the total number of immigrants from Austria-Hungary (US Immigration Commission 1911: 371).

Economic and social conditions common to most of southern and eastern Europe help to explain the emergence of emigration. The transformation of a predominantly agrarian society by capitalist industrialization, as well as the inability of the industrial and other sectors to absorb the newly formed working class generated an unemployed and mobile labor force.[6] Transportation facilitated population movement as well as economic change. Railways connected remote regions to cities and ports (Macartney 1968: 738), while transatlantic steamship companies offered inexpensive passage and spread tales of success on the other side of the Atlantic (Antić 1985: 244; Čizmić 1986: 255; Prpić 1971: 95). Emigration from Croatia-Slavonia acquired a political dimension under the governorship of Khuen-Héderváry (1883–1903), who carried out the brutal policy of magyarization, not only imposing the Hungarian language and culture on Croats but also subjugating them economically (Macartney 1968: 693; Jelavich 1987: 72, for a detailed account, see Šidak *et al.* 1968: 137–187). Emigration became a way to escape from the authoritarian rule that some Croats regarded as foreign and for young men to avoid serving in the military (Čizmić 1986: 255; Nejašmić 1989: 94).

At first the government did little to control emigration. In the late nineteenth century, the idea that the growth and movement of the population could be managed by the government was just emerging, as were efforts to gather statistical data about the population. The authorities became aware of emigration after 1880, when they started to collect statistical data on the phenomenon. Statistical surveys as a mode of political information began in Croatia-Slavonia during the 1850s, when chambers of commerce began gathering economic data for the monarchy (Karaman 1974: 38). Once emigration was acknowledged, it was not considered harmful but was seen by some circles in Vienna and Budapest as a solution to the problem of pauperization and the question of nationalities (Macartney 1968: 755; Banović 1987).[7] In the part of the empire ruled by Hungary, "the Liberal philosophy of the day favored the free operation of the law of supply and demand," and "for long years the regime spent far more effort on preventing [the people] from revolting against their condition than on trying to improve it" (Macartney 1968: 717, 719). At the same time, "the Magyar and Magyar-minded ruling class in Hungary had never in history regarded their State as either a-national or multinational," and their attempts to dominate other nationalities might be complemented by the departure of non-Magyars (Macartney 1968: 722).

Then, in response to public opinion and pressure from the military, measures were taken to restrict the flow of emigration. Until the widespread use of tools of governmental knowledge such as statistics, and therefore the conceptualization of migration in terms of trends and flows, emigration was seen mostly as an individual decision. The state attempted to control it at the individual level as well, primarily through legislation that was enforced by the police. On the Hungarian side, the first repressive *Law on Emigration in Croatia and Slavonia* was passed in 1883; it was revoked only in 1901 at the high point of emigration because of its obvious ineffectiveness (Čizmić 1986: 265; Holjevac 1968: 20–21). In 1891, the first "Service for sending persons of working and peasant class into overseas countries"[8] was founded, and in the following years, a Department for

Emigration was established within the Ministry of the Interior (Holjevac 1968: 40).[9] These bodies were complemented in 1898 by the Croatian Regional Statistical Office in Zagreb. Their role was mainly to collect information about emigration from harbor registers and steamship company records (Holjevac 1968: 41). On the Austrian side, in Dalmatia and Istria, although no law was passed restricting emigration (Antić 1985: 246), passports were introduced in 1881; since the authorities often refused to grant them, illegal emigration became common (Macartney 1968: 755 note 2). In addition, the law regarding obligatory military service tended to transform temporary into permanent emigration because young men feared imprisonment if they returned (Antić 1985: 246).

While intended to stop emigration, these police measures had very little effect on stemming the massive flow of departures. Newspapers and associations demanded government action to protect migrants from exploitation and abuse by travel agents and steamship companies. In 1905 the Emigrant Fund was established in the territories ruled by Hungary (Holjevac 1968: 41), and in 1909 it was complemented by the first dedicated Emigration Agency.[10] The role of the fund was to assist and protect emigrants during their journey and their stay abroad. An Emigration Act was passed in 1910 with the stated purpose of "regulating temporary migration." In fact the law had little effect, and many migrants stayed abroad (Čizmić 1990: 154). The real turning point in the control of emigration finally came with a 1913 law that reinforced the protection of emigrants from steamship companies and agents, forbade emigration by men under the age of 16, prohibited propaganda promoting migration and, to deter shipping companies, assessed a tax on each ticket sold, which reverted to the Emigration Fund.

By 1913, the question of emigration was being actively debated. Facing the looming prospect of war, military leaders in Vienna and Budapest grew concerned about the flight of potential soldiers. A letter to the editor of the newspaper *Domovina* said, "People wrote, spoke, shouted, begged—and nothing helped until the Minister of War realized that emigration from Austro-Hungarian monarchy was dangerous for the military power of the state."[11] The press, civil society organizations, and political parties reframed the issue of emigration as a matter of depopulation, which they presented as a danger to the economic development of the nation and to its biological survival. A 1904 article in Zadar-based *Narodni List*[12] declared that "from the economic and political point of view emigration presents a loss for the future development of Croatian life and should it continue in its present direction and numbers it will bring about the suicide of our nation." This view was shared by some émigrés. A 1910 article in the newspaper of the Croatian Fraternal Union based in Pittsburgh, Pennsylvania, states that "the emigration from Croatian lands to America during the last ten years was of such great proportions that it could become the chief danger for the survival of our nation."

Non-governmental organizations such as the Communal Council in Split, Dalmatia,[13] organized events and conferences on the question of emigration and passed resolutions to prevent emigration. In 1905, F. Lupis-Vukić, a Dalmatian activist, published a long article in *Narodni List* calling the attention of the authorities to the conditions endured by emigrants and arguing for measures to protect their welfare. In addition to those included in the Hungarian law of 1913, he mentioned the establishment of a residence for emigrants abroad (*dom za izseljenike*) and the creation of a social security fund for emigrants abroad. Consulates were accused of neglecting emigrants' hardships, and particularly for not having Croats or Croatian-speaking staff in areas where most Austro-Hungarian emigrants were Croats. A letter from a Croat living in Peru published in *Narodni List* in 1886 concluded plaintively: "We, Dalmatian Croats, known here as Austrians, ... cannot find anybody to help us.... We are therefore like orphans living under somebody else's mother."

Under Austro-Hungarian rule, the emphasis was not on the management of emigration as a social and economic phenomenon; the available statistical data was insufficient to enable the conceptualization of population trends. Rather, government policy aimed to give the authorities the ability to allow or forbid individual departures from the territory. The police were charged with preventing illegal emigration, a category which was itself produced by the criminalization of this act by the poorer classes of society. Here, as in other European counties, emigration policies were policies designed to get rid of the poor.[14]

The sudden awareness that emigration was a problem for military manpower rather than a solution to poverty and the nationalities question was not caused by a change in this framework. The years 1870–1914 manifested a governmental rationality based on the *raison d'etat*: emigration policies were shaped by considerations of defense, wherein the limit and scope of the exercise of power is the territory, and concern for the subjects is conditioned by the survival and empowerment of the sovereign.

At the same time, newspapers, associations, and politicians began formulating alternative conceptions of the question. Based on nationalist and socialist assumptions about the people as both the substance of the nation and its labor force, the fear of depopulation was primary. Although civil society organizations advocated an end to emigration, in practice they became increasingly involved in its practical benefits through the transmission of remittances and their monopoly on jobs linked to the transportation of emigrants. This situation, coupled with the increasingly circular pattern of emigration[15] and the crisis precipitated by World War I, dramatically changed the handling of the emigration question.

The Kingdom of Serbs, Croats, and Slovenes (SHS), 1919–1930

World War I brought about the dissolution of the Austro-Hungarian monarchy. Over the years before the war, nationalists from Croatia, along with activists from the newly independent Serbia and Montenegro, had formed a pan-Slavic movement aimed at bringing all South Slavic nationalities into a single federated state. During the war, South Slav activists from different regions of Austria-Hungary united in an exile organization called the "Yugoslav Committee." Its most prominent member was Dalmatian Croat politician and active Yugoslav militant Ante Trumbić. On 20 July 1917 in Corfu, the Yugoslav Committee reached an agreement with Serbian exiled prime minister Nikola Pašić for the creation of a Kingdom of Serbs, Croats, and Slovenes to be led by the Karađorđević royal family. The kingdom became reality in December 1918, at the end of a war in which Croatian emigrants had largely supported the "old country" in economic, humanitarian, and political terms (Ramet 2006: 42; Lampe 2000: 103).

The economic and social situation in the new state was dire. Because the economies of these territories had been oriented toward different networks (Austria, Hungary, and Serbia), the new country included four different rail systems, five currencies, and six customs areas (Lampe 2000: 118). The war severely damaged both agricultural and industrial production; regions of Croatia faced food shortages, and Serbia's industry was paralyzed. These and other factors led to a wave of peasant uprisings across Croatia (Ramet 2006: 49; Lampe 2000: 120). The state's inability to find immediate solutions to the economic crisis provided the structural conditions for unchecked emigration to continue. Although in previous decades most emigrants had come from the Dalmatian coast, increasing numbers came from inland areas of Croatia. From 1919 to 1930, the emigration flow was primarily directed overseas to the Americas or Australia, but during the last decade before World War II it was redirected to Europe (Holjevac 1968: 39).[16] It is estimated that between 1918 and 1938 approximately 75,000 Croats left the homeland, two-thirds going to the Americas and one-third going to other European countries.[17] Most departures were permanent, but the 1920s saw an increase in return migration, and gradually a circular pattern of migration developed (Čizmić and Mikačić 1974: 22; Holjevac 1968: 46).

The massive scale of emigration, which peaked at one-tenth of the SHS's total population, politicized the issue (Antić 1990: 229). The problem was divided into two separate issues: first, how to manage the state's relationship with pre-1914 emigrants (*iseljenici*); second, how to manage the new wave of emigration (Holjevac 1968: 36). The SHS adopted a very different policy than that of Austria-Hungary, which had aimed at stopping the flow. The goal now was to manage it: to direct emigrants to the right destination, to preserve their sense of national identity abroad, to facilitate their return, and to invest the foreign currency they sent home (Antić 1990: 229).

This perspective was articulated by Minister of Social Affairs M. Simonović in 1926 during a discussion in the National Assembly[18]:

Emigration ... is neither a new nor an extraordinary phenomenon. If one looks at the history of the world, one will inevitably come across the fact that there has always been movement.... We therefore cannot and should not try to stop emigration at any cost.... The emigrant goes to the world to make a living, and if he cannot make this living at home then it is more advisable that he look for it somewhere else, rather than allow his family to starve to death. It is, however, our duty to control and regulate this emigration.[19]

32 Seeing like an emigration state (1880–1991)

The new managerial view led to the creation of government departments exclusively devoted to emigration. Across different levels of the administration, bureaucrats formulated policies, prepared and organized statistical information, developed expert knowledge about who and where these populations were, and proposed better ways of dealing with the problem of emigration. But the results did not match their intentions.

The rapid centralization of authority in the SHS shaped the administration of the 1921 Law on Immigration and Emigration[20] (Holjevac 1968: 38; Čizmić and Mikačić 1974). As the bureaucracies and deliberative assembly of the province of Croatia-Slavonia were eliminated,[21] a Department for Immigration and Emigration[22] and an Interministerial Consultative Committee[23] were created within the ministry for social affairs[24] in Belgrade. Significantly, these institutions were located within ministries of domestic and not foreign affairs, although they dealt mostly with issues related to emigrants abroad. The most important institution was the General Commissioner for Emigration, based first in Zagreb then in Belgrade[25] (Jonjić and Lausić 1998; Antić 1990: 231; Hranilović 1987: 331; Holjevac 1968: 38), whose mission included death and burial insurance for emigrants, protection from fraudulent practices of transport companies, the restitution of properties confiscated during the war to citizens in the United States and British dominions, and the care of orphaned emigrants. The Commissioner was also in charge of keeping statistical records and processing emigrants' remittances (Antić 1990: 231). The 1921 law defined the emigrant (*iseljenik*) by a blend of class and geographic criteria as one who "emigrates to overseas countries to earn money through manual labor, or who emigrates with his family who previously emigrated under the same conditions."[26]

Due to a combination of lack of funding and bureaucratic inefficiency, the new policy was ineffective.[27] The decline of offices that were designed to manage and serve emigrants was confirmed in 1928 when their funding was shifted from the Ministry of Social Affairs to the Ministry of Foreign Affairs. This move signified an effort to get rid of these institutions and pretend the emigration problem did not exist (Hranilović 1987: 331; Antić 1990: 232).

In response to the laissez-faire policy of the SHS, non-governmental organizations demanded that the government take care of the emigrant population both "nationally," in terms of the survival of the Croatian language, culture and traditions abroad, and "socially," in terms of social welfare and protection. In 1924, important returning emigrants and former civil servants of emigration institutions, Ivan Frano Lupis Vukić, Milostislav Bartulica, and Milan Marjanović, founded the first Organization of Emigrants in Zagreb to provide assistance to emigrants and to publicize the emigrant problem in the country.[28] In 1926, these claims were expressed in a report to the National Assembly:

> The political-national phenomenon of emigration requires that emigrants are provided with special care. There is no need to talk at length about this, because it is clear to everyone that we in the homeland have a duty towards

Seeing like an emigration state (1880–1991) 33

our workers in the overseas lands, to support them in preserving the national spirit, to prevent them from becoming denationalized, and to try to bring their savings to the homeland.[29]

The concern for emigrants contradicted the interests of the government and drew on a different political-economical rationality for the management and regulation of emigration:

> Until today, our emigration policy has been limited to the delivery of passports and has left emigrants to their own devices. Our society benefits from emigration as it allows the discontented to leave, and inhabitants of poor regions to earn an income abroad and to return with capital and knowledge.[30]

Extraterritorial concern for the care of emigrants abroad posed new challenges to political sovereignty, citizenship, and nationality.

> We should not allow our national body (*naš elemenat*) to disperse without a goal in the world [because] our state ... would not be able to take care of them. Therefore the way should be cleared for them; they should be concentrated in one country elsewhere where our state, through its organs, could control them and keep them in constant contact with their homeland.[31]

Two important features of diaspora politics emerged for the first time in this discourse. First, the fate of the emigrants is the fate of the nation; the notion of nation is stretched outside the borders of SHS. Second, the central concern here is not for state limitation of emigration but for the care that the state extends to the members of the national body abroad. This care ensures the belonging of emigrants to the nation.

In the SHS, emigration was thought of and governed in new ways. It was recognized as an important political and social problem. The government categorized the good emigrant as a temporary emigrant. Circular migration was positive because it provided a safety-valve for the unemployed, sustained families, and was a source of remittances for the country. In contrast, the bad migrant, one who left permanently, was a loss for the nation economically, socially, and politically. Emigration was relocated from the realm of national defense and police rule to social policies. Nonetheless, governmental practices of control and management had few concrete results.

In contrast to governmental rationality and practices, which remained bound to the territorial borders of the SHS, some philanthropic societies formulated rather different claims. For the Organization of Emigrants in Zagreb, the population abroad was still part of the nation and should be offered social support. The emigrant's belonging to the nation was independent of territorial considerations, and the only danger of loss lay in processes of denationalization or assimilation. For the first time, the idea emerged among activist circles in Zagreb and Split that a population deserving state attention resided outside of the internationally recognized borders of the state. Since the nation had traveled across borders through emigration, state policies should extend beyond them as well.

The Kingdom of Yugoslavia, 1929–1941

Social and national tensions in the Kingdom of Serbs, Croats, and Slovenes took a new turn with the assassination of the Croatian nationalist leader Stjepan Radić.[32] King Alexander, fearing for the legitimacy and stability of the state, revoked the constitution, abolished the parliament, banned all political parties, and appointed a new government which disbanded the 33 provinces and designed a new territorial division with nine regional units (*banovine*). On 3 October 1929, the name of the country was changed to Kingdom of Yugoslavia (Ramet 2006: 74–77; Lampe 2000: 171).

The economic crisis of 1929 depressed the prices received for farm products, which was a serious blow because three-quarters of the population was in the agricultural sector. The value of exports declined as well, and the currency depreciated (Lampe 2000: 171). The public debt more than doubled, making Yugoslavia the most indebted country after Greece (Ramet 2006: 76).[33] In order to attract foreign capital, Yugoslavia implemented the economically liberal prescriptions followed by other European nations. The dinar remained on the gold standard to reduce inflation, the budget was cut, and government social services were reduced (Lampe 2000: 171–223).

By 1929, the serious flaws in the 1921 and 1923 laws were exposed. The restrictive laws passed by the US in 1924 dramatically increased the number of would-be emigrants who were refused admission. Canada, Australia, and Argentina soon adopted similar restrictions. The financial crisis gave the final blow to circular migration and signalled the beginning of the problem of return (Holjevac 1968: 38). Većeslav Holjevac estimates that 13,838 people left the *Savska Banovina* (which more or less covered Croatian lands) but 14,835 returned (Holjevac 1968: 51). The return of destitute migrants was considered shameful, however, and was largely ignored by the state. At the same time, the value of emigrants' remittances reached an unprecedented level (Čizmić and Mikačić 1974: 27).

At first the government of Yugoslavia did little to manage emigration. Some scholars suggest that the Serbian centralists who ruled in Belgrade were indifferent toward an outflow that was predominantly Croatian (Antić 1997: 81). Although emigration might not entirely cease, it could be temporary. A 1940 report expressed this view in terms that sound like wishful thinking.

> The Croatian emigrant does not come from the city proletariat, who is deprived of any means, and would emigrate with the intention of never coming back to the homeland. [He] is a poor peasant who has left his motherland. His income earned abroad through intense labour will be almost entirely saved in order to pay back debts and improve his business. He is, in

the full sense of the word, a temporary emigrant, who has the strong intention of coming back home. He is not vulnerable to assimilation and amalgamation and maintains, in almost every respect, a high moral and national conscience. The Emigration Agency in Croatia has, from its foundation, guided by its leaders, supported our temporary migrant morally and materially.[34]

Yet the fear of depopulation did not entirely recede. In 1933 Fedor Aranički, head of the Emigrants Agency, declared: "To be honest, if emigration had continued in the same proportions as it had up until 1918, America would have become our second Kosovo. Our country ... would have fallen into the hands of the foreigner" (Bartulica 1933: 23).

Following the 1939 Cvetković–Maček agreement, long-abandoned emigrant institutions were reorganized[35] and the government integrated some ideas proposed by civil society. A public fund was planned for the repatriation of poor emigrants. International agreements were signed for the employment of Yugoslav nationals abroad (mainly with Germany, anticipating the guest worker programs of the 1960s and 1970s) and for the social care of emigrants overseas. Statistical records were updated.[36]

Organizations that sought to assist and represent emigrants, especially SORIS, the Council of Emigrants' Organizations (*Savez organizacija iseljenika*), located themselves in a radically different configuration and articulated a complex relationship between territory, nation, and citizenship. In the discourses of the 1930s, these organizations appropriated the idea that Croats abroad formed a special form of colony, which did not require a state apparatus or a legal link of citizenship. The only necessary link was ethnic, cultural, and linguistic.[37] In a key Emigration Conference held in Sarajevo in 1933, SORIS president Milan Marjanović explained:

> In the past years we have started to commonly say that the emigrants are our Tenth Banovina. This is not just an expression.... Other countries fight and get involved in wars in order to acquire colonies.... We never had any territorial possessions or colonies, but because of involuntary and forced circumstances, we have hundreds and hundreds of thousands of our nation (*naš svijet*) dispersed in foreign countries around the world. We never realized that this in fact is somehow our colony, that there lives a part of our nation not only as an ethnic community, but our nation as a social and economic community and therefore as a political community.
>
> (Bartulica 1933: 15)

What Marjanović articulates in this statement is a meaning of colony that could be traced back to ancient Greece, in which emigration from the homeland generates transnational ethnic, social, and economic ties between the old country and the new populations. It is also a Herderian,[38] pre-Westphalian understanding of the term: the sense of allegiance and belonging is not dependent on attributes of statehood such as citizenship or formal sovereignty. What ties the homeland and the population abroad is the sense of shared origins, culture, language, and religion, independently of the nationality of the ruler whose territory it inhabits or the formal citizenship it holds.

Indeed, in contrast to the 1921–1923 laws designed to preserve national consciousness through the preservation of citizenship (Hranilović 1987: 328), SORIS argued in 1933 that the question of citizenship was irrelevant. Marjanović explained:

> I have heard people say, ... "our emigrants who take foreign citizenship are national traitors (*izdajice i odrodi naroda*) and should be treated as renegades of their nation (*pomadžareni*)."[39] This is a completely wrong understanding. It is a completely different thing to accept Hungarian, German, or Italian citizenship on the one side, and citizenship from South or North America on the other side. There [in America], denationalization is not expected from the migrants; citizenship is rather the precondition for emigrants to improve their status economically and socially, so that he can earn more and be a stronger economic factor. Moreover, future Croatian American citizens [will become] the representatives of a faraway land in Europe, and this [their American citizenship] will give them a stronger mandate in the country in which they reside, and it will come to our aid.
>
> (Bartulica 1933: 15)

Changing logics regarding emigration and modalities of governmentality

Between the turn of the twentieth century and World War II, Croatian émigrés not only increased in number but also gained political significance. Emigration was understood through statistical tools and treated as part of modern government. Two main logics, located in two different epistemes, can be distinguished in the practices adopted regarding emigration.

The first logic, which prevailed under the Austro-Hungarian rule, located in an economically liberal understanding of political rule, rested on safety-valve policies designed to remove undesirables, in particular the poor and ethnic or national minorities. Knowledge began to be gathered through statistics, but emigration was mainly conceived as a series of individual cases. The relationship between the government and those who left was defined through the law and enacted through policing techne; individuals were categorized as legal or illegal migrants, i.e., necessary or superfluous bodies. Police enforced the government's interest in emigration, which only extended to a concern that the basic functions and capacities of the state, particularly making war, were threatened by the departure of too many potential soldiers. Access to civic rights was tightly bound to the territory. Those who left evaded the scope of the state.

The second logic, which came to the fore after 1918 under the kingdoms of SHS and Yugoslavia, shows the emergence of a managerial approach to the question, representing a shift not only in the policies but also in the modality of government. In this epistemic frame, emigration is understood as an inexorable flow that can only be enhanced or reduced and oriented in particular directions. Control moves from the police to the government Ministry of Social Affairs and to ad hoc institutions that compiled statistical information and calculated population trends and emigration flows. Contrary to the individualizing logic of the safety-valve, emigration is considered a natural phenomenon to be governed, not a decision to be approved or denied. The benefits of managing migration appear most clearly when it is circular, or temporary rather than permanent. Once abroad, emigrants are independent; the state extends care to them only before they leave and after they return. In this new context, the categorizations of the state are not legal/illegal binary but temporary/permanent. The category of temporary emigrant fits the perceived benefits of circular migration; the category of the permanent migrant is considered damaging to the state.

The new paradigm of emigration as a natural phenomenon determined by social and economic conditions rather than individual decisions also shaped the ways in which nationalist and socialist movements framed the question. They articulated claims for social and national rights that extended beyond the territorial limits of the state. The fundamental assumption was that neither presence on the territory nor legal citizenship in the state justified this attention; rather, emigrants belong to the nation by reason of their shared ethnicity, culture, and language. In their view, emigrants should benefit from cultural services, education, healthcare, and social protection similar to those offered in the homeland. The rather startling perspective challenged spokespersons of the government, Croatian organizations, and émigré associations to try to fit this new conception of the relationship between the extraterritorial population and the homeland into existing categories of the nation-state. Before Yugoslavia itself was transformed by World War II, spokespersons elaborated two metaphors, the tenth banovina and the stateless colony. Although deterritorialized care for migrants was theorized, its concrete applications were yet to come.

The Federal People's Republic of Yugoslavia, 1946–1962

Initially, Tito's Yugoslavia resembled the Soviet Union. Its 1946 constitution was modeled on that of the USSR of 1936. It also adopted similar repression methods and political-economic organization (Lapenna 1972). In the 1945 elections, the communist-led popular front obtained 81.53 percent of the vote. Two important trials, of Četnik (Serbian nationalist) leader Draža Mihailović and Zagreb Archbishop Alojzije Stepinac (accused of having collaborated with the *Ustaša*, the Nazi-friendly movement who took power over the Independent State of Croatia between 1941 and 1945), were carried out as public condemnations of Serbian and Croatian nationalism (Ramet 2006: 165–169). More quietly, from 1946 to 1948 numerous political trials were carried out to silence opposition. In 1948, the Federal People's Republic of Yugoslavia (FNRJ)[40] broke its ties with the Soviet Union by refusing to comply with Stalin's leadership and insisting on taking its own route toward socialism (Banac 1988). By 1951, Yugoslavia had repositioned itself between the Eastern and Western blocs as a non-aligned country.

World War II devastated the country. At least 1,000,000 Yugoslavs were killed[41] during the war. Material destruction was widespread, including one-seventh of pre-war housing, two-fifths of industrial facilities, and half of all livestock and agricultural machinery (Lampe 2000: 233). To promote recovery, the Yugoslav authorities designed an ambitious, Soviet-style five-year plan (Vucinich et al. 1969: 204–205). The plan was a failure, but the economy revived because of international assistance. In addition to shipments of food, clothing, and medical supplies, the United Nations Relief and Rehabilitation Agency provided the federation with US$415,000,000, which financed the rebuilding of the transport infrastructure (Lampe 2000: 233).

In the face of these daunting tasks, emigration disappeared from political debate. The new state prohibited emigration, refusing to issue passports until 1962. This policy of closure was based on policy makers' belief that the older economic migrants had either died or had been assimilated and that younger workers who had gone abroad would return in response to the economic development of Yugoslavia. Accordingly, they organized a policy of return and reintegration (Čizmić and Mikačić 1974: 65).

At the same time, the authorities made a sharp distinction between the "old Yugoslav emigration" (*staro jugoslovensko iseljeništvo*) and the "fascist and extremist" emigration, which they initially identified as reactionary nationalists who had fled when the communists triumphed. It later expanded to include "Cominformists" who supported Stalin and dissented from the position taken by Yugoslavia.[42] These definitions are encapsulated in a 1985 manual on national security:

> The largest part of our old emigrants [*iseljenici*] are loyal citizens where they live, and have a positive attitude towards SFRY [Socialist Federal Republic of Yugoslavia].... Our state offers support to the activities of old emigrant associations and encourages an intense communication with the old country. This activity is [however] under heavy pressure from fascist and extremist organizations, who oppose it.... Enemy activity of fascist and extremist emigrant organizations has taken place continuously from the end of World War II until now. The main goal of all forms of enemy activity is to overthrow or subvert the social-economic and political system in SFRY, as well as to oppose the non-aligned orientation of Yugoslavia.
>
> (Đorđević 1986: 152–153, 183)

The new antagonist was labeled the Yugoslav Enemy Migration (*Jugoslavenska neprijateljska emigracija*). This group of exiled nationalists was closely monitored, controlled, and sometimes eliminated (Doder 1989).

Reflecting this dichotomy, two different policies were elaborated. For the old migration, policies aimed at normalizing the emigrants' situation according to a Westphalian understanding of sovereignty and citizenship. Those who wanted to return to the homeland were encouraged to do so, and in 1946 the Secretariat of Labour instituted a "first aid fund" for returnees. They also allowed Yugoslav citizens to claim the pensions they had been granted while abroad, which would facilitate the return of those who had been away for decades. This policy was a dismal failure, and between 1946 and 1951 only 16,128 people returned (Čizmić and Mikačić 1974: 65–69).

The Yugoslav Enemy Migration was handled by the state's security apparatus. The Department for the Protection of the People,[43] led by the powerful Alexander Ranković, spawned several agencies that carried out surveillance of emigrants at the federal level.[44] At the republic level, the Directorate for State Security was particularly dreaded.[45] Initially, opponents of the regime were exiled. The most horrifying moment of this policy is the May 1945 Bleiburg massacre, when prisoners of war, and Croats and Slovenes fleeing the advancing Partisans, were forced by British troops to return to Yugoslavia, where they were subjected to marches and executed because they were suspected of collaborating with the enemy.[46] During and immediately after the war nationalists from all sides, Četnici, Ustaše, and Domobrani,[47] fled the country with their families and took refuge in camps in Austria and Italy. As the nature of the regime became clearer, Catholics, anti-communists, and Cominformists also went into exile. An estimated 300,000 people left in the aftermath of the war (Bilandžić 1985: 99). Conflict continued inside the country as well. In 1945, the Yugoslav People's Army (JNA)[48] was still fighting small groups of former Ustaše soldiers (Križari) and Četnici hiding in the woods. The secret police agencies concentrated on uprooting the "internal enemy": "bourgeois and counter-revolutionary" elements, "religious," "nationalist-chauvinist," and "bureaucratic" forces.

The old emigration, which was not seen as a threat, attracted less attention. The semi-independent Foundation for Emigrants from Croatia (*Matica iseljenika Hrvatske*), founded in 1951, sought to preserve the link with the old migrants and improve the image of the new Yugoslavia. A 1958 report details its activities: organizing month-long visits to the home country; sponsoring traditional *tamburica* orchestra tours to and from Yugoslavia; distributing folkloristic and touristic material in America, Australia, and Argentina; and publishing a magazine, *Matica*, and a yearly calendar. Since the security spectre loomed, however, the magazine was intended to compete ideologically with political publications by emigrants:

> In the old migration today, there are about a hundred publications in Yugoslav languages (the majority in Croatian and Serbian). Most are printed by enemy elements ... who are doing everything to increase their influence on our old migrants.... In order not only to maintain but to increase the number of subscribers, we need to systematically target the new emigration. Not the enemy elements ... but those who left and were marked as refugees even if they are not enemies at all.... The second potential audience is the children of our old migrants.
>
> (M.I.H. 1956: 10)

In this perspective, the old migration is reconstituted as a friendly population whose allegiance is to be assured by combating the influence of the more recent enemy emigration.

The period between the end of World War II and the opening of the borders in 1962 was characterized by a disciplinary modality of control based on the territorial exclusion of dissenters and the intensive surveillance of this undesirable minority outside the state's borders by the security apparatus. In Ole Wæver's terms, the question of emigration was securitized.[49] The territorial state continued to function as the referent for relations between the state and its citizens elsewhere. The vast majority, the old migrants, were not given Yugoslav citizenship unless they returned, and the banned emigrants were denied a passport and citizenship rights once abroad. Similarly, debates concerning the national question centered on Yugoslavia's federal and socialist compromise—i.e., to what extent should a socialist country recognize national identities, or merge them in a broad, new socialist identity—in which the freedom of nationalities was inextricably linked to the freedom of the working class in the territory of Yugoslavia.[50]

The territorialized modality of emigration control is tied to a broader form of political economy which combines the political strategy of "oneness" and an economic strategy of autarchy, as Zolberg defines it, where in the pursuit of economic and military goals the no-exit policy is a means to an end of preserving a valuable asset, the population. By leaving, people endanger a greater political and economic goal. If one is to look at the techniques of control as a coin, no-exit policies are one side of it, while the other is (forced) expulsions (1981: 23).

The territorial management of workers temporarily abroad, 1962–1973

The fact that the political economy and modality of disciplinary control came to an end with the opening of the Yugoslav borders in 1962–1963 was an unprecedented step for a communist regime. This major shift was linked to the international context and the internal economic situation. As a non-aligned country, Yugoslavia accepted substantial amounts of aid from the Western bloc as well as the USSR (Rusinow 1977: 178). In 1965, in its search for a "Yugoslav way" to socialism, it undertook a series of political and social reforms, gradually accepting the principle of profit, allowing a degree of decollectivization, increasing the use of banks, and questioning the guarantee of full employment (Milenkovitch 1971, 1977: 55–56).

Unemployment was thought to be a result of these reforms, and looking for employment abroad became acceptable. The number of Yugoslavs seeking employment in other parts of Europe and beyond rose from 18,000 in 1960 to 210,000 in 1966 and peaked in 1973 at 860,000. Even though a small fraction of this wave of emigration left for the previous overseas destinations (US, Canada, South America, and Australia), the vast majority left for closer European countries: Austria, Germany, France, etc. Croatia's population was disproportionately

Table 2.1 Yugoslav migration flows, in thousands (1968–1981)[1]

Year	Departing	Returning	Abroad at the end of the year	Dependents living abroad[2]	Total abroad
1968	80	20	260		
1969	130	60	330		
1970	240	70	600		
1971	145	65	680		
1972	145	55	770		
1973	115	25	860		
1974	30	80	810		
1975	30	70	770	250	1,020
1976	25	70	725	355	1,080
1977	30	50	705	385	1,090
1978	35	45	695	395	1,090
1979	35	40	690	405	1,095
1980	30	27	693	415	1,108
1981	30	28	694	422	1,116

Notes
1 Source: Baskin (1986: 27). Reproduced with permission.
2 Data on the number of dependents living abroad is not available before 1975.

involved: according to the 1971 census 33.4 percent of the migrants were from the Socialist Republic of Croatia (SR Croatia), even though the republic represented only 21.6 percent of the Yugoslav population (Baskin 1986: 27).

In the early 1960s, Yugoslav policy makers regarded emigrants as falling into three categories: the old migration, the Yugoslav Enemy Migration, and the new socio-economic category officially called "workers temporarily employed abroad" (*Radnici na privremenom radu u inozemstvu*). Until 1966, the emigration of Yugoslav workers was not a political issue, although some officials were concerned that "Western capitalist countries employ ... tens of thousands of workers from Socialist Yugoslavia" (Baskin 1986: 78). After the 1965 reforms and the fall of Alexander Ranković the next year, Yugoslavia's political atmosphere became more open and liberal (Bilandžić 1985). By 1972, when the scale of emigration had become apparent, migrants began to figure in Yugoslavia's development strategy. In accordance with the development framework established by organizations such as the International Labour Organization (ILO), the Organization for Economic Cooperation and Development (OECD), and the UN, Yugoslavia revived the idea expressed in the 1930s that labor migration could prove useful to the national economy by alleviating unemployment, bringing in foreign currency, and raising the skill level of the work force. This situation was mutually beneficial, since Western countries were looking for a temporary labor force to fuel post-war economic development (Vedriš 1981: 441).

New quantitative and qualitative research on emigration began at the same time. Until the 1960s only the Employment Service kept migration records; then the Economic Institute of the University of Zagreb and the Institute for Social Research in Belgrade started tracking the phenomenon. International scientific collaboration began, in particular with German institutions who funded Yugoslav research on migration, and set up joint projects and conferences with Yugoslav scholars. In the 1970s, the Centre for Migration Studies in Zagreb became influential among Yugoslav policy makers (Baskin 1986: 79, 81).

Legislation concerning work abroad developed as this new migration grew. The 1963 Instruction on the Procedure for Employment Abroad[51] legalized workers who were already abroad, authorized their return, and allowed Yugoslav agencies to operate outside territorial borders to perform non-diplomatic tasks such as counseling migrants, teaching Yugoslav languages, and delivering job certificates. Passports were delivered the same year (Zimmerman 1987: 75–77). Special agreements with Western trade unions solved the "ethical question" regarding relations with capitalist countries (Baučić 1975). The 1965 Travel Permits of Yugoslav Citizens Act[52] and the 1966 Amendments of the Organization and Finance of Employment Act[53] eliminated restrictions on working abroad, regulated the way Yugoslavs could leave the country, and officially coined the term "workers temporarily employed abroad."[54] As reform-minded leaders encouraged labor migration, the state's managerial control of migration was strengthened; workers would seek jobs through the Bureaus for Employment, which regulated the flow. Bilateral agreements allowed populations abroad to be controlled by host states as well (Đorđević 1986; Godler and Pavić 1975).[55]

For the old migration, the cultural organization *Matica iseljenika Hrvatske* maintained what appeared to be an apolitical and folklore-centered program, offering concerts, trips, publications, and scholarships to connect pre-war migrants and their children with the homeland (M.I.H 1968). Yet its contacts with Yugoslav organizations abroad were also intended to combat the ideological influence of the Yugoslav Enemy Migration. With new migrants arriving in Europe, in 1965 it began publishing *Rodna gruda* for France and Belgium (Alfirević 1978: 607). Finally, the secret police continued their dreadful activities. Although the infamous Directorate for State Security was renamed, it continued monitoring and infiltrating Yugoslav organizations abroad. An estimated 22 extrajudicial executions outside the state took place between 1946 and 1969 (Vukušić 2002).

The open borders policy promoted by the reformers was challenged from three different quarters. First, conservatives within the establishment "saw no need to sponsor or support measures aiding those who would 'desert' Yugoslavia for the lure of hard currency" (Baskin 1986: 56). Second, the emigration of workers provided an occasion for internally marginalized religious organizations, in particular the Roman Catholic Church (Croats are predominantly Roman Catholic, while Serbs are in the majority Orthodox), to challenge the Yugoslav government. In 1969 it established a mission for Preaching for Croatians Abroad in Rome and a Council of the Bishop's Conference for Croatian Migration in Zagreb. Within a decade, the church had established 110 missions employing more than 200 clerical and lay staff abroad. In addition to religious ceremonies, they provided a broad range of cultural and social

Seeing like an emigration state (1880–1991) 43

services. They helped with employment, documents, housing, and relations with employers and authorities. They also directly competed with government-sponsored social and cultural events, bulletins, and newspapers for migrants (Vijeće BK za hrvatsku emigraciju 1982: 203–210).

The most direct contest began after the explosive events of the "Croatian spring" in 1971, when a heterogeneous movement of reform-minded communists, nationally oriented organizations, students, and the Catholic Church pushed for economic reforms, civil liberties, and national autonomy. The issue of workers abroad was a subject of heated discussion. Student organizations accused the authorities of selling the Yugoslav labor force to global capitalism, while nationalist movements re-enacted the fear of depopulation by claiming, among other things, that emigration policies were a Yugo-Serb plot to extinguish the Croatian nation.[56]

The reforms of the mid-1960s marked a sea change both in the way the economy was run and in the way governmental power was exercised. Liberal economic elements were introduced, and governmental rationality developed a socialist form of liberalism. At the same time, Yugoslavia still practiced de facto policing and elimination of political opponents in foreign territories[57] and exercised its cultural (and political) influence with *Matica iseljenika Hrvatske*. In these years, the massive transnational movement of workers was still regulated territorially.

As William Zimmerman observes,

> the picture for the years 1965 to 1972 is one of Yugoslav authorities governing the workers *prior* to their departure and negotiating with the Western European states and Australia about the ways *those states* would govern the

Table 2.2 National composition of emigrant workers and population (1971)[1]

Nationality	Number		Percentage		
	Migrants	Population	Migrants	Population	Migration rate
Montenegrins	5,260	508,202	0.8	2.5	1.0
Croats	261,721	4,516,466	39.0	22.2	5.8
Macedonians	38,298	1,194,188	5.7	5.9	3.2
Muslims[2]	40,565	1,727,171	6.0	8.5	2.3
Slovenes	46,856	1,576,253	7.0	7.7	3.0
Serbs	191,342	8,136,267	28.5	39.9	1.1
Albanians	34,748	1,308,528	5.1	6.4	2.7
Magyars	19,552	478,084	2.9	2.3	4.1
Others	33,566	942,267	5.0	4.7	3.5
Total	671,908	20,387,786	100.0	100.0	3.3

Notes
1 Source: Baskin (1986: 33). Reproduced with permission.
2 The category Muslims usually meant the Muslim population of Bosnia-Herzegovina, now referred to as Bošniak.

workers during their stay abroad ... informed by an implicit, rather conventional, view of the realms of domestic and foreign affairs, and of the role of the state domestically and abroad.

(1987: 109–110)

These forms of control were subtler than the heavy surveillance and brutal treatment of the Yugoslav Enemy Migration. Workers temporarily abroad were controlled through an ad hoc authority[58] under the direction of the League of Communists of Yugoslavia. Its main tools were the economic benefits and the system of insurance on which these workers depended. Any misstep or contact with the political opposition abroad could have meant the confiscation of their passport and the end of both the direct income they earned and the social benefits provided by the home state which they enjoyed in the host country. Yugoslav clubs and societies were set up and closely monitored by consulates and embassies (Heršak and Mesić 1990: 46).

Implementing long-distance governmentality in the Seventh Republic, 1973–1990

In the early 1970s, political and economic crises led to changes in Yugoslav policy toward workers temporarily employed abroad. The Soviet invasion of Czechoslovakia in 1968 empowered the security-minded conservatives within the establishment. The fear of Soviet invasion had been palpable during the Croatian Spring of 1971, with Brezhnev, the leader of the Soviet Union at the time, directly threatening Tito unless he established control over the events. The 1971 meeting in Karađorđevo sealed the destiny of the reformists within the party. Finally, when an economic crisis hit Western Europe in 1973–1974, guest workers suddenly became an unwanted surplus.

From 1968 on, criticisms of the Yugoslav laissez-faire attitude toward emigration were voiced from a variety of perspectives. To the conservatives, migration had only increased inequalities, and the fact that Socialist Yugoslavia was providing a subaltern labor force for European countries was shameful. Others faulted the lack of a consistent policy, the understaffing of consular institutions, and the state's inability to defend workers abroad. Critics pointed out its failure to fulfil advocates' promises: instead of improving workers' skills it had stimulated the departure of skilled labor; no effects could be seen in terms of foreign currency; and regional inequality had risen. Migration specialists concluded that the policy had not solved the problems it was set up to address but had actually exacerbated them (Baskin 1986: 96). In the media, a new public discourse based on psychology and sociology developed by the research institutions that were established to study migration emphasized its harmful effects on individuals and families, especially the traumas of separation and divorce for those who were left behind and the consequences of isolation and xenophobia in host countries (Baskin 1986: 91–99). The need for a new policy was clear: the state needed to provide better care for the migrants abroad and promote their return.

The reconceptualization of the Yugoslav population abroad as the "seventh republic" as Zimmerman calls it crystallized in 1973 (1987: 106–131). A 5 February 1973 joint meeting of the League of Communists of Yugoslavia and the Presidency of the SFRY pronounced migration to be a problem for national security and an obstacle to development.[59] Security concerns loomed large in the aftermath of the events of 1971 as the victorious faction labeled the dissenters "nationalist" and "chauvinist" and worried about possible connections between workers temporarily abroad and the enemy emigration. A member of the Socialist Alliance of the Working People of Yugoslavia (SAWPY)[60] explained in 1973 that workers employed abroad "are very vulnerable to the influence of foreign propaganda, in particular from the political emigration and some religious organizations."[61] Like the Austro-Hungarian generals in 1913, military officials warned that the Territorial Defense Forces[62] were endangered by migration. A trade union report estimated that 511,000 military reservists (10 percent of the national total) were employed abroad by 1973, making it impossible to form units in some areas (Baskin 1986: 98).

At the same time, emigration became an internal issue. As Ivo Baučić, a specialist in Yugoslav migrations, remarked, "The sociopolitical organizations and administrative bodies in Yugoslavia came to the conclusion that the foreign migrants are a specific category of the population" (Baučić 1976 in Zimmerman 1987: 113) With respect to this *Seventh Republic*, "Yugoslav decision makers acted increasingly as though they had to treat the workers, while abroad, as nearly as possible as a matter of domestic politics, namely to control, educate, and socialize them according to socialist principles" (Zimmerman 1987: 112).

Workers abroad were now considered an integral part of the Yugoslav working class[63] (Baskin 1986: 327) and became the objects of long-distance socio-economic management. The policy outlined in the laws of 1973 and 1974[64] was twofold. Yugoslavs living outside the state were extended services similar to those given to the domestic population. Through consulates and cultural centers in countries where substantial numbers of Yugoslavs worked[65] (Baskin 1986: 74) they were offered education in all Yugoslav languages, media content including newspapers, radio, and TV, social welfare programs, workers' assistance, and leisure activities. As Mark Baskin put it, officials "felt that the psychological, social and political expansion of official Yugoslav organizations in Western Europe would allow the average migrant to feel as if he or she had never left Yugoslavia" (Baskin 1986: 167).

The government also encouraged return and reintegration. The Federal Committee for Labour and Employment developed a program for return migrants (Baskin 1986: 173–174). Both the Party and the League of Communists of Yugoslavia (LCY) emphasized the need to build the kind of setting that would provide returning immigrants an opportunity to find employment at home and utilize the skills and knowledge gained abroad.[66] With the OECD and other international organizations, funds and initiatives promoted investment and small businesses, the country's new economic mantra. By 1980, however, the question had lost political urgency. Laws governing foreign investment and customs

46 Seeing like an emigration state (1880–1991)

duties were eased, but the impetus for development that was expected from migrant workers' remittances and savings did not materialize (Baskin 1986: 351).

In apparent contrast with the SFRY's propensity to intervene in the lives of workers employed abroad, Tito argued that dealings with the old migration should be based on the principle of respect for sovereignty, independence, and non-intervention in the internal affairs of other states. "We must develop our collaboration with all old migrant organizations, no matter the form of organization [mutual support, cultural, sport, professional, etc.] on a national, republican, provincial and Yugoslav basis."[67] In practice, though, *Matica iseljenika Hrvatske* attempted to monitor and control migrant political activity. Organizations such as the Croatian Fraternal Union were submissive to its direction. As late as 1989, the Directorate of *Matica iseljenika Hrvatske* reported one member saying:

> I think we had to finally get rid of our illusions, still present in some here, that the CFU is our branch in the USA. Once we get rid of that, things will look easier. We have to stick to our political cooperation with the old migration which has been decided, defined and which has its document. Let's stick to that and we won't have political problems.
>
> (M.I.H. 1989: 8)

Despite the progressive liberalization of the regime from the 1970s on, secret police operations continued. The federal intelligence agencies[68] remained loyal to the regime, investigating and punishing anti-Yugoslav activities,[69] but the allegiances of the intelligence services at the republican level were more ambiguous. Although their task was to monitor and report on nationalist activities, they often became embedded in the nationalist movements that were emerging in the 1990s, and surveillance of the political emigration soon became an important source of political contacts.

The period between 1973 and 1990 was the high point of the transnationalization of Yugoslav governmental power. Three different state attributes were exported, depending on the category of the population abroad: the monopoly of violence, through the surveillance and killing of the Yugoslav Enemy Migration; the monopoly of allocation of resources, through the monitoring of workers temporarily employed abroad; and the monopoly of symbolic violence, through *Matica iseljenika Hrvatske* and the Yugoslav education extended to the old migration. These three relationships were determined by the knowledge that the different state bureaucracies gathered about them: individualized police knowledge for the first, demographic and economic statistics for the second, and the vaguely defined constituencies of pre-war organizations for the third.

This schema is a program of power, not a diagram of what was done; it represents the problematizations in which these different populations were caught and the plans the state had for them. Resistance to these policies was strong. The Yugoslav Enemy Migration managed to escape police surveillance and coercion. Workers Temporarily Employed Abroad either joined the activities of political émigrés or disregarded the Yugoslav government's advice about investing their money and returning home. The old migration's links to the homeland became attenuated as the original emigrants aged and became integrated into their countries of residence. By the mid-1980s most of these transnational Yugoslav policies were withdrawn as the state was slowly succumbing to economic and institutional collapse.

Conclusion

The long twentieth century of Yugoslav migration witnessed three governmental categorizations of Croatian populations abroad, defined by three relationships of power. The enemy émigrés' was the most uncompromising. In this form of long-distance securitization (Bigo and Guild 2005), a section of the population abroad is considered as removed from politics within the country and dealt with through surveillance and execution by security forces linked to the ministries of interior, foreign affairs, and defense. These institutional bodies delimit this category by producing individualized knowledge on political activists and organizations abroad. Techniques of power are drawn from the coercive repertoire of the state: passports, law, tribunals, prisons, and judicial and extrajudicial executions. These governmental practices are deployed in a broader modality of government that can be defined, following Foucault, as a disciplinary-sovereign movement focused on exporting the state's monopoly of violence beyond territorial borders.

The second category is the economic migrant, relabeled the worker temporarily employed abroad. This category is subdivided, first between the temporary (good) and permanent (bad) migrant and then between the investing (good) and non-investing (bad) migrant. This shifting typology reflects the changing economic interests of the state; always an anomaly with regard to normal development, labor migration was sometimes encouraged and sometimes hidden as a shameful national condition. This category of the population is reduced to its bare productive function.

Aristide Zolberg pointed to the treatment of economic migrants purely as a labor force in his discussion of Hannah Arendt's considerations on minorities and stateless individuals:

> Refugees of the type she had in mind can be thought of as persons deprived of their humanity because they are considered in terms of one dimension only, their undesirability in terms of the political calculations of rulers in their country of origin somewhat as migrant workers are deprived of humanity as a consequence of unidimensional economic calculations.
> (Zolberg 1981: 19)

The function of workers employed abroad is to produce wealth and contribute to the well-being of the population. They are dealt with through the ministries of labor and social affairs, which produce knowledge in the form of demographic, economic, and financial statistics. The objective of the state is not to allow or prohibit emigration but to tap what appears to be an inevitable, almost natural phenomenon. It represents the management of what we might call a population-wealth, with the government as both the receptacle and the redistributor of wealth. In this sense, Socialist Yugoslavia is the epitome of the welfare state, a government that "had managed to connect [itself] to a diversity of forces and groups that in different ways had long tried to shape and administer the lives of individuals in pursuit of various goals" (Rose *et al.* 2006: 87).

The form of control exercised over labor migrants is much more subtle than that over enemy emigrants. It involves access to employment abroad and to social security and pension schemes that is conditional on good behavior. The modality of government at play here is what Foucault defined as governmentality, governance through freedom and the promotion of life (2004: 112). In circumstances in which national economies are deeply integrated, this government of the monopoly of the allocation of resources operates beyond territorial limits in a form of long-distance governmentality.

The third category, the old migration of the tenth banovina and the seventh republic, is defined through cultural and national ties and set in opposition to the enemy emigration. It is conceptualized as a part of us, but abroad. The relationship ranges from the familial sympathy of folklore and cultural heritage to policies of education and control targeted at workers temporarily employed abroad. On the side of the state these are a mixture of seduction and utilization. Although in the early 1980s this connection might have seemed useless, it unexpectedly provided the grounds for the elaboration of diasporic discourse and practice in the 1990s. Indeed, this cultural relationship was linked to the continual recreation of the presence of home abroad and to the idea that populations abroad represent a potential asset or modality of influence. At the very least, Croats abroad can serve as ambassadors of their nation in the world. At stake is the exportation of the monopoly of symbolic violence and the establishment of a link in which populations abroad are objectified, being seen as both the receptacle of the official culture and the vectors of governmental power oriented toward further goals.

The account of state practices presented in this chapter demonstrates, first, that transnational identities or processes of identification are conditioned and constrained by the sending state's practices. The legitimacy of the political emigration depended on their exclusion from the territory because of their political views. Their reactions to surveillance ranged from obedience or silence to the pursuit of political activities or even direct attacks on state institutions abroad, but they were always directed at the sending state. For workers abroad and the old migration, most resistance took the form of counter-conducts, subversive activities undermining the authority of the state. Opposition to Yugoslav policies was organized through various modalities that questioned the legitimacy of the government to lead. Religious organizations provided a crucial source for alternative identifications but could not avoid constraints imposed by embassies and consulates. The transnational condition is, thus, not a state-free condition.

Second, these categorizations enabled the government to justify practices of power abroad. Labeling a section of the Yugoslav migrants enemies (Ustaše, Četnici, Fascists, Nazis) justified transnational police practices domestically and internationally. Similarly, the need to extend care to migrant workers as a section of the Yugoslav working class justified deterritorialized welfare measures. Finally, the old migration category justified the cultivation of cultural bonds through schools and folklore programs. These categorizations do not account for the migrants' condition or status; they were mainly constructed to legitimize state practices. The "unproductive migrants" of the 1930s became the "friendly" old migration after the war. A worker temporarily abroad could easily fall into the enemy migration category if he adopted or expressed the wrong political views. The categories are rhetorical, yet practical, justifications for the particular kind of state practices to be deployed to produce specific effects.

Third, although these deterritorialized practices shift over time, they build a history of practices of state attention. They stipulate and reinforce the idea that state intervention outside the territory can be legitimate, outlining patterns for state policies and practices and of ways in which emigration is conceptualized and inserted into governmental strategies.

Fourth, in these strategies we can see correlations between the transnationalization of state practices toward populations abroad and broader programs of government. The transnationalization of policies regarding emigrants is connected primarily to security practices and concerns. These concerns often come into conflict with ideas about economic development, particularly the progression from a state-controlled autarchic political economy Zolberg talks of (1981: 23) to a self-managed economic liberalism.

Finally, the level of attention given by the government to populations abroad is closely linked to matters of citizenship and national identity, in particular the tension between republican versus ethnic conceptions of belonging.

Yet, we must acknowledge, the Croatian diaspora policies of the 1990s were planned and carried out by a government that claimed to be fundamentally different from communist Yugoslavia and took power through a radical rupture of the former state. In order to understand the deterritorialized nationalist policies of the 1990s, we must look beyond earlier institutional state practices. These practices laid down a blueprint for the legitimization of claims to extraterritorial power. To understand the program and ideological agenda of the group of political actors that came to power in 1990–1991, we must investigate the transnational political field of Croatian politics, the social space generated by various actors who sought to define what Croatia should be and how Croats should be governed. That field was structured by actors who were located both inside and outside the territorial borders of Croatia and Yugoslavia.

Notes

1 I draw here on Hobsbawm and Ranger's classic title, *The Invention of Tradition* (1983), which has since been applied to other non-technological innovations, e.g., *The Invention of the Social* (Donzelot 1994), *The Invention of Populations* (Lebras and Bertaux 2000), *The Invention of the Passport* (Torypey 2000).
2 I also rely on several other scholars: Østergaard-Nielsen 2001, 2003; Basch *et al.* 1995; Glick Schiller and Fouron 1998, 1999; Levitt and de la Dehesa 2003; Smith 2003a, 2003b; Fitzgerald 2006; Schmitter Heisler 1985; Legg 2005: 148–149; Scott 1998.
3 Yugoslavia was officially called the Federal People's Republic of Yugoslavia in 1946 and changed its name to the Socialist Federal Republic of Yugoslavia in 1963.
4 Croatia-Slavonia was administered by a royal governor (Ban) appointed by Hungary. It also had a diet (Sabor), which exercised most deliberative functions. Limited executive functions were assigned to the Croatian Territorial Government (*Hrvatska zemaljska vlada*).
5 Some immigrants were recorded as Austro-Hungarians, while others were given more specific regional or ethnic labels.
6 During the *Vormärz* period which ended with the revolutionary upheaval of March 1848, in Austria alone 75 percent of the population made their living from agriculture in 1790. This number declined over the years to 71.7 percent in 1850, and to just under 50 percent by 1910 (Good 1984: 45). In Hungary, in 1780, 72 percent of the population made their living from agriculture (Macartney 1968: 167), and by 1910 the share of the agricultural population in the total population reached 62.5 percent (Good 1984: 45).

In Croatia-Slavonia, the traditional form of communal farming, the Zadruga, gradually declined under the pressure of the market economy (Tomasevich 1975: 188; Biondich 2000: 21; Lampe and Jackson 1982: 287; Jelavich 1987: 77; Čizmić 1986: 257–255). In Bosnia and Herzegovina, too, rural laborers had increasing difficulty finding employment (Lampe and Jackson 1982: 287). In Dalmatia, the situation was worsened by Phylloxera, which devastated the vineyards (Colaković 1973: 23; Nejašmić 1989: 83).
7 Zolberg noted a similar pattern in the United Kingdom starting in the mid-1820s regarding the Irish question (Zolberg 2007: 45).
8 *Služba za otpremanje osoba radničkog i seljačkog stališa u prekomorske zemlje.*
9 Following the establishment of the Service in 1891 (see note above), pursuant to the 1893 *Naredba Kraljevske hrvatsko-slavonsko-dalmatinske zemaljske vlade* [Order of the Royal Croatian-Slavonian-Dalmatian Territorial Government] an under-department for emigration, *podosjek*, was formed in the *Hrvatska zemaljska vlada* [Croatian Territorial Government], and then a section for emigration, *Odsjek za iseljavanje*.
10 By decree number 8391 of 28 February 1909. See Čizmić (1986: 264), Holjevac (1968: 40), and Banović (1987: 321).
11 This letter was published in the Croatian emigrant newspaper based in Puntarenas, Chile, *Domovina* [Homeland], 25 December 1913, in Antić (1985: 249).
12 *The National Gazette*, directed by Juraj Biankini.
13 *Zadružni savez u Splitu*.
14 In Italy, for example,

> Emigration was seen as a painless solution to the southern question: the northern elite had their liberal policy, the southern elite had their land, and emigrants were assisted in leaving, as outlined in the Faina report of the 1907–09 Parliament.
> (Cinel 1991, quoted in R. C. Smith 2003a: 738)

15 Circular migration designates a pattern of emigration, return migration, and renewed emigration over a short period of time. In this sense, circular migration encompasses several cycles of temporary migration.

16 The Croatian and Slovenian population of Istria, which after 1920 fell under Italian sovereignty, became the object of a proactive policy of nationalization; emigration of the non-Italian population was encouraged by the Fascist government (Krmac 2006: 12–13; Purini 2003).
17 The statistical data is very unreliable, in part because the category "Croats" was not used at the time. Većeslav Holjevac, a political figure and student of emigration, described the categorization for statistics after 1924: "One of the most important categories, the number of emigrants per nationality, is not recorded any more. A new term is introduced, 'Yugoslavs,' which encompasses all nationalities of the state. Foreign nationalities, Germans, Hungarians, Romanians, and Albanians are still recorded separately" (Holjevac 1968: 45–46).
18 *Narodna skupština*.
19 *Novi iseljenik* [The New Emigrant], Zagreb, 1 April 1926, in Antić 1990: 232.
20 *Zakon o iseljavanju, 30 December 1921*, and *Pravilnik o izršavanju Zakona o iseljavanju, 3 August 1922*. Its enforcement was defined by a decree of 1923.
21 According to Sabrina Ramet, "Out of 11 departments in the provincial government for Croatia and Slavonia in 1918, eight were eliminated by the king. Belgrade authorities also severely reduced the competency and powers of the Croatian Ban (governor). Later, on November 30, 1920, a royal edict dissolved the Croatian Sabor, stripping Croatia of a vital factor and symbol of its statehood" (Ramet 2006: 52).
22 *Odsjek za iseljavanje i doseljavanje*.
23 *Iseljenički interministerijalni savjetodavni odbor*.
24 *Ministarstvo socijalne politike*.
25 *Iseljenički komesarijat*.
26 "Koji se seli u prekooceanske zemlje radi zarade telesnim radom, ili koji se seli svojim rodjacima, koji su se ranje iselili pod istim uslovima." *Zakon o iseljavanju, Policijski propisi iseljavanja član 7 i 8* [Law on Emigration, Police Reports on Emigration], "Iseljenički propisi," *Svezak I*, Zagreb 1922, p. 7, in Holjevac (1968: 41). Emigrants were defined according to multiple criteria in other European countries: in Italy, Austria, and Spain by their intention to stay abroad; in France and Portugal by social class as indicated by their steamship tickets (Čizmić and Mikačić 1974: 3).
27 For example, the Kingdom of SHS had only two consulates, one in New York City and one in Chicago to cover the United States, Australia, and New Zealand (Hranilović 1987: 331; Čizmić and Mikačić 1974: 33).
28 The stated goals of the organization were

> to maintain the links with emigrants through organization or consulates, to publicize the problem of emigration, to unify emigrants and increase their solidarity for their benefit and the benefit of the homeland and finally to inform potential emigrants about opportunities, migration and return.

Debates about emigration were regularly published in the association's newspaper, *Iseljenik* (Emigrant); see "Organizacija iseljenika u Zagrebu," *Iseljenik, Službeno glasilo organizacije iseljenika u Zagrebu*, Zagreb, 1 January 1925, p. 1.
29 *Izvještaj Narodnoj skupštini za 1926/27 godinu*, Beograd 928, p. 6 (in Holjevac 1968: 42).
30 "Pitanje naše emigracije," *Iseljenik, Službeno glasilo organizacije iseljenika u Zagrebu*, Zagreb, 1 April 1925, p. 1. This view was echoed by the 1929 Emigration Conference in Split (Bartulica 1929).
31 Ibid.
32 For more about Stjepan Radić, see Biondich (2000).
33 For a broader picture of the economic situation of the Kingdom of Yugoslavia, see Lampe and Jackson (1982: 429–472).

52 *Seeing like an emigration state (1880–1991)*

34 "Iseljenička politika" (1940) [The Emigration Policy], *Godišnjak lasti Banovine Hrvatske (1939–26 olovoza 1940)* [Annual Record of the Government of Croatia], 244 (emphasis added).
35 The *Sporazum Cvetković-Maček* (Cvetković-Maček Agreement) was signed on 26 August 1939 by Yugoslav prime minister Dragiša Cvetković and Vladko Maček, the head of Croatia's Peasant Party, which was the main Croatian political force at the time. The agreement resulted from Croatian politicians' pressure for more autonomy within the institutions of the SHS. The agreement's main outcome was the reorganization of the administrative units of the SHS, including the creation of the Banovina of Croatia, which grouped most of Yugoslavia's Croats under one administrative unit. For more on these reforms and political changes, see Ramet (2006: 104–109).
36 "Iseljenička politika" [The emigration Policy] (1940), *Godišnjak banske vlasti Banovine Hrvatske (1939–26. kolovoza 1940)* [Annual Record of the Government of Banovina Croatia], 244 (emphasis added).
37 These organizations formalized ideas that had been circulating for a long time. Stjepan Radić himself had devoted a book to the emigrant question (Radić 1904).
38 This definition of nation has more in common with the view of national belonging that is traceable to J. G. von Herder (1784), which emphasizes ethno-cultural ties, and contrasts with the view identified with Ernest Renan (1882), which emphasizes common citizenship in the polity.
39 The term in Croatian refers to those Croats who chose to become Hungarians during the Austro-Hungarian domination of Croatia, Istria, and Dalmatia.
40 *Federativna Narodna Republika Jugoslavija.*
41 The last census before the war took place on 31 March 1931 registering 13,934,038 people living in Yugoslavia. According to projections published by the General State Statistics Bureau on 31 March 1945, the population of Yugoslavia would have been 16,601,493 had it not suffered the losses of World War II. See *Demographic statistics, Calculation of population of Yugoslavia for 1941 and 1945*, Series II, Issue 2 (1945). Belgrade: State Statistics Bureau of the Federation of Yugoslavia (electronic library of the Statistical Office of the Republic of Serbia, Available: http://pod2.stat.gov.rs/ObjavljenePublikacije/G1945/pdf/G19454001.pdf (accessed 29 May 2016).
42 The Cominform was the international communist organization from which Yugoslavia withdrew and was then expelled.
43 *Organ zaštite naroda.*
44 Federal agencies included the Military Intelligence Agency (*Vojna obavještajna služba*) and the Counter-Espionage Agency (*Kontra-obavještajna služba*), later called the Security Agency of the Yugoslav People's Army (*Služba sigurnosti JNA*), part of the Secretariat for National Defense (*Savezni sekretarijat za narodnu obranu*), and the Agency for Intelligence and Documentation (*Služba za istraživanje i dokumentaciju*), part of the Secretariat for Internal Affairs (*Savezni sekretarijat za unutrašnje poslove*).
45 At the republic level, operations were conducted by the *Uprava državne bezbednosti*, which was later called *Služba državne sigurnosti* in Croatia and *Služba državne bezbednosti* in Serbia.
46 During the 1990s, the memory of Bleiburg was politicized to portray Croats as the victims of "Yugo-Serb" oppression during World War II. On competition for victim status, see MacDonald 2002.
47 The Domobrani were the regular army of the Independent State of Croatia (1941–1945).
48 *Jugoslovenska narodna armija.*
49 For the concept of securitization, see Wæver (1995). For an overview of the literature on Critical Approaches to Security in Europe, see c.a.s.e. collective 2006.
50 On this question, see Hudelist 2004: 450.
51 Uputstvo o postupanju pri zapošljavanju u inostranstvu, *Službeni list SFRJ* [Official Gazette of SFRY], n° 613, 42/1963. See also Zaključci Predsjedništva SFRJ i

Predsjedništva SKJ o problemima zapošljavanja u inozemstvu (1977), *Zapošljavanje i udruženi rad*, II (3–4).
52 Zakon o putnim ispravama jugoslavenskih državljana, *Službeni list SFRJ*, n° 224, 12/1963.
53 Zakon o dopunama Osnovnog zakona o organizaciji i financiranju zapošljavanja, *Službeni list SFRJ* [Official Gazette of SFRY] n° 566, 47/1966.
54 "Radnici na privremenom radu u inozemstvu"; see the provision in *Zakon o dopuni Zakona o privredno-planskim merama u 1965 godini* [The Act Amending the Act on the Economic Plan Measures for the Year 1965] *Službeni list SFRJ* [Official Gazette of SFRY] n° 291, 15/1965 and *Zakon o dopunama Osnovnog zakona o organizaciji i financiranju zapošljavanja* [The act amending the act on the organization and finance of employment], *Službeni list SFRJ* [Official Gazette of SFRY] n° 566, 47/1966.
55 Bilateral agreements were signed with France (1965), Austria and Sweden (1966), Federal Republic of Germany (FRG) (1969), and Belgium, Holland, Luxembourg, and Australia (1970). Similar agreements regarding social security were signed earlier with France (1950), Belgium and Luxembourg (1954), and Switzerland (1962), and later with Sweden and FRG (1969) and Norway (1974).
56 The 1971 Croatian Spring echoed other social movements in Europe and in the Communist bloc. For more on the ideas put forward in 1971, see Šošić (1994) and Brleković (2002). The movement was crushed by Tito, but its claims were taken into account. See Tanner (1997) and, for a participant's perspective, Tripalo (1989).
57 In an interview with *Der Spiegel*, Muammar Gaddafi expressed his envy of the Yugoslav privilege: "Tito sends agents to Germany with the order to eliminate the Croatian opponents that live there. Nevertheless, Tito's reputation in Germany isn't damaged at all. Why does Tito have the right to do what I am not allowed to?" (Babić 1990).
58 Opunomoćstvo za jugoslovenske radnike na privremenom radu u inozemstvu (Žunec and Domišljanović 2000: 36).
59 Zaključci Predsjeništva SFRJ i Predsjedništva SKJ o problemima zapošljavanja u inozemstvu, *Zapošljavanje i udruženi rad,* II (3–4/1977), pp. 1–4.
60 SAWPY, initially the People's Front, was a para-political mass organization set up by the League of Communists of Yugoslavia (LCY) to counterbalance and complement the party's control of government, federal, and national institutions.
61 "Doznake radnika i za otvaranje novih radnih mjesta," *Vjesnik*, 16 February 1973, p. 4.
62 The Territorial Defense (*Teritorijalna obrana*) was a regional military corps not unlike the Home Guard during World War II in Britain. It was set up after the 1968 Soviet invasion of Czechoslovakia. See Đorđević (1986).
63 In line with the official formulation characterizing migrants as "an internal part of the Yugoslav working class" and not as permanent emigrants, migration policy is treated both in the Commission on Employment as well as in the Commission for International Activity.
64 "Zakon o osnovnim uslovima za privremeno zapošljavanje i zaštitu jugoslovenskih građana u inozemstvu [The act on the basic conditions for temporary employment and protection of Yugoslav citizens employed abroad]," *Službeni list SFRJ* [Official Gazette of SFRY] n° 414, 33/1973 and "Društveni dogovor o privremenom zapošljavanju jugoslovenskih građana u inozemstvu i vraćanju jugoslovenskih građana sa rada u inozemstvu" [Social Agreement on the Temporary Employment of Yugoslav Citizens Abroad and Return of Yugoslav Citizens from Employment Abroad], *Službeni list SFRJ* [Official Gazette of SFRY] n° 758, 39/1974.
65 Between 1969 and 1975 Yugoslavia opened 17 new consulates (13 in FRG) and five cultural information centers.
66 The LCY, a body politically stronger than the Party, urged in 1982 "quicker creation and improvement of conditions for domestic employment of our citizens who are temporarily employed abroad" (Migracije, XI (11), p. 406 in Baskin 1986: 335).

67 Predsjedništvo Savezne Konferencije SSRNJ (1977) "Osnove daljnje suradnje s iseljenicima i njihovim potomcima" [Basis of Further Collaboration with Emigrants and their Descendants] in Krsnik (1989).
68 The Agency for Information and Documentation (SID) within the Secretariat of External Affairs, as well as the two military agencies under the umbrella of *Uprava sigurnosti/ bezbednosti*.
69 For example, in 1985, 70-year-old Mirko Sunić, a retired judge, was sentenced to four years in jail and his daughter Mirna Sunić to ten months for possession of the emigrant journal *Nova Hrvatska* (Kušan 2000: 205).

References

Alfirević, P. (1978) "Publikacije matica iseljenika Jugoslavije i informisanje iseljeništva" [Publications of the emigrant Foundation of Yugoslavia and Information for Emigrants] in *Iseljeništvo naroda i narodnosti Jugoslavije* [Emigration of Nations and Nationalities of Yugoslavia] (pp. 605–610), Zagreb: Zavod za migracije i narodnosti.

Antić, L. (1985) "Prilog istraživanju austrijske iseljeničke politike i zakonodavstva kao činilaca masovnog iseljavanja iz dalmacije pred prvi svjetski rat," *Zadarska revija*, 34(2–3), pp. 242–254.

Antić, L. (1990) "Iseljenička politika stare Jugoslavenske Države" in Šehić, N., ed., *Migracije i Bosna i Hercegovina* (pp. 229–235), Sarajevo: Institut za istoriju u Sarajevu—Institut za proučavanje nacionalnih odnosa.

Antić, L. (1997) *Croats and America*, Zagreb: Hrvatska sveučilišna naklada.

Babić, J. (1990) "Ubojice na službenom putu" [Killers on a Business Trip], *Danas*, pp. 26–27.

Banac, I. (1988) *With Stalin against Tito: Cominformist Splits in Yugoslav Communism*, Ithaca: Cornell University Press.

Banović, B. (1987) "Emigracijska politika Austro-Ugarske i iseljavanje iz Hrvatske u razdoblju 1867–1914," *Migracijske teme*, 3(3–4), pp. 313–323.

Bartulica, M. (1929) *Iseljenička konferencija u Splitu*, Zagreb: Savez organizacija iseljenika u Zagrebu.

Bartulica, M. (1933) *Iseljenički kongres u Sarajevu*, Zagreb: Savez organizacija iseljenika u Zagrebu.

Basch, L. G., Glick Schiller, N., and Szanton Blanc, C. (1995) *Nations Unbound: Transnational Projects, Postcolonial Predicaments, and Deterritorialized Nation States*, Basel; UK: Gordon and Breach.

Baskin, M. A. (1986) "Political Innovation and Policy Implementation in Yugoslavia: The Case of Worker Migration Abroad," PhD dissertation, University of Michigan, 1986.

Baučić, I. (1975) *The Social Aspects of External Migration of Workers and the Yugoslav Experience in the Social Protection of Migrants*, Zagreb: Center for Migration Studies.

Bigo, D. and Guild, E. (2005) "Policing at a Distance: Schengen Visa Policies" in Bigo, D. and Guild, E., eds., *Controlling Frontiers: Free Movement into and Within Europe* (pp. 234–263), Aldershot, UK; Burlington, VT: Ashgate.

Bilandžić, D. (1985) *Historija Socijalističke Federativne Republike Jugoslavije: Glavni Procesi 1918–1985* [History of the Socialist Federal Republic of Yugoslavia: Main processes 1918–1985], Zagreb: Školska knjiga.

Biondich, M. (2000) *Stjepan Radic, the Croat Peasant Party, and the Politics of Mass Mobilization, 1904–1928*, Toronto; Buffalo: University of Toronto Press.

Brleković, J. (2002) *Hrvatski Tjednik, Bibliografija* [The Croatian Weekly, a Bibliography], Zagreb: Matica Hrvatska.

c.a.s.e. collective (2006) "Critical Approaches to Security in Europe, A Networked Manifesto," *Security Dialogue*, 37(4), pp. 443–487.

Cinel, D. (1991) *The National Integration of Italian Return Migration, 1870–1929*, New York: Cambridge University Press.

Čizmić, I. (1974–1975) "O iseljavanju iz Hrvatske u razdoblju 1880–1914," *Historijski Zbornik (Zagreb)*, 27–28, pp. 27–46.

Čizmić, I. (1986) "Emigration from Yugoslavia Prior to World War II" in Glazier, I. A. and De Rosa, L., eds., *Migration Across Time and Nations: Population Mobility in Historical Contexts* (pp. 255–267), New York: Holmes & Meier.

Čizmić, I. (1990) "Emigration from Croatia, 1880–1914" in Puskás, J., ed., *Overseas Migration from East-Central and Southeastern Europe, 1880–1940* (p. 246), Budapest: Akadémiai Kiadó.

Čizmić, I. and Mikačić, V. (1974) *Neki suvremeni problemi iseljeništva iz SR Hrvatske, Teme o iseljeništvu*, Zagreb: Centar za istraživanje migracija Instituta za geografiju Sveučilišta u Zagrebu.

Colaković, B. (1973) *Yugoslav Migration to America*, San Francisco: Rand & Research Associates.

Doder, M. (1989) *Jugoslavenska neprijateljska emigracija* [The Yugoslav Enemy Migration], Zagreb: Centar za informacije i publicitet.

Đorđević, O. (1986) *Leksikon Bezbednosti* [Lexicon of Security], Beograd: Partizanska knjiga.

Fitzgerald, D. (2006) "Inside the Sending State: The Politics of Mexican Emigration Control," *International Migration Review*, 40(2), pp. 259–293.

Foucault, M. (2004) *Sécurité, territoire, population: Cours au Collège de France (1977–1978)*, Paris: Gallimard, Seuil.

Glick Schiller, N. and Fouron, G. (1998) "Transnational Lives and National Identities: The Identity Politics of Haitian Immigrants" in Smith, M. P. and Guarnizo, L., eds., *Transnationalism from Below* [electronic resource] (pp. 130–161), New Brunswick, NJ: Transaction Publishers.

Glick Schiller, N. and Fouron, G. (1999) "Terrains of Blood and Nation: Haitian Transnational Social Fields," *Ethnic and Racial Studies*, 22(2), pp. 340–366.

Godler, V. and Pavić, S. (1975) "Pitanja radno-pravne zaštite jugoslovenskih radnika na privremenom radu u inostranstvu" [Labor and Legal Questions Concerning the Protection of Yugoslav Workers Temporarily Employed Abroad], *Socijalna politika i socijalni rad* [Social Policy and Social Work], XI(1–2), pp. 7–22.

Good, D. F. (1984) *The Economic Rise of the Habsburg Empire, 1750–1914*, Berkeley, Los Angeles, London: University of California Press.

Heršak, E. and Mesić, M. (1990) "L'espace migratoire de Yougoslavie: historique des migrations yougoslaves," *Revue Européenne des Migrations Internationales*, 6(2), pp. 27–64.

Holjevac, V. (1968) *Hrvati Izvan Domovine*, Zagreb: Matica Hrvatska.

Hranilović, N. (1987) "Iseljenička politika i služba u Jugoslaviji između dva rata," *Migracijske teme*, III(3–4), pp. 325–334.

Hudelist, D. (2004) *Tuđman, Biografija* [Tuđman, a Biography], Zagreb: Profil International.

Iseljenička Politika [The Emigration Record] (1940) *Godišnjak banske vlasti Banovine Hrvatske (1939–26, kolovoza 1940)* [Annual Record of the Government of Banovina Croatia], Zagreb: Narodne Novine.

Jelavich, B. (1987) *Modern Austria: Empire and Republic, 1815–1986*, Cambridge; New York: Cambridge University Press.
Jonjić, P. and Lausić, A. (1998) *Izvješća Iseljeničkog komesarijata u Zagrebu 1922–1939*, Zagreb: Institut za migracije i narodnosti.
Karaman, I. (1974) "Osnovna obilježa razvitka industrijske privrede u sjevernoj Hrvatkoj do Prvoga svjetskog rata," *Acta historico-oeconomica Iugoslaviae (Zagreb)*, I, pp. 37–60.
Kann, R. A. (1950) *A History of the Habsburg Empire, 1526–1918*, Berkeley, CA: University of California Press.
Krmac, D. (2006) "Dalla Jugoslavia all'Argentina: il travaso delle direttrici migratorie nel caso istriano (1918–1939)," translated by Università degli studi di Pavia, Facoltà di Scienze Politiche, Lombardy, Italy.
Krsnik, V. (1989) "Previše improvizacija" [Too Much Improvisation], *Danas*, 3 November 1989.
Kušan, J. (2000) *Bitka za novu Hrvatsku* [The Struggle for the New Croatia], Rijeka: Otokar Keršovani.
Lampe, J. R. (2000) *Yugoslavia as History: Twice There Was a Country*, 2nd ed., Cambridge; New York: Cambridge University Press.
Lampe, J. R. and Jackson, M. R. (1982) *Balkan Economic History, 1550–1950: From Imperial Borderlands to Developing Nations* (The Joint Committee on Eastern Europe Publication Series; no. 10), Bloomington: Indiana University Press.
Lapenna, I. (1972) "Main Features of the Yugoslav Constitution 1946–1971," *The International and Comparative Law Quarterly*, 21(2), pp. 209–229.
Legg, S. (2005) "Foucault's Population Geographies: Classifications, Biopolitics and Governmental Spaces," *Population, Space and Place*, 11(3), pp. 137–156.
Levitt, P. and de la Dehesa, R. (2003) "Transnational Migration and the Redefinition of the State: Variations and Explanations," *Ethnic And Racial Studies*, 26(4), p. 25.
Macartney, C. A. (1968) *The Habsburg Empire, 1790–1918*, London: Weidenfeld & Nicolson.
MacDonald, D. B. (2002) *Balkan Holocausts? Serbian and Croatian Victim Centred Propaganda and the War in Yugoslavia*, Manchester: Manchester University Press.
M.I.H. (1956) *Matica: iseljeniécki kalendar*, Zagreb: Glavni odbor Matice iseljenika Hrvatske.
M.I.H. (1968) *Izjestaj o radu glavnog odbora za vremensko razdoblje 1966–1968* [Report on the Work of the Head Committee during the period 1966–1968], Zagreb: Matica Iseljenika Hrvatske.
M.I.H. (1989) *Zapisnici sa 23. do 28. sjednice predsjednistva (1988–1989)* [Minutes from the 23rd to the 28th Meeting of the Presidency (1988–1989)], Zagreb: Matica Iseljenika Hrvatske.
Milenkovitch, D. D. (1971) *Plan and Market in Yugoslav Economic Thought*, New Haven: Yale University Press.
Milenkovitch, D. D. (1977) "The Case of Yugoslavia," *The American Economic Review* 67(1) (Papers and Proceedings of the Eighty-ninth Annual Meeting of the American Economic Assocation), pp. 55–60.
Nejašmić, I. (1989) "Depopulacija-značajke prostorno-demografskog procesa," *Zapošljavanje i udruženi rad*, 14(2), pp. 169–181.
Østergaard-Nielsen, E. (2001) *The Politics of Migrants' Transnational Political Practices*, translated by Ssrc/Esrc/Princeton University, New Jersey, USA.

Østergaard-Nielsen, E. (2003) *International Migration and Sending Countries: Perceptions, Policies, and Transnational Relations*, Basingstoke, UK; New York: Palgrave Macmillan.
Prpić, J. (1971) *The Croatian Immigrants in America*, New York: Philosophical Library.
Purini, P. (2003) "L'emigrazione non italiana dalla Venezia Giulia tra le due guerre" in Cecotti, F. and Mattiusi, D., eds., *Un'altra terra un'altra vita. L'emigrazione isontina in Sud America tra storia e memoria 1878–1790* (pp. 87–107), Gradisca d'Isonzo: Centro isontino di Ricerca e Documentazione storica e Sociale "Leopoldo Gasparini."
Radić, S. (1904) *Moderna kolonizacija i Slaveni, Poučna knjižnica Matice hrvatske*, Zagreb: Matica Hrvatska.
Ramet, S. P. (2006) *The Three Yugoslavias: State-Building and Legitimation, 1918–2004*, Woodrow Wilson Center Press, Bloomington, IN; Chesham: Indiana University Press; Combined Academic Distributor.
Rose, N., O'Malley, P. and Valverde M. (2006) "Governmentality," *Annual Review of Law and Social Science*, 2(1), pp. 83–104.
Rusinow, D. (1977) *The Yugoslav Experiment*, Berkeley, CA: University of California Press.
Schmitter Heisler, B. (1985) "Sending Countries and the Politics of Emigration and Destination," *International Migration Review*, 19 (3rd Special Issue: Civil Rights and the Sociopolitical Participation of Migrants), pp. 469–484.
Scott, J. C. (1998) *Seeing Like a State: How Certain Schemes to Improve the Human Condition Have Failed* (Yale Agrarian Studies), New Haven: Yale University Press.
Šidak, J., Gross, M., Karaman, I., and Šepić, D. (1968) *Povijest hrvatskog naroda*, Zagreb: Udžbenici Sveučilišta u Zagrebu.
Šošić, Hrvoje (1994) "Hrvatski tjednik i 1971. Godina" [Croatian Weekly and 1971], *Kolo Matice Hrvatske*, 11/12, pp. 1163–1190.
Smith, R. C. (2003a) "Diasporic Memberships in Historical Perspective: Comparative Insights from the Mexican, Italian and Polish Cases," *The International Migration Review: IMR*, 37(3), pp. 724–759.
Smith, R. C. (2003b) "Migrant Membership as an Instituted Process: Transnationalization, the State and the Extra-Territorial Conduct of Mexican Politics," *International Migration Review: IMR*, 37(2), pp. 297–343.
Tanner, M. (1997) *Croatia: A Nation Forged in War*, London: Yale University Press.
Tomasevich, J. (1975) *Peasants, Politics, and Economic Change in Yugoslavia*, New York: Kraus Reprint Co.
Tripalo, M. (1989) *Hrvatsko Proljeće* [Croatian Spring], Zagreb: Globus.
US Immigration Commission (1911) *Reports of the Immigration Commission (1907–1910)*, Washington: Government Publishing Office.
Vedriš, M. (1981) "Pozitivni i negativni učinci vanjskih migracija" [Positive and Negative Effects of International Migrations], *Migracije*, X (12), pp. 439–444.
Vijeće BK za hrvatsku emigraciju (1982) *Crkva i hrvatsko iseljeništvo* [The Church and Croatian Emigration], Zagreb: Kršćanska sadašnjost.
Vucinich, W. S., Tomasevich, J., and Stanford University (1969) *Contemporary Yugoslavia: Twenty Years of Socialist Experiment*, Berkeley, CA: University of California Press.
Vukušić, B. (2002) *Tajni rat Udbe protiv hrvatskoga iseljeništva*, Zagreb: Klub hrvatskih povratnika iz iseljeništva.
Wæver, O. (1995) "Securitization and Desecuritization" in Lipschutz, R. D., ed., *On Security*, New York, Chichester: Columbia University Press.

Wank, S. (1993) *The Nationalities Question in the Habsburg Monarchy: Reflections on the Historical Record*, Working Paper No. 93-3, University of Minnesota Center for Austrian Studies.

Zimmerman, W. (1987) *Open Borders, Nonalignment, and the Political Evolution of Yugoslavia*, Princeton, NJ: Princeton University Press.

Zolberg, A. (1978) "International Migration Policies in a Changing World System" in McNeill, W. H. and Adams, R., eds., *Human Migration: Patterns and Policies*, Bloomington, IN: Indiana University Press.

Zolberg, A. (1981) "International Migrations in Political Perspective" in Kritz, M. M., Keely, C. B., and Tomasi, S. M., eds., *Global Trends in Migration: Theory and Research on International Population Movements*, 1st ed., Staten Island, NY: Center for Migration Studies.

Zolberg, A. (2007) "The Exit Revolution" in Green, N. L. and Weil, F., eds., *Citizenship and Those Who Leave: The Politics of Emigration and Expatriation* (p. 318), Urbana: University of Illinois Press.

Žunec, O. and Domišljanović, D. (2000) *Obavještajno-sigurnosne službe Republike Hrvatske: stanje i načela preustroja za razdoblje konsolidacije demokracije* [Security and Intelligence Agencies of the Republic of Croatia: State and Principles of Reorganization During the Period of Democratic Consolidation], Zagreb: Naklada Jesenski i Turk.

3 Croatian diaspora nationalism and the transnational political field (1945–1987)

The previous chapter focused on state categorizations and on the establishment of differentiated relations between the Croatian and Yugoslav governments and its population abroad. Over the course of the twentieth century, these relations occupied transnational spaces of power; entire sections of the population living abroad were governed as if they were still located within the territory of Yugoslavia. Yet every practice of government is met by forms of resistance, every attempt to organize conducts is matched by what Foucault defined as "counter-conducts," namely "struggles against the ways to conduct others" (2004: 205). In this chapter, I analyze counter-conducts to long-distance governmentality, and highlight alternative rationalizations that developed in the Croatian transnational political field. More precisely, I analyze elements of the general relationship between "diaspora" and "nationalism," and the emergence of what I term "post-territorial nationalism."[1] The evolution of the Croatian transnational political field demonstrates that one of the responses to Yugoslavia's deterritorialized policies has been the elaboration of a nationalist synthesis, which takes into consideration the transnational dimension and transcends territorial borders.

This chapter puts forward two main ideas. First, it shows how the diaspora policies of the 1990s in Croatia are firmly rooted in the right and extreme right political traditions. This tradition has progressively evolved throughout the second half of the twentieth century partly under the influence of long-distance Yugoslav policies described in the previous chapter, and partly through other international political evolutions.

Second, and again, contrary to what can be found in the literature on the links between exile, diasporic experience, and nationalism, is that a "diaspora's" degree of nationalism is defined not by the diasporic condition as such, nor the integration or the missed integration in the host society. What is key is the interaction between the *habitus* of social agents and an objectively structured field, with its rules, its divisions, and its legitimate and illegitimate modes of carrying out politics. While most of the literature understands the Croatian diaspora as the paradigmatic "nationalist diaspora,"[2] a detailed analysis of Croatian diasporic institutions highlights much more complex and contradictory dynamics. I thus show that, until approximately 1987, a snapshot of the Croatian transnational political field would have led to the anticipation of a peaceful democratic transition from communism—similar to the one that took place in Poland or in Czechoslovakia in the 1990s—rather than the violent nationalist politics and subsequent war. It is therefore most of all through field effects, through a set of relationships of power which have structured transnationally the possibility of the actors in question, that the idea of a transnational nationalism emerged.

Whereas the majority of the literature on the Croatian "diaspora" follows the bureaucratic categorizations of the state or the actors themselves, for instance limiting the study of the transnational political field to organizations that are self-defined as "political" or described by the state as "economic," this chapter includes the "old migration," the "political emigration" and the "workers temporarily abroad," arguing how these categories are mutually constituted. Chapter 1 showed that the political evolution of the different actors in the transnational political field can only be explained in a relational way. Contrary to those who affirm the primacy of the actor's rationality or political project and those who emphasize only the structural conditions for the possibility of politics, I show that the evolution of diasporic actors can be understood only through a sociology (1) of the positions and position-taking of diasporic actors; (2) of sending and receiving states' structuration of the field and (3) of the interactions between the *habitus* and the evolving structures of the field.

1945–1962: a field marked by the ideological divide

From 1945 to 1962, the Croatian transnational political field was structured around the division between communists and anti-communists. This opposition was structured by two main elements. First, the inner political field—that is the political field circumscribed by Yugoslavia's borders—and the outer political field—i.e., the political field located outside these borders—were strictly divided. This division was linked to an autarkic policy of the early years of the regime, enforced through strict police rule. Second, the outside field was structured around two main positions, which broadly corresponded to waves of migration and socio-demographic groups: on the one hand supporters of Tito's Yugoslavia, composed largely of pre-1945 migrants, on the other hand Ustaše and moderate nationalists, mostly the new migration wave from Yugoslavia.

In 1945, when the first émigrés fleeing communism arrived in Argentina or the United States, they often encountered an already established and numerically strong Croatian presence. Smaller numbers were present in Australia, Canada, and European countries (Antić 1997; Holjevac 1968). Nearly all pre-1945 migrants came from rural areas of today's Croatia and Bosnia-Herzegovina, and occupied a low rank in their countries of arrival, mostly as industrial workers (Nejasmić 1989).[3] By 1945, most of these Croats had acquired citizenship, and some of them were already children of the first migration wave of 1880–1914.

The new emigrants had a different socio-professional background. Most of them were educated, and had been doctors, lawyers, professors or religious dignitaries back in the homeland. Some of them came from Croatia itself, but many came from Herzegovina. They mostly left because they were anti-communist or linked to the

Ustaša regime, or because staying in Yugoslavia was too risky. As legally "displaced persons," they fled Yugoslavia over land toward refugee camps in neighboring countries from which they moved to other destinations. It is now known that the Catholic Church helped many *Ustaša* dignitaries to flee. Krunoslav Draganović in particular is known to have organized the trip to Buenos Aires for Ante Pavelić, the Nazi puppet leader, along with Nazis and fascists from Germany, Italy and other European countries (Aarons and Loftus, 1991). Countries accepted them according to different quotas, and gave them different possibilities of engaging in politics.

However, not all opponents of Tito's Yugoslavia fled. Some maintained hope that military operations would topple the newborn communist regime. Some military formations launched rear-guard guerrilla operations from Austria and Italy, but by 1946–1947 these *Križari* (crusaders) units were ambushed by Yugoslav secret services and imprisoned (Hockenos 2003: 29). By those years, the international context had closed the window of opportunity for anti-communist forces to come back to power. The West was behind Tito, and had largely supported him in the last phase of the war. In this sense, political emigrants from Yugoslavia—unlike other emigrants from the Eastern bloc—were not an asset for Western regimes (Glamočak 1997: 58, 62).

The Yugoslav authorities officially divided Yugoslavs abroad into the two monolithic categories of the "old migration" and the "Enemy Yugoslav Emigration." But the sociological reality of the groups abroad was complex and dynamic. Croats abroad had a long history of contentious political mobilization for the homeland.[4] For example, internal division struck the Croatian Fraternal Union (CFU) in the United States (the largest Croatian association, with more than 50,000 subscribers).[5] The CFU was a traditional "old migration association," whose leaders "were often middle class people with minimal education from the ranks of the working men and women, tradesmen or students" (Čizmić 2000: 255). On top of the inner divisions, the hostland's authorities closely monitored these associations. In the United States, although Tito was "a friend," it was hard to support a communist organization in the midst of the McCarthyist persecutions. Communist organizations such as the American Slav Congress (ASC) or Louis Adamić's Yugoslav Relief Committee (YRC) were disgraced. In what was left of the communist movement in the USA, the Tito–Stalin break further marginalized the Yugoslavs within the CPUSA.[6]

Therefore, at the end of the war, the political position of the CFU was uncomfortable. In 1949, the CFU was openly accused of pro-Yugoslavism, and as an organization caught up simultaneously in two political fields it had to address multiple constituencies in a difficult exercise:

> We recognize but one Flag and but one authority and that is the Flag and the Constitution of the United States [...]. We have a tender regard, too, for the homeland of our fathers, but in any test of allegiance, in any question of loyalty, we assure you all that we stand unswervingly behind this Country and will prove it again as we have in the past.
>
> (Prpić 1971: 316)

Throughout its post-World War II history, the CFU embraced a clear position in the transnational political field. First, as it could not engage in politics under its "fraternal union" legal status, it was officially apolitical, although one of the central organizations in the field. But second, and more importantly, it was first and foremost an *American* association. Its loyalty and the loyalty of its members was with the USA, and apart from a "tender regard" toward the homeland, it relied on the clear division between borders and allegiances.

What Yugoslavia considered as the Yugoslav Enemy Migration (YNE) was actually composed of two rival camps who both self-defined as "political exiles." The stake of the struggle was the representation of the "legitimate" authority abroad. Democratically-minded nationalists already had a voice in the pre-1945 émigré circles, but the shock of the communist massacres (such as Bleiburg) and the first signs of authoritarianism brought new sections of the "old migration" to a more suspicious attitude toward the newborn Federal People's Republic of Yugoslavia (FPRY). In March 1946, the United Croatians of America and Canada was founded in Cleveland as a reaction to the wave of pro-Yugoslavism. It united, among others, the Croatian Catholic Union (CCU), the CFU (paradoxically), *Hrvatsko Kolo*, and the American Branch of the Croatian Peasant Party (HSS-I). The CFU, led by Ivan Butković remained the most influential group in the umbrella organization and reached 71,000 members in 1947, with access to more than $15 million.

But the post-1945 wave of migration had brought new players to the political field, who considered themselves to be different from the old migration because of their "refugee" status. They did not consider themselves as migrants, but rather clung to the group identity of "political exiles." This transnational group of educated exiles who had fled the country gathered mostly around journals and clubs. One of the major journals of this group was *Nova Hrvatska* (New Croatia), established by Jakša Kušan in London. The establishment of a bulletin in 1958 and then a monthly review was intended to challenge the dominance of the *Ustaša* organization's propaganda in the refugee camps in Europe (Kušan 2000: 22). It gathered various nationalist intellectuals[7] disappointed by the brutality and failure of the *Ustaša* regime. *Nova Hrvatska* was quickly accepted by the majority of groups as one of the most respected Croatian publications abroad, and was supported by both pro-Yugoslav and pro-*Ustaša* leaders.[8] Whereas most émigré papers hardly reached 4,000 subscribers, at its height it reached 20,000 worldwide (Kuzmanović 1990: 41).[9]

As the editor Jakša Kušan explained, the journal did not have a single political line and worked more as a platform than an ideological organ. It managed to gather views from the democratic left (a rare occurrence in the political emigration groups) to the anti-Ustasha nationalists.[10] A good example of such stances is Kušan's 1962 *Open Letter to the Croatian communists*,[11] directly addressed to the Croatian members of the communist party in Yugoslavia. The letter published in *Nova Hrvatska* raised several points which would become central to most moderate Croatian nationalists in the following decades. Kušan hence argued,

We don't want to underestimate the meaning of ideological commitment for the individual man, but we believe that today the ideological struggle is a secondary problem. The most important thing is that all Croats work for Croatia.

(2000: 173)

It further called Croatian communists "not to forget the vital interests of their nation,"[12] by halting, for example, the "financial exploitation" of Croatia by Serbia and Montenegro. It also formulated another central idea of Croatian nationalism, that "strong forces push Croatia towards the West, while they push Belgrade the other way,"[13] and called for a democratic, independent Croatia to join the European nations. However, contending that ideological divides were secondary and that it was possible to distinguish Croatian and Serbian communists was an idea which, even in 1962, was too much to stomach for many, and Kušan was flooded with letters expressing this disagreement (2000: 174).

Those who could not agree with Kušan's positions were a small, distinct group in *Ustaša* émigré circles, composed of the dignitaries of the Pavelić regime and their sympathizers. After the 1945 defeat they were marked by excessive factionalism, and divided into three groups. In Argentina, after several attempts, Ante Pavelić and his loyalists founded with Stjepan Hefer the Croatian Liberation Movement (HOP—*Hrvatski Oslobodilački Pokret*) in 1956. Although it claimed to be the only legitimate Croatian organization and the continuation of the Independent State of Croatia (NDH), its political activities soon shrank to nostalgic gatherings and celebrations of 10 April (the anniversary of the Bleiburg massacre) and the anniversary of the pro-Nazi independent state (Čizmić 2000: 427; Meštrović 2003: 158). In 1950 the *Ustaša* circles published the political and literary journal *Hrvatska Revija* (Croatian Review), founded by Antun Bonifačić and Vinko Nikolić. Nikolić would later on abandon his support for *Ustaša* organizations, and acquire the reputation of a moderate. Bonifačić migrated to the USA and founded a branch of HOP under the name "Croatian Guardians of Liberty, Inc. for the United States of America." As in Argentina, the small organization was centered around a few rituals, such as the 10 April celebration and annual public demonstrations against Yugoslavia (Čizmić 2000: 428–429). Bonifačić then moved to Chicago and joined a group of Franciscan friars from Herzegovina organized around Dominik Mandić, to edit their journal, *Danica* (Meštrović 2003: 57, 158). This group openly claimed the lineage of the *Ustaša* regime, and sported an ideology that had not changed since 1941: they advocated an independent, *Ustaša*-controlled "Great Croatia,"[14] sharing an anti-Serbian resentment but putting their hatred of communism above all.

A second openly *Ustaša* organization, the Croatian National Council (HNO-j *Hrvatski Narodni Odbor*), was led by Branko Jelić[15] in Germany. Although his role in active politics was limited, he was respected as an intellectual figure of the movement in the 1930s, and his journal *Hrvatska Država* (the Croatian State) enjoyed a large diffusion (4,000) among radical émigré circles, sharing almost the same ideas as its counterparts in Latin and North America (Meštrović 2003: 58).

64 Croatian transnational nationalism (1945–1987)

Finally, in Spain, a third heir of the *Ustaša* regime, Vjekoslav "Maks" Luburić, created the Croatian National Resistance (*Hrvatski Narodni Otpor—* HNO-1, or Otpor) and the journal *Drina* in 1955. Luburić was a dark figure in the *Ustaša* regime, gaining notoriety as the director of the concentration camp at Jasenovac, where between 70,000 and 500,000 Serbs and Jews died.[16] Yet Luburić had been disappointed by the *Ustaša* regime, and considered the other organizations useless and corrupt (Meštrović 2003: 57, 174).

While Pavelić's HOP and Jelić's HNO had very much maintained and reproduced the principle of division of the Croatian political field, namely the fundamental opposition to communists and Ustaše, Luburić had developed two different ideas. First, impressed by Spanish dictator Francisco Franco's policy of national reconciliation after the Spanish civil war, Luburić elaborated the idea of an all-Croat national reconciliation of communists and Ustaše (what he defined the "Croatian pacification"; *hrvatsko izmirenje*). Second, for the first time in the course of Croatian nationalist thought, Luburić formulated the thesis of an "all-Croat political organization across the world which would bring all Croats at home and abroad in one single movement for the creation of the Croatian national state" (Hudelist 2004: 513). But for the moment, Luburić was only a marginal voice in the field.

Therefore, during the first fifteen years that followed the fall of the Independent State of Croatia (NDH), the Croatian transnational political field was characterized by four main features. First, there was an effective and very concrete line of demarcation between the "inner" political field in Yugoslavia and the "outer" political field abroad; the Yugoslav territorial logic described in the previous chapter had produced concrete effects. Second, what Bourdieu would term the field's "principle of vision and division," namely what organized the actors' categories, was the ideological divide between pro-Yugoslav communists and anti-communists, and it was stronger than the democratic/non-democratic or violent/non-violent divide. It was linked to a third feature, which was the coexistence, within the "outer" Croatian political field, of two demarcated subfields, mostly determined by the status of its members in terms of socio-economic background, education, wave of emigration, and legal status[17]—the political fields of the "old migration" and the "political exiles." Whereas the "old migration" field was composed of second- and third-generation members mostly coming from a working-class background, firmly located in the hostland's political field, the "political exile" subfield was almost entirely autonomous: it was not engaging in the political field of its country of residence, but it was also entirely cut off from its homeland "constituency," functioning therefore as what Stéphane Dufoix has defined as an "exopolitie."[18] While this subfield was divided again in two camps, which we could define as "democratic nationalists" on the one side and "nostalgic Ustaše" on the other, the similarities of education and socio-professional backgrounds explain the constant dialogue and interaction between the moderates and the radical exiles.[19] Finally, while the "old migration" subfield was deeply rooted in the hostland's political field and held regular elections to renew its institutions, the "exiles'" autonomization and legitimacy struggles increased over the years for the "exile" political subfield. This last aspect became evident when new organizations emerged. These 15 years were therefore dominated primarily by an ideological divide: on the one hand a neutral to warm feeling of the "old migration" organizations (which represented the large majority of Croats abroad) toward the newly created state; on the other, a strong anti-Yugoslav, anti-communist, often nostalgic nationalism which maintained the NDH as its horizon; all advocates for "national reconciliation" were marginalized.

In 1960, a new organization emerged and began a new era in Croatian politics abroad. The Croatian Revolutionary Brotherhood (*Hrvatsko Revolucionarno Bratstvo*—HRB)[20] burst into the field, dismissing the "elders" as "talkers" and calling for violent action. It considered the old *Ustaša*, those directly linked to the historical NDH, as outdated, and advocated armed struggle as the only efficient form for the liberation of Croatia.[21]

1962–1978: from the ideological divide to the violent/ non-violent divide

The evolution of the Croatian transnational political field is marked by two important changes between 1962 and 1978. First, with the opening of the borders of Yugoslavia and the liberalization of the domestic political field, the "inner" and "outer" regions of the field came increasingly in contact. Political émigrés were able to connect with nationalist groups at home, and the wave of workers' migration brought a great number of Croats in direct contact with the political emigration. This had a second consequence, the increased level of reaction to the homeland's political processes among the exile groups. So while the relation of power of the previous years in the exiled field was bringing about a marginalization of the old organizations directly linked to the *Ustaša* legacy, the 1971 repression rapidly legitimized neo-*Ustaša* radical organizations in their competition with the moderate groups for the monopolization of the transnational political field. As a consequence, the ideological divide was dropped and the idea of an all-Croat national reconciliation became a taken-for-granted assumption in the different camps.

Some structural factors inside the transnational field brought significant changes to the structure of power relations that had been established. First, the "domestic" Yugoslav political field, in particular in the Socialist Republic of Croatia, was changing. At the 8th Congress of the LCY, Croatian reformist Miko Tripalo, along with Savka Dabčević-Kučar, criticized Yugoslavia's economic and political centralism. This had an economic dimension (more federalism was demanded) but it also referred to the national question (Tripalo 1989: 37, 42). In 1962, the borders were officially opened, and a large number of "workers temporarily employed abroad," the official title for guest workers, went to work in Western Europe. However, at home, what started as a reformist movement inside the party in the mid-1960s was soon taken up by students, workers frustrated by the rising unemployment caused by the 1965 reforms, scattered nationalist intellectuals,[22] and elements of the Catholic Church. By 1969–1970, a full-scale social movement was in motion, formulating increasing demands on the authorities, often with nationalist overtones.[23] However, the Prague Spring was freshly remembered, and Nixon's support[24] for the movement convinced Tito of the danger of a Soviet intervention (Tripalo 1989: 149). The Croatian leadership was removed at the 1971 meeting in Karađorđevo, and the following year was marked by a wave of police repression and farcical political trials, giving Yugoslavia its own "Croatian spring" (*Hrvatsko Proljeće*). The repression created further waves of radicalized *Proljećari* (members of the Croatian Spring) emigrants. But before the repression, two semi-autonomous institutions were crucial in connecting the homeland and the "outer" political organizations: Franjo Tuđman's Institute for the History of the Worker's Movement in Croatia (*Institut za Historiju Radničkog Pokreta u Hrvatskoj*—IHRPH) and Većeslav Holjevac's *Matica iseljenika Hrvatske* (Society of Emigrants from Croatia) (Salaj 2002: 9). For the first time, important links were created between the inside and the outside in the transnational political field.

Despite the spectacular and violent actions of some organizations, most of the Croatian population and their descendants abroad kept a fair distance from right-wing organizations' politics. With the election of John Badinovac in 1967, the CFU, who continued to grow as the main Croatian association in the US and in Canada, moved from neutral to openly pro-Yugoslav (Prpić 1971: 412).[25] The CFU became one of the best allies of the Yugoslav government abroad by negotiating an important agreement: abroad, the CFU would not upset the Yugoslav political line and promote a depoliticized folkloric "homeland" culture, mostly based on tamburica (traditional mandoline-style small guitars) orchestras, food and folk culture[26]; in return, the SFRY government would allow the CFU to promote a "soft" Croatian folklorism during immigrants' visits back home in which usually forbidden symbols of the Croatian national culture, such as the national flag and traditional songs, could be displayed publicly.[27] The CFU established privileged links with the para-governmental institution *Matica iseljenika Hrvatske* (Society of Emigrants from Croatia) and became for the government a model "old migration" association. Unofficially, Yugoslav government officials in charge of the emigration used the CFU-SFRY link to neutralize anti-Yugoslav propaganda.

The pro-Yugoslav turn of the CFU deepened the rift that existed inside the "old migration" microcosm and the "political emigration" groups. In 1921, the CCU had been created to counterbalance the left-wing orientation of CFU's predecessor, the National Croatian Association (Čizmić 2000: 47). In 1967, the CCU's journal *Nada Naša* (Our Hope) and CFU's *Zajedničar* (The Fraternalist) exchanged violent insults. But the biggest rift was between the pre-1945 majority's democratic views and the proliferation of groups and movements in the microcosm of the Croatian political emigration.

Between 1962 and 1978, the "political exile" subfield was marked by a double process: the quasi-extinction of orthodox *Ustaša* organizations, and the progressive convergence of their heirs toward moderate nationalist positions. The economic and political development of Yugoslavia and its liberalization had helped marginalize groups who were in full opposition to the regime. In 1969, after more than twenty years of exile in Valencia, Spain, Maks Luburić was assassinated by the Yugoslav secret police. Leadership of his HNO-1 movement, which had small branches in West Germany, Sweden, France, Australia, and the US, was transferred to Dinko Šakić in Argentina until 1974, but it remained marginal (Meštrović 2003: 257). Similary, Branko Jelić's HNO-j became increasingly isolated, and was infiltrated by UDBa agents; in 1970 he was assassinated among a moderate indifference (Meštrović 2003: 173).

On the other hand, post-fascist groups such as the intellectuals of *Hrvatska Revija* broke with their *Ustaša* past[28] and committed themselves to democratic values.[29] Along with the journal *Nova Hrvatska*,[30] *Hrvatska Revija* established itself as an "all-Croat, independentist and democratic publication, which wants to work for the affirmation of Croatia in the world and obtain Croatian national freedom through culture" (Nikolić 1990: 636). These groups closely followed the unfolding events occurring at home, and actively supported the Croatian causes. Their agenda mirrored that of the movement emerging at home: more autonomy—ideally independence—for Croatia, better government positions for Croats, a better financial redistribution of resources between republics, and increased linguistic and cultural rights. In 1967, *Hrvatska Revija* reprinted one of the founding texts of the Croatian nationalist claim to a distinct language[31] and promoted similar initiatives abroad.[32]

But with the opening of the political field at home in 1968 (through the opening of the border), the very existence and legitimacy of these democratically-minded nationalists was unexpectedly challenged. Readership was shrinking as free and fresher news was now coming from the homeland through Zagreb-based publications such as *Hrvatski Tjednik* and *Hrvatski Književni List* (Kušan 2000: 80). The de-differentiation of the "inside" and the "outside" of the transnational political fields in fact made their positions redundant.[33] This was reinforced by increasing contact with the homeland movement; while the editors of the émigré journals had founded their legitimacy on their perceived contribution to "the cause," messages from Zagreb explicitly revealed that the Yugoslav public ignored the existence of *Nova Hrvatska* or *Hrvatska Revija*. Moreover, it was said that their support was unwanted: links with the emigration were a delegitimizing burden for the movement at home (Kušan 2000: 84). The delegitimizing effect proved to be very real with the 1971–1972 repression. As Kušan admitted in his memoirs:

> The events [...] contradicted my belief that our writing abroad [could] not be used against the homeland opposition. Amongst the first "evidence" against the Croats accused of leading a counterrevolution led from abroad, extreme nationalism and links with the "*Ustaša*" emigration, the Yugoslav press quoted excerpts of *Nova Hrvatska* in which I was questioning our existence as a journal, provided we [had] better newspapers and magazines in the homeland.
>
> (2000: 91)

Other invented plots were used to accuse the demonstrators of links with anti-Yugoslav elements abroad.[34] However, after the repression of 1971, the legitimacy and *raison d'être* of both publications was re-established. Flocks of freshly emigrated students and intellectuals came to join the ranks of the moderate nationalist circles. They were reinforced by the increasing presence of "workers temporarily abroad" in Germany, Austria, Sweden and other European countries, who were initially regarded with suspicion and contempt by the political emigration. The newcomers were generally of working-class backgrounds, had a passport and were entitled to return. Sometimes they were pejoratively called *pasošari* ("those with a passport"). Yet as Branko Salaj, a political exile in Sweden at the time, noted, the new wave of "workers temporarily employed abroad" did not change the structure of the political field. Instead, Croatian organizations abroad managed to "recruit" some of the newcomers; and for the émigré newspapers, they contributed to a substantial increase in sales (Salaj 2002: 16).

Young, radical organizations convinced of the necessity of a guerrilla-style armed struggle for the liberation of Croatia soon filled the void left in the transnational political field by the moribund *Ustaša* organizations. Some groups such as the HRB had emerged before 1971 and had gained popularity through spectacular actions. In 1963, the HRB sent a group of young men known as the "Tolić-Oblak" group into Yugoslavia's territory, with the aim of sabotaging the rail tracks between Zagreb and Rijeka and Zagreb and Belgrade. The nine men were caught before even going into action and were sentenced to between 12 and 13 years in prison.[35] Subsequently, several members of the HRB group would be executed by the secret services abroad.[36]

But most were attracted to armed struggle after the 1971 repression, convinced that, although the methods of the old Ustaše were outdated, their radical political positions were right—there was no possibility for democratic change in Yugoslavia (Salaj 2002: 6).

The most charismatic leader to emerge from this generation was a former aide to Franjo Tuđman in the IHRPH, Bruno Bušić. Bušić, along with Zlatko Markus and Mladen Schwartz,[37] had a three-part platform: first, he had recuperated Luburić's idea of national reconciliation (*hrvatsko izmirenje*), arguing that Croatian fighters from both sides of the ideological divide were now suffering from the oppression of the Serbian-dominated Yugoslavia; former communists and former Ustaše had to cooperate in order to liberate Croatia. Second, under the strong influence of Che Guevara and Régis Debray, Bušić believed in the "foco theory" of armed struggle: only armed insurrection would launch the revolution. Third, he put the ideal of Croatian independence and the Croatian state above all other conditions, including democracy, tacitly endorsing the NDH.[38] As political exile Ivan Babić later said of him:

> Bušić thought that the support for our cause in America and in Europe could be transformed in concrete actions only if something constantly happened in

Croatia, showing the impossibility of maintaining the *status quo*. That is, that the homeland undergoes a revolution.

(Meštrović 2003: 178)

Bušić became the new icon of the radical émigrés' circles nostalgic for Pavelić and Luburić, who saw armed struggle as a new possibility for Croatia's independence. And the 1970s saw the multiplication of "terrorist" actions. In 1971, the Yugoslav ambassador was murdered by Miro Barešić and linked to the structures of Pavelić's HOP (Popović 1995: 49; Zebić 1991a, 1991b, 1991c, 1991d). Bušić's adoption of the "foco" theory was allegedly behind another spectacular operation in 1972, in which a group of 20 young émigrés from Australia, Germany, and Austria penetrated the Raduša mountains in southern Bosnia-Herzegovina, only to be killed along with 13 members of the Territorial Defense and two military police officers. Only the youngest member was sentenced to 20 years in jail (Koričanić 1991: 18; *Feral Tribune* 2004). Another spectacular action took place in 1976, when Zvonko Bušić, a cousin of Bruno Bušić, along with his wife Julienne Eden and other activists, hijacked a TWA New York–Chicago flight. The intention was to fly over Croatia and drop revolutionary flyers written by Bruno Bušić, thus raising political consciousness and preparing for the revolution. The plan failed, a US police officer was killed and Zvonko Bušić and his wife were given heavy sentences in the USA (Meštrović 2003: 185; Bušić 2000). The Croatian "cause" became famous, but it failed to engender the expected sympathy.

The effects of these actions on the transnational political field were immediate. The established pro-Yugoslav associations felt threatened for both their relation vis-à-vis SFRY (where anti-nationalist groups within the Communist party could use the radicals' actions as an argument to sever ties) and with their "hostlands" (where anti-immigrant groups could use the climate to attack their legitimacy). The moderate organizations realized how these actions could potentially delegitimize their position as figures of the democratic opposition. Steps were therefore taken to "muster" the radicals through an all-Croat representative body.

While the "old migration" subfield was dominated by pro-Yugoslav positions and a satisfaction with the status quo in Yugoslavia, the "political exile" subfield was greatly divided by the violent tactics of some. As the moderate nationalist poet Boris Maruna commented:

There existed two distinct sides in the Croatian emigration. The first one was Ustaša, the second those around the HSS. Neither had a pluralist political agenda [...]. These people [*Ustaše*] with their stone-age ideas did not mean anything to people who came in the emigration [...]. The majority of them knew how to think and they did not even think about mingling with the Luburić supporters. These people did not see a solution in the Ustaša revolution nor in the HSS legitimacy. They are the ones who created the

Croatian American Academy, Studia Croatica and the Hrvatska Revija [...] these people wanted something modern, something which could go somewhere for Croatia.[39]

Yet both groups agreed to create an all-Croat exile representative body, all sides probably hoping it could strengthen their position. In 1974 in Toronto, the Croatian National Council (*Hrvatsko Narodno Vijeće*—HNV) was founded by both *Ustaša* and moderate nationalist organizations. One of the initiators of the Council was Mate Meštrović, the son of the famous sculptor Ivan Meštrović. Meštrović had understood the catastrophic effects of the violent tactics and the importance of broadening the coalition to isolate the ideologically sterile groups. As he stated in a 1967 letter:

> Croatian politics cannot be led from Argentina, the current headquarters of what survived from the Ustaša leadership of NDH, because it is too far away from Croatia. What is important is the link between people and the homeland [...]. It is important to work with the so-called "*pasošari*" in Europe. In the current situation it is only possible to change the course of things through actions in the homeland.
>
> (2003: 154)

"Old migration" associations were not represented in order to maintain their relationship with Yugoslavia. At the first elections of the Council's assembly in 1975, the "moderate" nationalist and old Ustaše won the majority among the 3,270 members. Members of HOP, HNO-j, HNO-l and other organizations were elected to the executive organ.[40] But the second general election, in 1977, brought a different result. After the TWA hijacking, the list presented by Bruno Bušić obtained the majority, with 3,742 votes, marking a hard defeat of the moderates. Figures like Vinko Nikolić or Boris Maruna did very poorly (Meštrović 2003: 257). So the plan to organize and moderate backfired, and the election of the radicals marked the high point of the "*Proljećari*" monopoly of the "political exile" subfield. However, with less than 4,000 members worldwide compared to the 100,000 and more members of the CFU in the US and Canada, the HNV's assembly was hardly representative of anyone but the émigrés' circles themselves.

Therefore, the evolution of the positions and organizations of the transnational political field from 1962 to 1978 can be explained by the power relations linked to internal and external processes. A first apparently paradoxical element is the discrepancy between the large numbers of pre-1945 organizations such as the CFU and their absence in the later political scene. This is mainly explained by the structuration of the transnational field by the Yugoslav government: in order to carry out their social activities in Yugoslavia "old migration" organizations could not delegitimize themselves by collaborating with organizations that were considered by Belgrade as open enemies. In fact, on more than one occasion, supporting the CFU's activities was precisely seen by Yugoslav authorities as an indirect way of countering the influence of anti-Yugoslav organizations.

Second, the power structure inside the "political exile" subfield is directly linked to Yugoslav policies. Before 1971, the liberalization of the domestic political field delegitimized the most radical organizations, splitting them between a minority of die-hard illegitimate extremists and a majority who moved toward democratic positions. However, after 1971 the process of re-differentiation re-legitimized exile organizations and the repression in Yugoslavia restarted the familiar process of escalating violence, which marginalized the moderates and empowered the most radical groups.[41] This radical space was occupied by members of a new wave of migration who brought with them two important elements of "symbolic capital": proximity to the homeland constituency and the legitimacy of having participated in the movement. Moreover, they brought with them an ideological choice of violence which mimetically corresponded to the structure imposed by the Yugoslav authorities' escalation. Besides these obvious changes, a more subtle change had occurred: the focus on the violent/non-violent debate had obscured the fact that the division of the field had brought about a new *doxa*,[42] namely that the division was no longer ideological but national. It was not between communists and anti-communists, but between Croats and Serbs. This was a new principle of division that presumed that all Croatian organizations abroad must participate in an equal representative body.

1978–1987: the prospect of a democratic transition

Everything in the evolution of the Croatian transnational social field from 1978 (the year of the death of Bruno Bušić) would have led to a prediction of the dominance of a democratic, moderately nationalist position in 1990. By the mid-1980s, the positions in the political field were indeed divided into two. A first option advocated for autonomy (or independence) for Croatia, repudiated violent methods and favored a democratic, independent state. It advocated for the collaboration of moderate elements from within the Communist party with nationalists outside the party and abroad to form a broad democratic platform. Structurally, this resulted from two evolutions: the passage of the "old migration" from a pro-Yugoslav to an increasingly pro-Croatian position and the banishment of violent groups, leading to the dominance of moderate nationalist organizations. In terms of territory, there was still dissension about the borders of Croatia—some were ready to accept the 1946 (AVNOJ) borders, some still believed in a large Croatia. The question of minorities (Serbs and Muslims) was to be solved democratically, a line supported by prominent emigrants such as Jakša Kušan, Mate Meštrović, Branko Salaj, and Bernard Luketich.

The second option, almost entirely defeated politically, was the ideological line running from Maks Luburić to Bruno Bušić: a line that similarly called for "national reconciliation," and for the collaboration of all Croats abroad and in the homeland, but which advocated violence, did not think much of democratic principles and put statehood above all. Moreover, this line strongly believed in a "greater Croatia," including all Bosnia-Herzegovina, cleansed of all Serbs.

After the death of Tito in 1980, Yugoslavia continued toward the liberalization and decentralization of the economic system, infusing the market economy into the moribund economic system. Politically, the federation slowly affirmed national and ethnic identities, in part because of the 1971 Croatian events. Although the movement was repressed and its leaders jailed, the SKJ understood the need to concede some of the claims. So, after the reforms and the proclamation of the 1974 constitution, an increasing number of federal prerogatives were delegated to the republics, including education and security. On the other hand, underground, the *Proljećari* left at home were slowly reorganizing with the help of the emigration organizations they had neglected back in 1971. Led by 1971 figures such as Vlado Gotovac, Marko Veselica, Šime Đodan, Dražen Budiša and Franjo Tuđman, they were forming a democratic and liberal political opposition similar to that of Poland with Lech Walesa's Solidarnosc and of Czechoslovakia around Vaclav Havel.

But the 1987 events in Serbia reshaped the Croatian transnational political field. A strong Serbian nationalist push emerged from different parts of society, from the "bureaucratic revolution" initiated by Milošević to the Memorandum of the Academy of Arts and Sciences of Belgrade.[43] Instead of repressing them, however, then leader Slobodan Milošević took the option of building politically on this mobilization in order to promote his own agenda. Many foresaw rising tensions within the federation. In Croatia, parallel to the democratic opposition that was gaining political ground, a covert "objective alliance" was formed between radical members of the security forces, excluding "nationalist" party officials and radical right-wing organizations abroad. In 1987, Franjo Tuđman was given his first passport to travel to Europe, Canada, and the United States.

One of the signs that the Yugoslav idea was dead at home and abroad was when the traditionally pro-Yugoslav CFU turned pro-Croatian, as Ivana Djurić shows in her systematic study of CFU's newspaper *Zajedničar* (The Fraternalist), between 1980–1990. The traditionally pro-Yugoslav fraternal union involved itself in homeland politics to defend the language, religion, and a distinct Croatian "culture." Although by the mid-1980s the fraternal union's constituency spoke almost only English, the organization strongly supported a campaign against the proposed language change in the Socialist Republic of Croatia's constitution from "Croatian Literary Language" to "Croato-Serbian" (Djurić 2003: 117).

Throughout the world "grassroots" organizations took peaceful steps to advocate for the Croatian cause outside of the intricacies of the Croatian "political émigré" subfield. From November 1977 to December 1979, at 34 Canberra Avenue, one of the busiest streets of the Australian capital, a group of Croats led by Marijo Despoja opened an unofficial "Croatian Embassy" (Despoja 1996: 175). In response to official Yugoslav pressure on the Australian government to close the embassy, Despoja positioned his initiative in multiple and conflicting political fields: "The statements of the Yugoslav ambassador are nothing less than interferences in the domestic affairs of Australian citizens of Croatian origin and are as such in complete contradiction with his diplomatic status" (Despoja 1996: 176). But the peaceful, legal initiative was also intended to erase the image of right-wing terrorists that had been stuck to Croats abroad As Despoja later explained: "We knew the Embassy would be closed down, but we wanted to turn its closing down in a Croatian victory—we wanted to show that Croats are not terrorists; that we respect the laws of this country" (1996: 168). Croats abroad supported the democratic (and national) forces that were pushing for change in Yugoslavia, but never did these groups advocate for an all-encompassing conception of the Croatian nation, nor for a specific "alliance" between groups at home and abroad.

In the "political emigration" subfield, the passage from the 1970s to the 1980s was marked by the high point and also the rapid delegitimizing of violent organizations in the transnational political field. The first enormous blow to the violent movement was the 1978 killing, by Yugoslav secret police, of the charismatic leader Bruno Bušić in Paris. As one of the leading members of the HNV, his death was a clear message to the political emigration as a whole. The effect was the further division of the political émigrés' circles between hardened radicals and convinced democrats. Old *Ustaša* organizations came back to life, and in particular Luburić's HNO-Otpor, with its violent, anti-democratic and expansionist all-Croat ideology.

HNV "moderate" members became specifically targeted by violent attacks. In 1978, Croatian moderates Ante Cikoj and Križan Brkić were killed by unknown gunmen (*Narodni List* 1992: 14). In 1980, bombs exploded in a Manhattan bank in February, in the house of a Yugoslav embassy official, and in a New York museum in June (Meštrović 2003: 236). In 1982, the Croatian community in the United States received letters from Paraguay imposing a revolutionary tax, with death threats to those who would not pay (Meštrović 2003: 231). The escalation continued with the Yugoslav secret police abroad. In 1983, Stjepan Đureković, a former highly-ranked civil servant, fled the country and published several books about the corrupt "red bourgeoisie." He was murdered a few months after his arrival in Germany.[44] By then, "host states" had entered the repression, too. In 1978 Germany banned the Otpor and the HRB (Meštrović 2003: 228). In 1980, two Yugoslav citizens were arrested and charged with attempted murder on behalf of the Yugoslav police (OHR 1995: 53). Otpor moved to the United States, whose government was rapidly irritated by its activities: undercover agents infiltrated the organization, and in 1980 three members of Otpor were arrested.[45] In 1982, ten Otpor Croats were brought to trial and given sentences of between 20 and 40 years on charges of violence toward the Croatian community and extortion, mostly against the "mild" faction of the HNV (*Narodni List* 1992: 14–15).

The violent activities of the most radical émigré groups were partially caused by the death of Bušić and a logic of escalation with Yugoslavia and its perceived supporters, but they also had an institutional explanation. While Bušić's list had been successful in 1978, the third Sabor (assembly session) of the HNV held in London in January 1980 returned the organization to moderates (Meštrović 2003: 166).[46] The dominance of a moderate HNV executive on the political émigré scene was reinforced by the departure of the radical group from the council, and its apparent return to the margins of the subfield. The defeated Bušić list, as well as the traditional *Luburićevi*, left the HNV in order to fund a new party, the Croatian Independentist Movement (*Hrvatski Državotvoreni Pokret*—HDP) in 1981 (Meštrović 2003: 166). While the HNV was pushing an independentist but democratic agenda, the radicals advocated an ethnically cleansed Croatia. As Mate Meštrović explains:

> Radical independentist Croats hated Milovan Djilas more than Tito himself, because Tito, despite all the crimes he had committed, was a Croat, while Djilas, even if after the dispute with Tito he became the promoter of a democratic Yugoslavia, he was still a Serb and a Montenegrin!
>
> (2003: 125)

According to one of his members, Mladen Schwartz: "The specificity of HDP was extremism, radicalism and maximalism."[47] But HDP leaders, particularly Nikola Štedul, a former HOP and HNO member, understood that the organization had to gain legitimacy by renouncing terrorist methods.[48] The group gathered a small group of veterans of extremist organizations, such as Miro Barešić (the famous Yugoslav ambassador killer), Tihomir Orešković and others.[49] The HDP was closely linked to another marginal organization, HNO-Otpor, whose very president in 1980, Marin Sopta, was a member of HDP. According to Yugoslav police sources, the HDP and HNO members combined did not exceed 500 people in 1990 (Drobnjak 1990). As another "moderate nationalist" Boris Maruna explained: "The *Luburićevi* were a completely marginal group who never had, for the clever people, independently of their background and reasons for emigration, meant anything good, nor had any political perspective."[50]

The only support of this marginalized political faction was a small group of Franciscan friars based in the suburbs of Toronto. The friars had traditionally occupied the premises of the Croatian Ethnic Institute in Chicago, but with the arrival of Fra Častimir Majić, their support for Otpor ended (Meštrović 2003: 231). After unsuccessfully challenging the Toronto parish to oust Vatican-backed Croatian Roman Catholic Church priests in 1969, the Herzegovinian Franciscans established in 1977 the Croatian Social and Cultural Center in Norval, a few kilometers from Toronto. In the late 1960s, the Herzegovinian friars—traditionally anti-communist, especially after the massacre of many of them by the Partizans in the immediate post-war period—had espoused Luburić's ideas of "Croatian pacification," convinced that it was the only way to efficiently oust the regime. The Norval center became an excellent place for the few radicals still linked to Otpor to gather, among them future central figures of 1990s Croatian politics such as Ante Beljo, Marin Sopta, and future Defense Minister Gojko Šušak (Hudelist 2004: 624). Paradoxically, it was by relying on this marginal group's credo and funds that Franjo Tuđman and the HDZ would organize its access to power. As Mate Meštrović later commented:

> Many among us in the diaspora formulated the idea of an all-Croatian reconciliation. Jakša Kušan, in the London-based *Nova Hrvatska* constantly spoke about it. But in a completely different way. Kušan called for a collaboration of all democratically oriented Croats in the homeland, outside the Croatian league of communists and inside it; as he called for the collaboration of all expatriates, leaving aside all non-democratic heirs of the violent Ustaša regime. The call for reconciliation, the way Luburić understood it, without any accent on democracy—was enacted twenty years later by Franjo Tuđman in the foundation of the Croatian state.
>
> (2003: 226)

Conclusion

In 1998, Guarnizo wrote, "identities forged from below are often no less essentialized than the hegemonic projects of nation states. Identities forged 'from below' are not inherently subversive or counter hegemonic" (Guarnizo and Smith 1998: 23). The primary objective of this chapter was to trace the emergence of a form of "transnational nationalism," a new evolution of the old territorialized conception of the nation into a conception that includes all Croats, no matter where they live. As we see from the evolution of the ideology in the Croatian transnational field, the elaboration of the Croatian diasporic ideology— namely the idea that an Emigrant Croatia and a Homeland Croatia, together, form the Croatian nation—can be directly traced to an adaptation of the World War II *Ustaša* ideology, even if this ideology is marginal in the Croatian transnational field until the mid-1980s.

Thus, arguing that the "Croatia diaspora" as a whole had a negative role in the war can only be done at the cost of indulging in certain intellectual dishonesties: first, by conflating a group of wealthy but politically marginal diasporic groups with the rest of the organizations in the transnational political field; and second, by ignoring 50 years of evolution in the Croatian transnational field and assuming that the hierarchy of these organizations in 1990 had been historically constant.

More broadly, this chapter has demonstrated the usefulness of approaching diaspora politics through a transnational political field perspective, for four main reasons. First, the transnational political field approach includes both homeland and hostland bureaucratic institutions in the analysis, accounting for the important power of state policies over diasporic institutions; through the choice of immigration policies, refugee policies, and multicultural or assimilationist policies, "hostland governments" are critical in allowing or preventing ethnic identification and mobilization, access to citizenship, and the right for refugees to engage in political activities. The relation between homeland bureaucratic institutions and diasporic groups is crucial in defining, legitimizing, and delegitimizing groups in the transnational social space. The structuration by governmental agencies is further complicated by the relations between hostland and homeland institutions, in which diasporic institutions and groups are caught up. Second, the approach allows us to do away with the monolithic concept of "diaspora," and highlight the social differences of the actors in terms of traditional socio-professional markers such as cultural (education, diplomas), economic (wealth), and social (social networks) capital; but also forms of capital that are specifically important in *transnational* social fields, such as the "wave" of migration, legal status (refugee, illegal migrant, visa holder, citizen), homeland region of origin, and political socialization prior to migration. Furthermore, it helps us understand the diasporic political field both as united yet heterogeneous: united by the common stakes of the social actors, but conflicting in the constant symbolic and material struggle that takes place among the different actors for the monopoly of the representation of the field. Third, the concept of transnational political field is crucial in allowing us to understand the *habitus* of social agents and their political behavior within changing structures of the transnational political field, and in particular to understand how changes in the structure always produce effects of classification and declassification, legitimization and delegitimization of certain groups over others. Finally, in positing the transnational political field as a field of positions but also a field in which representations acquire a specific social value as principles of "vision and division" of the social world, the concept of transnational political field allows us to look "underneath" categories of practice such as "diaspora" and "political exile" and examine the politics that take place for the formulation and definition of who is "inside" and "outside" these categories, as well as the conflicting social and political effects of using these categories over others.

Notes

1 See in particular the analyses of Nina Glick Schiller (Basch *et al.* 1995) and Riva Kastoryano (2006).
2 See for example what Benedict Anderson says about it:

> consider the malign role of Croats not only in Germany but also in Australia and North America in financing and arming Franjo Tuđman's breakaway state and pushing Germany and Austria into a fateful, premature recognition [...]. Emblematic is the figure of Canadian citizen Gojko Šušak. A successful Ottawa-based pizza millionaire, he built over the years a huge right-wing network of "overseas" North American Croatians, used the ample funds he extracted from them to buy Franjo Tuđman his first election as Croatia's president, and obtained as his reward Croatia's Ministry of Defense (aka War).
>
> (1998: 62 and footnote 31)

3 A study shows that about 73 percent of the pre-1945 migrants had attended up to four years of high school and only 15 percent went to school in the United States (Colaković 1973: 57).

Croatian transnational nationalism (1945–1987) 77

4 See "Croats" in the *Harvard Encyclopedia of American Ethnic Groups* (Thernstrom 1980)
5 The division within the union was represented by the conflict at the top between then president Ivan Butković, who opposed Tito's Yugoslavia, and the union's journal editor Filip Vukelić who supported it (Čizmić 2000: 252–253).
6 Pro-Yugoslav *Narodni Glasnik* (circulation 10,000) in Cleveland. Council of American Croatians founded in 1943 at the Congress of American Croatians (Čizmić, 2000: 414).
7 Around Jakša Kušan gathered at different periods in time Gvido Saganić, Željko Tomčić Tothm Tihomir Rađa, Branko Salaj, Vlatko Pavlinić. (See Meštrović 2003: 57; Kušan 2000: 18.)
8 In *Hrvatski Bilten* of 1958, Karlo Mirth, editor of the first post-World War II bulletin *Croatia Press*, expressed his high opinion of the journal, along with the CFU and the journals *Danica* and *Hrvatska Država* (Kušan 2000: 25–26).
9 A similarly-minded publication in the United States was Karlo Mirth's *Croatia Press*, founded in Cleveland in 1952 (see Mirth 2003: 73). These publications were still dwarfed by the circulation of CFU's journal *Zajedničar*, which fluctuated between 70,000 and 100,000.
10 If one political party was to represent this group's views, it was the Croatian Peasant Party (HSS), led by its leader elected in Croatia in 1941, Vlado Maček, then Juraj Krnjević (Meštrović 2003: 157). The HSS, which based its legitimacy on a "legalist" argument, contending that it was the last legal representative of the Croats since 1939, very quickly lost any legitimacy and both Maček and Krnjević came to be considered as passive and marginal by most of the other groups. Its main publication, the *Hrvatski Glas* (Croatian Voice) diffused mostly democratic ideology oriented mainly toward Croatia's independence and center-right politics (Meštrović 2003: 57).
11 *Nova Hrvatska*, September 1962.
12 Ibid.
13 Ibid.
14 As it can be read in the Founding Declaration of the Croatian Liberation Movement (HOP): "Its purpose is the immediate and unconditional freedom for all Croatian people, and to restore the Independent State of Croatia in all her territory, fully comprised of all Croatian lands defined as that between the Mura, the Drava, the Dunava, the Drina and the Adriatic Sea" (HOP 1956).
15 Branko Jelić was a historical figure of the *Ustaša* movement. He was among the founding fathers of the movement and founded in 1933 the fascist *Hrvatski Domobran* (the Homeland Defender) political group in Buenos Aires. With the establishment of the Croatian Independent State he was meant to occupy an important hierarchical position, but on his way to Croatia he was arrested by the British authorities and forced to spend the war in a prison cell (see Čizmić 2000: 427).
16 The exact number of deaths is still under historiographical debate, and has been the stake of political struggles in the 1980s and the 1990s (see MacDonald 2002).
17 Raditsa 1958 quoted in Čizmić 2000: 192.
18 Dufoix defines "exopolitie" or "exile polity" as: "A political space that is both national and transstate, formed by groups who refuse to recognize the legitimacy of the current regime in their country of origin, or who consider the country to be under foreign occupation" (Dufoix 2008: 63). Read more about the concept in Dufoix 2002: 23–30.
19 There are several examples of this dialogue: Maks Luburić published letters in Kušan's *Nova Hrvatska*, while Branko Jelić was in regular contact with Kušan and even invited him (unsuccessfully) to become the editor of the *Ustaša* journal *Hrvatska Država*. See Kušan (2000: 58).
20 The organization was founded by two Australian-Croats, Geza Pašti and Josip Senić Pepo (Rogošić 1995: 53).

21 Franjo Goreta, interviewed in *Globus* (Rogošić 1995: 52).
22 Around *Matica Hrvatska* and its journals *Hrvatski Tjednik* (Croatian Weekly) and *Hrvatski Gospodarski List* (Croatian Economic Newspaper). The main figures around *Matica Hrvatska* were Vlado Gotovac, Šime Đodan, and Marko Veselica. See Salaj 2002: 10.
23 In *Hrvatski Tjednik*, authors went as far as demanding the formation of a Croatian Army, and the "unification" of Croatia and Herzegovina, as well as the exclusion of Serbs as constituent peoples of the Socialist Republic of Croatia from the constitution. See Tripalo 1989: 164.
24 Richard Nixon, on his visit to Yugoslavia, famously first visited Zagreb before Belgrade as a symbolic gesture of support for the movement. See Čizmić (2000: 442).
25 In its 1963 congress, the CFU announced a new peak: 108,000 members and a capital of 28 million dollars. For the first time, in 1963 the CFU congress became dominated by US-born Croats, and one of them was elected president in 1967 (Prpić 1971: 412).
26 See Dalbello (1999) for a systematic study of Croatian diaspora almanacs.
27 Ibid.
28 Upon his arrival in Argentina, Vinko Nikolić had first enrolled in Pavelić's organization *Hrvatski Domobran*. See Nikolić (1990: 632).
29 "The founding idea of the upcoming journal is described in its name. *Hrvatska Revija* (The Croatian Review) is an all-Croat, independentist and democratic publication, which wants to work for the affirmation of Croatia in the world and obtain Croatian national freedom through culture" (Nikolić 1990: 636).
30 See "Otvoreno Pismo Hrvatskim Komunistima" [Open Letter to Croatian Communists], *Nova Hrvatska*, October 1962, on the need to forget ideological differences and work for an independent Croatia; "Ne Rat Nego Rad" [Not War but Work], *Nova Hrvatska*, October 1963, on the rejection of armed struggle and the advocacy of political and economic confrontation with Yugoslavia; "Što je važnije za naše desničare?" [What Is Important for Our Right-Wingers?], *Nova Hrvatska*, no. 5–6, 1964, on the need for all right-wing Croatian organizations to unite.
31 The document was the "Declaration on the Name and Position of Croatians' Literary Language" ("Deklaracija o nazivu i položaju hrvatskog književnog jezika") *Hrvatska Revija*, 17 March 1967. See Bašić 2000: xiv.
32 For example by publishing a "Call to Croatian Writers Abroad from the Circle of the Croatian Review" ("Apel hrvatskih pisaca I knjievnika u iseljeništvu iz kruga Hrvatske Revije") *Hrvatska Revija*, 30 April 1967. See Bašić 2000: XIV.
33 On the notion of de-differentiation of the field, see Bigo and Guild (2005).
34 Branko Jelić, the editor of Berlin-based *Hrvatska Država*, was accused of establishing links between the Soviet Union and some members of the League of Communists of Croatia (LCC). Although there is no evidence that the central committee of the LCC was ever in contact with Jelić nor the Soviets, it helped conservative elements of the LCC to discredit the moderates. See Glamočak (1997: 81) and Meštrović (2003: 171).
35 Anonymous, "Bratstvo and Ubojstvo" [Brotherhood and Murder], *Feral Tribune*, 23 July 2004, p. 7. It is considered that the Yugoslav secret police knew of the whole operation long before, but let it happen to use the publicity that the arrest would generate (Koričanić 1991: 18).
36 Pašti was killed in France in 1965, Marija Šimundić in 1967, and Josip Senić and Stjepan Ševo in 1972.
37 Dujmović (1991).
38 See Bušić and Mijatović (2005).
39 Boris Maruna interviewed in *Feral Tribune* (Jergović 1998).
40 See Glamočak (1997: 172) for more details.
41 This phenomenon has been analyzed under the label of "ethnic outbidding" by Chip Gagnon. See Gagnon Jr, 1994–1995.

42 Bourdieu defines "doxa" as that "which goes without saying because it comes without saying [...] because the subjective necessity and self-evidence of the commonsense world are validated by the objective consensus on the sense of the world" (Bourdieu 1977). It refers to the set of beliefs and principles of the field shared by all actors as taken-for-granted assumptions.
43 For more on the historical unfolding of Serbian nationalism, see Ramet 2006.
44 On the charges and on the case *Vijesnik* (1999: 3), *Globus* (1991), Babić (1990).
45 In 1980 the police arrested Franjo Ivić, Nedo Sovulj, and Stipe Ivkošić. Ivić was charged with extortion, conspiracy, the attempted bombing of the Yugoslav "Republic Day," and the attempted murder of Hrvoje Lun. See Butković 1992: 14.
46 Mate Meštrović was in charge of foreign relations, Ivan Babić was nominated for political questions, and Jakša Kušan went back to the media office and information.
47 Mladen Schwartz interviewed in Dujmović 1991: 8.
48 Nikola Štedul, interviewed in *Feral Tribune* (2000).
49 The group also had a branch in the homeland: Antonio Lekić, Ivan Drviš, and Nikola Kristo were operating illegally at home (Klancir 2000: 42).
50 Boris Maruna, interviewed in *Feral Tribune* (Jergović 1998).

References

Aarons, M. and Loftus, J. (1991) *Ratlines: How the Vatican's Nazi Networks Betrayed Western Intelligence to the Soviets*, London: Heinemann.

Anderson, B. (1998) *The Spectre of Comparisons: Nationalism, Southeast Asia and the World* (Long Distance Nationalism, p. 374), London: Verso.

Antić, L. (1997) *Croats and America*, Zagreb: Hrvatska sveučilišna naklada.

Babić, J. (1990) "Ubojice na službenom putu," *Danas*, pp. 26–27.

Basch, L. G., Glick Schiller, N., and Szanton Blanc, C. (1995) *Nations Unbound: Transnational Projects, Postcolonial Predicaments, and Deterritorialized Nation States*, Basel; UK: Gordon and Breach.

Bašić, N. (2000) "Pedeset godina Hrvatske revije 1951–2000," *Hrvatska Revija* 4, vii–xix.

Bigo, D. and Guild, E. (2005) "Policing at a Distance: Schengen Visa Policies," in Bigo, D. and Guild, E., eds., *Controlling Frontiers: Free Movement Into and Within Europe* (pp. 234–263), Aldershot, UK; Burlington, VT: Ashgate.

Bourdieu, P. (1977) *Outline of a Theory of Practice*, Cambridge, UK; New York: Cambridge University Press.

Bušić, J. E. (2000) *Lovers and Madmen: A True Story of Passion, Politics and Air Piracy*, New York: Writers Club Press.

Bušić, B. and Mijatović, A. (2005) *Jedino Hrvatska!: sabrani spisi*, Mostar; Zagreb: Fram-Ziral.

Butković, D. (1992) "Pismo s eksplozivom uručiti franjevcu," *Globus*, pp. 14–15.

Čizmić, I. (2000) *From the Adriatic to Lake Erie: A History of Croatians in Greater Cleveland*, Zagreb: Institute of Social Sciences Ivo Pilar.

Colaković, B. (1973) *Yugoslav Migration to America*, San Francisco, CA: Rand & Research Associates.

Coric, D. (1999) "Raskol u Hrvatskom kanadskom kongresu," *Hrvatska Revija* 49, pp. 534–536.

Dalbello, M. (1999) "Croatian Diaspora Almanacs: A Historical and Cultural Analysis: A Thesis Submitted in Conformity with the Requirements for the Degree of Doctor of Philosophy," Toronto: University of Toronto, Faculty of Information Studies.

Dešpoja, Š. M. (1996) "Hrvatsko poslanstvo u Australiji (1977–1979): Pogled unatrag i naša sadašnjosti," *Hrvatska Revija* 1, pp. 168–205.

Djurić, I. (2003) "The Croatian Diaspora in North America: Identity, Ethnic Solidarity, and the Formation of a 'Transnational National Community'," *International Journal of Politics, Culture and Society*, 17(1), pp. 113–130.

Drobnjak, V. (1990) "Mi nismo ustaše," *Danas*, pp. 11–12.

Dufoix, S. (2002) Notion, concept ou slogan: qu'y a-t-il sous le terme de "diaspora"? *Colloque 2000 ans de diasporas*, International Conference, Poitiers, France.

Dufoix, S. (2008) *Diasporas*, Berkeley and Los Angeles, CA: Berkeley University Press.

Dujmović, T. (1991) "U HDP-u nije bilo agenata UDBE," *Globus*, pp. 8–9.

Feral Tribune (2000) "Sindičić je pucao iz auta," *Feral Tribune*, pp. 34–35.

Feral Tribune (2004) "Bratstvo & Ubojstvo," *Feral Tribune*, p. 7.

Foucault, M. (2004) *Naissance de la biopolitique: Cours au Collège de France (1978–1979)*, Paris: Gallimard, Seuil.

Gagnon, Jr. VP. (1994–1995) "Ethnic Nationalism and International Conflict," *International Security*, 19(3), pp. 130–166.

Glamočak, M. (1997) *Koncepcije Velike Hrvatske i Velike Srbije u političkoj emigraciji*, Uzice: KPZ.

Globus (1991) "Đurekovića je ubio Arkan," (anonymous), pp. 13–14.

Guarnizo, L. and Smith, M. P. (1998) "The Locations of Transnationalism," in Smith, M. P. and Guarnizo, L., eds., *Transnationalism from Below* (pp. 3–34), New Brunswick, NJ: Transaction Publishers.

Hockenos, P. (2003) *Homeland Calling, Exile Patriotism and the Balkan Wars*, Ithaca; London: Cornell University Press.

Holjevac, V. (1968) *Hrvati Izvan Domovine*, Zagreb: Matica Hrvatska.

HOP (1956) *Founding Declaration of the Croatian Liberation Movement (HOP)*. Available at: http://pavelic-papers.com/documents/pavelic/ap0037.html (accessed 12 February 2008).

Hudelist, D. (2004) *Tuđman, biografija*, Zagreb: Profil International.

Jergović, M. (1998) "Hrvati nisu dobar narod," *Feral Tribune*, pp. 8–10.

Kastoryano, R. (2006) "Vers un nationalisme transnational. Redéfinir la nation, le nationalisme et le territoire," *Revue Française de Science Politique*, 56(4), pp. 533–555.

Klancir, D. (2000) "HDP: Politicka stranka ili teroristicka organizacija?" *Globus*, pp. 42–46.

Koričanić, D. (1991) "Terorizam i renesansa." *Feral Tribune*, pp. 18–19.

Kušan, J. (2000) *Bitka za Novu Hrvatsku*, Rijeka: Otokar Keršovani.

Kuzmanović, J. (1990) "Urednik za odstrel," *Danas*, pp. 41–44.

MacDonald, D. B. (2002) *Balkan Holocausts? Serbian and Croatian Victim Centred Propaganda and the War in Yugoslavia*, Manchester, UK: Manchester University Press.

Meštrović, M. (2003) *U vrtlogu hrvatske politike: kazivanje Peri Zlataru*, Zagreb: Golden Marketing.

Mirth, K. (2003) *Zivot u Emigraciji*, Zagreb: Matica Hrvatska.

Narodni List (1992) "Odluka o Uspostavi Hrvatske Zajednice Herceg-Bosna," *Narodni List HZ H-B* 1/1992.

Nejasmić, I. (1989) "Depopulacija-Značajke prostorno-demografskog procesa," *Zapošlavanje i Udruženi Rad*, 14 (1989), pp. 169–181.

Nikolić, V. (1990) "'Hrvatska revija': cetrdeset godina jednog casopisa u egzilu," *Hrvatska Revija* 4, pp. 632–640.

OHR (1995) *The General Framework Agreement for Peace in Bosnia and Hercegovina*. Available at: www.ohr.int/?page_id=1252 (accessed 8 March 2017).
Popović, E. (1995) "Miro Barešić nije poginuo u okršaju s četnicima ...," *Globus*, pp. 18–19.
Prpić, J. (1971) *The Croatian Immigrants in America*, New York: Philosophical Library.
Raditsa, B. (1958) "Clash of Two Immigrant Generations," *Commentary* 25(1), pp. 8–15.
Ramet, S. P. (2006) *The Three Yugoslavias: State-Building and Legitimation, 1918–2004*, Bloomington, IN, Chesham: Indiana University Press; Combined Academic Distributor.
Rogošić, Ž. (1995) "Sreo sam u Splitu Dragana Barača ...," *Globus*, pp. 52–53.
Salaj, B. (2002) "Proljeće i dijaspora," *Hrvatska Revija* 2, pp. 6–22.
Thernstrom, S., ed. (1980) "Croats," *Harvard Encyclopedia of American Ethnic Groups* (pp. 247–256), Cambridge, MA: Belknap Press of Harvard University.
Tripalo, M. (1989) "Hrvatsko Proljeće," *Globus*.
Vijesnik (1999) "Đurekoviću presudili Dolanc, Planinc, Špiljak i Ljubičić?" *Vjesnik*, p. 3.
Zebić, B. (1991a) "Kako je UDBA obećala da će me ubiti," *Globus*, pp. 41–42.
Zebić, B. (1991b) "Kako sam kockao za Rolivićevu glavu," *Globus*, pp. 43–44.
Zebić, B. (1991c) "Kako smo pronašli Miroslava Barešića," *Globus*, pp. 13–14.
Zebić, B. (1991d) "U Paragvaj okovan kao zvijer," *Globus*, pp. 43–44.

4 Croatia, a diaspora forged in war (1987–1993)

In the small community of political exiles known as the "Norval" group, discussions focused primarily on ways to achieve Croatia's independence. All means were considered legitimate, including the most violent ones. Very few in the late 1980s would have given credit to this rather obscure group of radical exiles, which included the likes of an excommunicated priest, a pizza booth owner, and an electrician turned political essayist. The group itself probably could not imagine that most of its plans would come to fruition. Within three years, the group would move from a marginalized faction excluded not only from Croatia but also from the émigré circles abroad to become the center of the new sphere of power in Croatia. Instrumental to the group's rise to power was its alliance with Franjo Tuđman, a general of the JNA turned historian and political dissident—an intellectual who moved from the shadows of the 1971 uprising to the forefront of the underground political opposition. Both sides—and certainly Tuđman—thought of this encounter as providential. Domestic and international journalists who covered the story later in the decade often described it as a "Faustian pact," a "conspiracy" between Tuđman and the obscure group to garner financial, moral, and political support for an electoral victory against the promise of aggressive nationalist and expansionists policies.[1] An in-depth study indicates however that this encounter resulted from longer-term trends and a particular structuring of the transnational political field. At the center of this alliance for power was a strong mobilization of Croats abroad and the support for an independence movement that crafted a new brand of nationalism—one that included all Croats regardless of territory to reconcile an "expatriate" and a "homeland" Croatia and imagine ethnic homogeneity outside of a strictly territorial referent.

The mainstream literature on diaspora and conflict takes for granted the category of diaspora, constructing it as an analytical concept[2] or even a statistical category[3]—as if diasporas could be recognized, delimited, and counted a priori. Quite representative of this trend is the work of Paul Collier and Anke Hoeffler (Collier 2000; Collier *et al.* 2002; Collier *et al.* 2000), which uses diasporas as one variable among others to explain civil strife. From this perspective, the presence of diasporas is a strong indicator of the likelihood of further conflicts. Their research has concluded:

If the country has an unusually large American diaspora its chances of conflict are 36 percent. If it has an unusually small diaspora its chances of conflict are only 6 percent. So, diasporas appear too dangerous in post-conflict situations.

(Collier 2000: 6)

This chapter questions these theoretical assumptions through an empirical study of the Croatian case. Are borders of a diaspora given or dependent on social actors' definitions? When do diasporas "appear" as political subjects? This chapter explores how the diaspora as a category of practice emerges as a complex process of deterritorialized national mobilization. In this case, the war proved to be—even if only for a few years—a crucial spark that launched the movement of transnational national unity. Therefore, by reversing the traditional understanding of the relationship between diasporas and war, it can be said that it is not the diaspora that "created" the war, but the war that created the diaspora. This mobilization produced specific effects linked to the repertoires of meanings and blueprints for actions that it contained: the previously divided groups and categories of the population created the illusion of a homogenous population, entitled to speak and act in the name of a distant homeland. Following the premises of Chapter 1, the first half of the chapter retraces the logics of identification produced by different factors that led to the emergence of the diaspora as a mobilization category in the transnational field; the chapter then moves to the different ways these repertoires materialized in the early 1990s and led to specific repertoires of diasporic action. Due to the practical necessity to limit this empirical research, this second part of the chapter essentially deals with the case of Croatians in North America. The discussion will try, as much as possible, to refer wherever possible to Croatians elsewhere in the world. However, the empirical case of the United States is sufficient for the theoretical argument put forward herein concerning the "invention" of the diaspora and the competition among diaspora associations to be the exclusive legitimate representative of Croatians abroad.

Logics of identification: creating the diaspora (1987–1989)

As demonstrated in the previous chapters, over the years the Croatian political transnational field witnessed variations in its principles of vision and division. Yet social and group boundaries were progressively fixed—on the one hand by the practices of the Yugoslav government and its bureaucratic categories, and on the other hand by the willing or unwilling acknowledgment of these boundaries by Croats abroad as well as their institutions. However, this social, political, and linguistic stabilization was to be completely overturned due to major changes in the domestic and international context. At the end of the 1980s, a certain number of structural factors led to a shakeup of these established understandings—what Bourdieu defined as a "practical *epochè*." As the French sociologist put it, the heretic rupture with the established order and with the dispositions and the representations that it generates among the agents shaped according to these structures, supposes itself the conjunction between the critical discourse and an objective crisis, able to break the immediate concordance between the incorporated structures and the objective structures they are the product of, and to institute a sort of practical *epochè*, a suspension of the primary approval of the established order.

(Bourdieu 1982: 150)

In the Croatian case, three main structural factors brought the established social order to a profound crisis.

First, and most evidently, Slobodan Milošević's policies marked a fundamental change in ethnic relations in Yugoslavia. Since the creation of communist Yugoslavia, Yugoslav political life had been marked by several lines of division on the "national question" between promoters of a unitary Yugoslav identity—"unitarists" such as Stjepan Iveković or Ferdo Culinović—and promoters of a milder, federal understanding of the nationalities question, such as Vladimir Bakery, Kernel, or Tito himself (Ramet 1992). The doxa of the established regime was that ethnic mobilization or the stirring up of ethnic tensions—dubbed "chauvinism" in communist parlance—could only be an anti-Yugoslav activity, usually attributed to the Yugoslav Enemy Migration. Yet Serbia's repression of the Albanian strikes in 1981, Milošević's 1987 "anti-bureaucratic" revolution, and the progressive development of outspoken Serbian nationalism up to the 1989 speech of Kosovo Pole contributed to the radical questioning of this doxa. From Tito's death and throughout the 1980s, more and more sections of the ruling elite as well as society at large in Croatia—as in the rest of the federation—felt that ethnicity progressively structured everyday political life in a country destabilized by major economic problems (Gagnon Jr. 2004).

These developments accelerated a larger trend running much deeper within the Yugoslav institutions—namely, the "centrifugal" dynamic of the Yugoslav federation. Since the initial unitary attempts in the 1950s, Yugoslavia had indeed experienced a series of reforms that gave greater weight to the different republics. Among these, the post-1971 reforms were critical in devolving powers in diverse fields such as culture and education, policing, or national defense. The progressive "republicanization"—i.e., the devolution of bureaucratic prerogatives from the federal level to the republics—of Yugoslav political life progressively tightened affinities on an ethnic basis (Schöpflin 2005: 189–195).

Finally, the third element of the crisis was the fall of the Berlin Wall and the subsequent disappearance of the Communist bloc as such. Although Yugoslavia itself was not tied by the Warsaw Pact, the privileged position of the country as a leader of the non-aligned world was built precisely on this interstitial location within the East–West divide. Not only did Yugoslavia benefit from being both inside and outside both camps, but its very integrity as a country was also seen by both the Soviet Union and the United States as a fact of utmost priority.

Croatia; diaspora forged in war (1987–1993)

As Brezhnev's and Nixon's attitude attested in the 1971 Croatian Spring, neither bloc would have let Yugoslavia disintegrate. With the end of the Berlin Wall, this constraint at the international level no longer existed.

The connected and the disconnected

These three structural elements provided, however, only the conditions of possibility for the political mobilization and "invention" of the diaspora to take hold. What these changes provoked, indeed, was a restructuring of the field by removing the barrier that had existed between actors abroad and those within the country, progressively bringing separated political subfields together to embrace the principle of vision and division of Croatian transnational nationalism. Indeed, in the late 1980s, historical leaders of the Croatian dissident movements of 1971 were sensing that the possibility for change was within reach once again.

As in any political mobilization, these movements were in urgent need of—among other things—funding. The main dynamic that the progressive abolition of the domestic–expatriate divide brought about was precisely access to the funds of Croats abroad. In this race, political groups within the country that had already established links with networks abroad managed to organize efficiently; meanwhile, unconnected groups became marginalized. Thus, this section will first explore the formation of a nationalist group within the Yugoslav party structure, the contacts it failed—or willingly refused—to establish with the moderate exiles in the last years of the 1980s, and finally the importance of the Norval networks in shaping the future HDZ policies.

In the context of a late-1980s ethnicized Yugoslav political arena, the most empowered actors were those individuals who had occupied positions in the party and in the official institutions who had been "nationally aware." A certain number of high figures in the party protected and gave opportunities to likeminded members in order to occupy positions in which they could have influence. As Josip Manolić, a preeminent figure in the early days of HDZ commented in 1996, people such as Ivan Stevo Krajačić were central in this sense.[4] Krajačić, a central figure of the revolutionary guard and often suspected of nurturing nationalist tendencies, actively supported individuals such as Većeslav Holjevac, a popular mayor of Zagreb and scholar of the Croatian emigration, marginalized after the Croatian Spring for "nationalist deviation." Holjevac himself created the Institute for the History of the Worker's Movement (Institut za Historiju Radničkog Pokreta)—a historical research institute—and called the young Franjo Tuđman from Belgrade to head it. Future dissidents such as Bruno Bušić would come and go in these institutions (Glavaš 1996: 26). Franjo Tuđman's personal trajectory is particularly illustrative of how one strand of the Croatian nationalism of the 1990s—and subsequently the leaders to promote it—did not come from outside, but from within the Communist party itself.

A dedicated communist and young member of the Yugoslav People's Army during World War II, Tuđman occupied several positions in the Yugoslav bureaucracy and earned a doctorate in history. At the Institute for the History of the Workers Movement, Tuđman obtained the privilege of having access to the so-called Yugoslav Enemy Migration "propaganda," journals, and reviews published abroad. Another position also provided him with the material conditions to travel abroad: in 1967, Tuđman was appointed head of the North American section of Matica Hrvatska, one of the few Croatian cultural institutions tolerated by the regime. By traveling abroad, he got to know individuals who were already or would soon become classified as "enemies" by the Yugoslav secret services: Mate Meštrović, Stanko Vujić, Karl Mirth, Bogdan Radica, and George Prpić (Hudelist 2004: 459).

However, with the outbreak of the Croatian Spring, as a member of Matica Hrvatska and a participant in the movement, Tuđman was brought to trial and, in 1972, found guilty of having connections to the enemy migration (Hudelist 2004: 484). This marked the end of his contacts with emigration for a while and the beginning of his political marginalization in the homeland. Tuđman was however only a secondary figure of the Croatian Spring—certainly secondary to the young reformist leaders of the Croatian League of Communists Savka Dabčević-Kučar and Miko Tripalo, the student leader Ivan Zvonimir-Èièak Čičak, and the heads of Matica, such as the brothers Veselica and Vlado Gotovac. After his release from prison, Tuđman was marginalized by the dissident groups for his ideas, which were deemed to be too radical. With the political field inside Croatia closed to him, his only ideological partners were in groups in exile. Therefore, from that moment on, Tuđman intensified his relations with the exiles, particularly through his protégé Bruno Bušić as well as through illegal travels in Western Europe. During 1977 and 1978, he came to meet more important figures of the "Expatriate Croatia," such as Vinko Nikolić and Bernard Luketich (Hudelist 2004: 494–495).

In 1981, Tuđman progressively managed to position himself outside of the acceptable domestic political opposition and yet be the center of attention of nationalist radical organizations abroad. In a series of interviews given to the domestic and international press, Tuđman openly criticized the Yugoslav authorities, rehashing the mix of human rights, economic, and nationalist arguments that had constituted the bulk of the Croatian Spring's claims. Yet he went a step further, openly attacking Yugoslav official history—particularly by questioning the number of deaths from the World War II Croatian-run concentration camp Jasenovac.[5] Tuđman was brought to court in February 2001 on the grounds of "falsely representing the position of the Croatian nation and the freedom of citizens in the SFRY" in addition to contradicting the established official history (Okružno Javno Tužilaštvo Zagreb 1980: 391). The case was badly prepared by the prosecution, the accusations poorly grounded, and the entire situation offered him a perfect arena in which to publicize his ideas. His response to the accusations was published in several editions abroad, making him a hero for many in the radical circles there; while for many at home, he had crossed a line in condoning the NDH (Hudelist 2004: 517). Tuđman and his supporters argued for the unification of all Croats in one territory—a Great Croatia. Furthermore, by rekindling Luburić's idea of unity between the old Partizans and communists, he subsequently parted with the rest of the opposition movement of 1971 represented by Gotovac, Dabčević-Kučar, and Budiša, who instead advocated a small-Croatian, anti-communist liberal democratic agenda (Hudelist 1999: 85).

Tuđman's first important trip abroad after his 1981-1983 incarceration reflected the ambiguous position he occupied in the Croatian transnational political space, and marked the failed connection with the moderate elements of the Croatian transnational field abroad. Most probably with the support—or at least the permission—of sympathetic security authorities in Croatia, Tuđman received a passport in 1987[6] that allowed him to travel to North America officially in order to attend the annual meeting of the American Association for the Advancement of Slavic Studies (AAASS) in Chicago. In reality, Tuđman met with Croatian leaders abroad. As a former member of Matica Hrvatska, his natural alliances were with the intellectual, usually nationally moderated, political emigration circles.

Since the 1970s, he had been in touch with figures such as Branko Salaj in Sweden, Vladimir Pavlinić in the UK, Gojko Boric in Germany, and Tihomil Rađa in Switzerland (Hudelist 2004: 501)—emigrants who had in the 1970s organized sections of Matica Hrvatska abroad, followed by independent organizations that were "friends of" Matica Hrvatska. Similarly, Mate Meštrović's Croatian National Council, expunged of its violent and anti-democratic elements, was Tuđman's natural contact.[7] Tuđman visited the Croatian Fraternal Union's leader, Bernard Luketich, several times to find support among the members of the largest Croatian American organization. However, within these various moderate intellectual nationalist exiles, Tuđman was treated as one dissident among many. More problematically, he did not see among these circles the strong political and economic support he needed for his political project.

To the surprise of many, upon their return to Croatia two years later, at the turn of 1989, most of these exiles such as Mate Meštrović, *Nova Hrvatska*'s editor Jakša Kušan and others, found a strongly established movement—both abroad and in the homeland—that had managed to establish itself without them.

In Toronto, in 1987, Tuđman had indeed come into contact with different networks. The radical Norval group might not have possessed the same sophisticated manners, but it had three main strengths that other networks did not offer (Hudelist 2004: 582). First, it was organized around a religious institution, the Franciscan friars, that had developed a large number of Catholic missions abroad since the 1960s. The group could directly reach an estimated 600,000 Croats abroad. Second, the Norval group was composed primarily of Croats coming not from Croatia proper, but from Herzegovina, a region of Bosnia-Herzegovina known for widespread pro-*Ustaša*, strongly anti-communist feelings, strong family relations, and tight social networks (Lovrenović 2001). The mobilization of a few would have meant the involvement of many. Third, Tuđman understood that the Herzegovinian community of Canada and America counted wealthy individuals among its members, ready to actively contribute to the most radical projects.

Upon his return to Croatia, Tuđman became confident that he could organize a strong political movement with the support of his allies in Canada; he only needed to coordinate better with the Norval group, raise funds, and found the movement. By 1989, the evolution of the situation—both internationally and within the Yugoslav federation—encouraged several businessmen whom he had encountered between 1987 and 1989 to finance the political campaign of the party he founded on 17 June 1989: the HDZ.[8] Thus, an exchange of social capitals was organized through the alliance: Tuđman offered "reputational" capital, contact with the homeland, and future positions in the administration; in return the Norval Croatian businessmen,[9] marginalized radical circles (including the famous future Minister of Defense Gojko Šušak),[10] and the Franciscan friars offered a network ready to be mobilized as well as financial capabilities. Consequently, Tuđman's alleged support from the "diaspora" initially came primarily from this extremely small section of the transnational political field. The dominant moderate sections of the HNV (Mate Meštrović, Jakša Kušan, Boris Maruna, etc.) were de facto excluded from the process, and the silent majority represented by the CFU watched from a distance.[11]

Meanwhile, Tuđman's early trips from 1987 to 1990 led the mobilization within the diaspora—in part orchestrated by the HDZ, in part spontaneous—to reach unprecedented levels, as the majority of Croats abroad aligned behind whomever was standing for an independent Croatia. With the end of SFRY, the distinctions between the "old migration," the "political emigration," and "workers temporarily abroad" vanished, in favor of a larger, homogenizing category. At this point, the Croatian diaspora became, for the first time, a widespread representation of a unified, transnational political field.

Thus, the end of the Cold War, the end of communism in Yugoslavia, and the imminent independence of Croatia fundamentally restructured, declassified, and reclassified the positions and representations of the Croatian transnational political field (Bourdieu 2000: 62). The "declustering" of specific sectors of the Croatian transnational political field consequently served as the main condition allowing for the diasporic mobilization to emerge—one that placed Tuđman's HDZ in relation to wealthy radical groups, marginalizing the moderate elements of the political field.

"Iseljena Hrvatska" in Tuđman's transnational nationalism

The success of the alliance between Franjo Tuđman, the HDZ, and the Norval networks can be measured by their ability to reconstruct a political space around a specific, nationalist doxa. This is to say that the taken-for-granted assumptions that defined the very transnational political field in the 1990s had progressively moved from the moderate platform of the HNV and moderates such as Dabčević-Kučar and Gotovac to a radical nationalist one that could no longer be discussed for fear of being accused of not being "a good Croat" or "Croat enough."[12] At the center of Tuđman's nationalist doctrine was the development of the thesis about a single, unified category for Croats abroad as an integral part of the nation: the "expatriate Croatia" (*Iseljena Hrvatska*)—an idea that became, for many Croats abroad, the diaspora.

As with every national movement, the HDZ in the late 1980s and early 1990s was composed of a heterogeneous mix of political positions, represented by different political actors who had partially intersecting, often conflicting stakes in the political game; however, the free elections of 1990 represented a political juncture in which these positions coalesced behind the figure of Tuđman. Therefore, the HDZ's ideological positions did not originate from the thought of a single man, although Tuđman's writings are a privileged site of analysis of the doxa of this more expansive group of political actors who came to power in 1990.

The first important concept for Tuđman was the one of "national reconciliation" (*pomirba*). This idea, which was subsequently repeated by Bruno Bušić in exile, was allegedly inherited from Tuđman's reading of Maks Luburić's review during his days as the head of the Institute for the Workers Movement. The idea behind *pomirba* was that the traditional division within the Croatian nation between the left and the right, between the *Ustaše* and the communists, had to be transcended to achieve the higher goal of national independence. In this sense, heritages from all historical figures of Croatian history—from Ante Pavelić, the *Ustaša* leader, to Josip Strossmeyer, the tolerant cleric, and from Stjepan Radić, the populist peasant party leader, to Ante Starčević, the father of Croatian anti-Serb nationalism—were mobilized in a glorification of a trans-historical Croatianness, which would prevail in the realization of the state (Ramet 2006: 421). Hudelist's argument holds that Tuđman's idea derives directly from Luburić's experience of Franco's policies. While he fails to demonstrate exactly how the passage is done, our research found elements to support this thesis, such as this statement by the Croatian presidential candidate in 1990:

> Whoever is for an independent Croatia, from the right wing to the left wing, must be with us, in our Program, and must express our demands. Let us in Croatia be today clever like one general Franco 30 years ago in Spain when he said: "Spanish falangists and Spanish communists both fought for Spain, let us bury them together, each one under his flag, to build a democratic Spain!" And today Spain is indeed democratic. With this in mind, let us pull out this positive energy and work together, with no regard to which ideological and political camp we or our parents once belonged.[13]

Second, Tuđman's nationalism was based on a firm anti-Serb sentiment complemented by an all-encompassing definition of Croatianness intellectually inherited from the influential Franciscan friar Dominik Mandić. Croats were understood as radically different than Serbs and certainly unfit to live in the same country—ignoring years of pan-Yugoslav tradition.

> Under the influence of the Western Church and Western European nations, with whom they lived in European unity and state vicinity or alliance, Croats have continuously built their national culture in a Western spirit, and

thus become a nation of the European Western culture [...]. With the religious dispute of 1054, Serbs followed the Eastern church [...]. From there, all the Serbian religious and cultural life, ecclesiastic and state law, Serbian literature and art developed under the strong influence of the Eastern church and Byzantine culture. As such, Serbs, through their culture and in spirit have become markedly an Eastern nation of Byzantine type [...]. But when the Kingdom of Serbs, Croats and Slovenes (SHS) was founded in 1918, based on this fictive (Yugoslav) idea, it has been shown in essence that Croats and Serbs are not a single but two different nations, with opposite cultural, legal and moral ideas.

(Mandić 1971: 277)[14]

The final strikingly original aspect of Tuđman's nationalism was its transnational nature. Re-enacting the fear of depopulation from the beginning of the century (see Chapter 2), as early as 1977 Tuđman designated Serbian nationalism inside the Yugoslav institutions as reasons for the massive emigration of Croats (Tuđman 1995: 347). Because of the "catastrophic" circumstances of their departure, it was the mission of any independent Croatian state to bring back to the homeland this "exiled" part of the nation.[15] Thus, Tuđman's vision of the Croatian "Corpus"—the totality of the Croatian nation—was constituted not only by the Croats in Croatia, but also by a three-layered geographical distribution including the Croats from the Socialist Republic of Croatia, the Croats from the Socialist Republic of BiH, and other Croats from Yugoslavia as well as Croats living in exile (in Europe, the Americas, Australia). The minorities (Serbs, Hungarians, Italians, etc.) within Croatia were excluded from this repartition. As such, Tuđman had formulated not only a form of territorial nationalism (which would have implied the necessary realization of the Croatian nation as an independent state within its borders), but also a political cosmology in which the concept of "nation" transcended territorial borders, although it needed to be reunited: the national corpus was in fact the union of a "homeland Croatia" (*Domovinska Hrvatska*) and an "expatriate Croatia" (*Iseljena Hrvatska*) (Hudelist 2004: 455).

Based on this three-fold foundation of its political ideology and program, Tuđman and the HDZ established the foundation for a wide platform of transnational political mobilization of Croats abroad. The objective was simple: the three categories of Croats abroad (old emigrants, Yugoslav political emigrants, and guest workers) as well as ideological (*Ustaše*, Nationalists, communists) or even regional (Croats from Croatia/Croats from Herzegovina) differences were to be merged, culminating in the historical reunion of the "Expatriate Croatia" and the "Homeland Croatia" for Croatia's statehood and independence.

Financing the HDZ (1987–1990)

Between 1987 and 1989, Tuđman organized several trips to the United States, Canada, and Europe, attending conferences and fundraisers organized for him.

He came into contact with industrialists and influential Croatian Americans such as Ivan Nogalo, Domagoj Šola, Steve Bubalo, Anthony Maglica, and Pero Novak. Most were from Herzegovina, had recently emigrated to North America, and shared his radical ideas. One of the most influential figures of Croatian political life during the 1990s would certainly be the Canadian emigrant Gojko Šušak.[16]

On 17 June 1989, the Croatian Democratic Union was founded in Zagreb, although Tuđman would often say that it was de facto born in Canada. Among his political competitors, Tuđman did not have a head start.[17] His history as a general of the Yugoslav People's Army created resentment among Croats abroad, particularly in radical circles that had still not met him. Yet he had the right connections in Toronto, and a clear message. As former Ambassador to Canada Andrija Jakovčević explained:

> The HDZ was well implemented among the diaspora because their slogan was something that nobody could disagree with: "We want independent Croatia." Which member of the diaspora would disagree with that? No one! At that time, other parties also had some representation abroad, but none of them had the popularity of HDZ, and it's pretty simple to understand why: there was no time for liberal or mild ideas, you could not mobilize or create any emotional reaction! There was only place for strong patriotic ideas, and that was what HDZ was offering.[18]

Thus, during 1989, in the most important cities of the Croatian emigration—namely, Toronto, Vancouver, Pittsburgh, Cleveland, Chicago, New York, Stuttgart, and Paris—the HDZ set up offices and received funds from Croats abroad. When Tuđman gathered the first congress of the HDZ on 24 and 25 February 1990, the time for semi-confidential reunions had passed as the party had acquired real support. More than 2,500 militants from Croatia, Bosnia-Herzegovina, Montenegro, Hungary, and more surprisingly—without being hassled by the police—the United States, Canada, and Germany were present in the Lisinski concert hall to sing *Ljepa Naša Domovina*.[19] Žarko Puhovski, a professor of political philosophy in Zagreb, remembered the 1990 campaign in these terms:

> We were shocked. Tuđman at this point was just a retired general sitting in a cafe, and suddenly he had more money than anybody. It dominated everything.[20] Šušak remarked: "It was maybe a couple of million dollars, but here it was like it was a trillion. We had posters all over."[21]

On 30 May 1990, Tuđman won the elections with a relative majority, but the electoral law gave him almost complete control of the Sabor, the Croatian parliament, with 206 of 351 seats. The first objective of the HDZ—changing the regime—had been achieved.

Making the community appear: 26 July 1991, and other demonstrations

Thanks to the electoral victory, the structure of the Croatian transnational political field changed radically. The hostile government in the homeland was replaced by a nationalist party, the HDZ, composed (among others) of the very core group of political émigrés who constituted the "political exile" subfield.

This led to the emergence of new organizations abroad. In the United States, for example, the Croatian American Association (CAA), funded mainly by the rich Croatian American businessman Ilija Letica, was set up with the specific purpose of creating a Croatian lobby group.[22] It was also the association closest to the HDZ (most of its members and leaders were members of the HDZ) and seemed the most "Croatian." It opened a Washington branch to pursue its lobbying activities (its headquarters were in Chicago) and, from the very beginning, served as an unofficial Croatian embassy until the opening of the Office of the Republic of Croatia (the permanent office of the government in Zagreb before the international recognition of Croatia). Meanwhile, the CCU, close to the CAA, took a more distant stance, even though its members were actively involved in the CAA's activities as well as various humanitarian aid programs. The CFU, seen as too pro-Yugoslav, was considered suspect, but it quickly mobilized, implementing its humanitarian aid program as early as 1991.[23]

On 26 July 1991, the CAA marked one of the key moments in Croatian activism in the United States when it assembled a 35,000-strong protest in Washington. From California, Pennsylvania, Illinois, Texas, Georgia, Arizona, and even Canada, Croatian and Slovenian protesters spilled by the busloads onto the lawns of Capitol Hill, marching in a long procession of red-and-white-checked traditional dress, banners, and Croatian, Slovenian, American, and Canadian flags. The logic behind a demonstration is simple: convert identity construction into something palpable, measurable, and real.

> Officialization is accomplished through *demonstration*, a typically magical act (which does not mean to say devoid of efficiency) by which a group that is practical or virtual, ignored, denied, or repressed, engages in protest for the benefit of other groups and *for itself*, and attests to its own existence as a known and recognized group, aspiring to institutionalization.
>
> (Bourdieu 1982: 142)

Thus, protesting created a dual effect. First and foremost, it made the group's existence known to all—in this particular case, to United States "public opinion," the White House, and Congress. Second, it allowed the illusion of *diasporic construction* to be refined, giving it physical shape and acting as a means to "make people aware of its existence."[24] Thus, 26 July 1991 was a significant moment for both identification with the Croatian diaspora and the organization of its political agenda. Finally, looking more precisely at the struggles taking place among the various organizations to monopolize representation of the diaspora, it is apparent that 26 July 1991 also marked the beginning of the CAA's exclusive role as the organization for Croatian Americans in Washington.

The aims of the protest were simple: to plead for the recognition of the independence of Slovenia and Croatia, declared by Ljubljana and Zagreb on 25 June 1991; for the implementation of the ceasefire negotiated by the European Community; and for an end to fighting in Croatia. Bob Dole, who had already spoken out in favor of the Croatian cause, was among an improvised delegation of members of Congress—none of whom had predicted the scale of the event.[25] In his speech, Dole provided an illustration of how the Croatian cause could be recast in the language of American, anti-communist, anti-interventionist politics:

> No doubt, many of you gathered here today, left your homeland to escape communist oppression and to build a new life in America, so that you could speak freely, worship freely and meet freely, as you are doing right now [...]. While the immediate future appears dangerous and uncertain, I am confident that the Croatian people will, in the end, triumph over communism in all of its forms. And, I believe that your presence here will send a message around the globe that Croatia is ready to join the free world.[26]

The organizers' speeches were also based on three fundamental points determined to be the argument most likely to have an impact on the American public: defense of human rights, the right to self-determination, and anti-communism:

> Promotion of peace, prosperity, human rights and self-determination as an American issue and an American duty which should not be denied to the peoples of the Republic of Croatia.[27]

The entire leadership of these Croatian American organizations was present on the platform: Franck Politeo (CAA), Ivan Mihaljević (CAA), Frane Golem (Croatian representative in Washington), Bernard Luketich (President of the CFU), Anthony Petrušić (President of the CCU), Ilija Letica (President of the CAA), and Slavko Jambrušić (Croatian Academy of America). However, the protest also aimed to take a stand against Milošević—specifically, to show that this was not an "ethnic" conflict, but an actual war of aggression waged by Milošević against the Balkan peoples as a whole. Thus, during a similar protest a few months later, Max Primorac, head of the Croatian Democracy Project, stated:

> now the White House can no longer say that they can't do anything because the conflict in Serboslavia is ethnic. Our togetherness here is undeniable proof that the problem and cause of the conflict is Serbia.[28]

Clearly these protests served both to mobilize the diaspora and to make it real— real in the eyes of the Croatian Americans who were becoming aware of its existence at the time as well as equally real for the American political leaders who were simultaneously beginning to take stock of its sheer size. The involvement of senators, House representatives, and other politicians in the majority of these protests also served to provide direct access to the centers of decision-making by speaking the language of Washington. However, lobbying Congress and the White House was an activity in itself to which CAA members dedicated their efforts.

Logics of mobilization: a "diaspora" at war, the Croatian-American example (1989–1992)

The construction of a "Croatian identity" by the HDZ and other nationalist organizations depended on the writing of an authorized history to sketch out the unique traits of the Croat nation—its origins, language, religion, and cultural traditions—that legitimately led to the nation's claim to independence. Yugoslavia, according to this interpretation of Croatian history, was nothing but a manipulative tool constructed by Western powers and Serbian rulers to subjugate the 1,000-year-old Croatian people. In its collective dimension, discourse on the Croatian diaspora was thus the representation and expression in political terms of these natural cultural traits: if indeed the Croat nation matched this description and if—as a member of the diaspora—people felt that they belonged to that nation, then it was legitimate to rally for the natural achievement of the nation's goal of independence.

Therefore, the collective dimension of the diaspora incorporated this process of mobilization, which was itself the product of identification with a particular authorized version of the nation's history. However, within the context of dispersal, for diasporic institutions this allegiance posed a major problem related to the simultaneously universal (right to self-determination) and particular (each nation is unique) aspects of the nation-state project—namely, how could they persuade American, Canadian, and German citizens to rally to the Croatian cause? How could they ensure that this mobilization would not be considered a subversion of the principles of the states in which these second- and third-generation Croatians were living? How could they ensure that this political rallying would deploy in those channels where it would be the most effective?

Croatian associations could justify their action by grounding their treatise in legitimate values both in the dominant political discourse of their hostland and in the dominant political discourse of the transnational Croatian political field. Indeed, in this intersection of symbolic repertoires of mobilization such associations would be able to develop the most persuasive argumentation. Therefore, this discussion questions the optimistic hypothesis put forward by Yossi Shain, who states that political diasporas are not a threat to foreign politics and the American democratic ethos, insofar as to be understood and achieve their demands they are forced to comply with the conventions of their hostland (1999: 8). The argument is based on the idea that institutions claiming to represent various diasporas will only use their host country's channels for political protest and comply with the host country's norms in formulating their demands if these demands are sufficiently adapted to the norms of the host country. This last variable is highly dependent on the *habitus* of members of these institutions as well as on how useful they perceive the various American institutional channels to be. If members of diaspora institutions did not think that channels for American political protest suited their protests because, for example, their system of values contradicted that of the United States, then it would be a safe bet that their action would be organized through different channels, such as confrontational action or violence. The action of radical Croatian organizations in the 1970s can be explained in this way.

While members of the Norval network—allied with ex-communists turned nationalists—were gradually organizing the institutions of the new independent state-to-be, Croatians abroad began to mobilize (the next chapter deals with the diaspora policies drawn by the new government in place). The second part of this chapter is concerned with what is without doubt the most important place in the first years of history of the new state—and one that is widely neglected in official history grounded in methodological nationalism: the transnational arena. As Daphne Winland comments:

> Those who acknowledge the importance of transnationalism focus mostly on the refugees who fled their homes. Seldom does the discussion gravitate toward consideration of the role of diasporas before, during, or after the wars of succession, which, in the Croatian case, were formidable.
>
> (2007: 17)

Indeed, in the United States, mobilization of the CFU, through the *Zajedničar* newspaper, was organized based on political values that were legitimate in the hostland as well as through the institutional channels of American politics.

The beginning of the war: humanitarian aid (1990–1991)

Following the 1990 elections, tensions began to flare within the country—most notably in Knin, the capital of the Krajina region. The Serbian minority saw the election of Tuđman in a bad light: the highly nationalist program, the introduction of a new flag, the reintroduction of the Croatian checkerboard shield, and the newly opened office of the President of Croatia were all cause for concern. Moreover, the Serbian nation's change in status from a "constituent population" to a "minority" aroused anger (Tanner 1997: 234). During the summer of 1990, the recently established National Serbian Council published the "Declaration on the Sovereignty and Autonomy of Croatian Serbs." The Serbs began to arm themselves, with the support of the JNA and the police.[29] The Croatian government, for its part, had already begun to purchase arms. Blockades were erected on roads between Zagreb and the coast; skirmishes between the Popular Defense Council and Croatian forces multiplied. On 17 August, following an attack by Croatian police special forces on the Serb-controlled Benkovac police station, the Serbs seized weapons from the police reserves and barricaded the roads. Thus began the Serbian uprising in Croatia.[30]

With both the onset of the confrontations and the Knin rebellion, clubs and associations, cultural circles, and Croatian Houses across the United States and Canada took to the cause. The "suffering from afar" of the Croatian diaspora was a significant moment in their mobilization. This unification with the "suffering masses," this moment of identification *par excellence* on the part of the "hyphenated Croats" with their brothers back home, was one of the most powerful moments of both the mobilization and the construction of identity of the diasporic unit. Thus, the sense of *hrvatstvo* came to the fore, even for second- or third-generation Americans of Croatian origin:

> The interesting thing to me is that when this war of aggression was started by the Serbs how our patriotism or I should say Croatian patriotism came to life in all of us, not just myself, and I only came here as a twelve-year-old so really what did I know, but I was surprised myself that I had such strong feelings as I did about it, and maybe unconsciously I knew about the oppression and suppression of everything Croatian, but I didn't really realize it until it came to the forefront and until they tried to destroy everything Croatian.[31]

Humanitarian aid also became one of the main objectives of persons feeling they were part of the diaspora. Here, the CFU played a central role for several reasons. First, as Tony Peraica[32] explains, the CFU had long since had Yugoslavs[33] among its members. Now, when the time came to choose those who would lead the support for the Croatian cause, a number of Serbian or Yugoslav members had left. On the other hand, as previously discussed, CFU members—the majority of them Americans of Croatian origin—were generally somewhat removed in their political convictions from the radical political exiles. Finally, the legal status of the CFU—namely that of a fraternal union—prevented it (in theory) from engaging in political campaigns.[34] For this reason the CFU was, in its leadership in the field of humanitarian aid, to hit upon a situation felt to be extremely satisfactory at the heart of the diaspora. Its members were simultaneously committed to their country, but without denying their political (or apolitical) credo or getting involved in radical organizations. Moreover, the CFU, organized around an insurance fund structure, had both the bureaucratic wherewithal and technical ability to best organize the humanitarian aid.[35]

Aid in Croatia, in the form of clothing, food, various goods, or simply money, was organized early on. The catastrophic fall of Vukovar in October 1991 surely sent sufficient shockwaves to spur people into action. Aid had probably already begun in the form of individual shipments from family to family and to close ones still "back home." This aid—although impossible to quantify—played a crucial role in offering both material and moral support alike.[36] Approximately 300 local organizations were spontaneously established during the early 1990s for the principal aim of supplying humanitarian aid. Such initiatives included, for example, the American Croatian Relief Project (St. Louis, Missouri).[37]

The greatest collective effort came from the CFU. One CFU report (Luketich 1999) puts the total value of aid sent at over 24 million dollars, shipped in more than 141 containers between 1991 and 1999—or, to put this into perspective, a value equivalent to just less than one-tenth of the total European Community aid sent to Croatia over the same period via the ECHO aid program.[38] Similarly, the Dora Fund, set up to help war orphans, has offered support to more than 650 children since it was founded, providing a total of more than 1.2 million dollars in aid.

The CFU's humanitarian aid fund was set up after the president of the Croatian parliament, Stjepan Salimanac, contacted Bernard Luketich directly,[39] asking him for aid in the form of medical equipment. The fund also took charge of supplying food aid as well as clothes to refugees. Thus, the pages of the *Zajedničar* newspaper often carried specific appeals, giving a description of the medicines being sought.[40] Most of the time, goods were collected through local churches, clubs, and cultural associations and then categorized and packaged up at the CFU's Pittsburgh offices, which subsequently shipped them to Croatia via the port of Baltimore.

Most of the costs were covered through CFU donations and the names of donors were regularly published in the CFU newspaper, along with the amount given.[41] Croatian transport workers also helped ensure shipments made it to their intended destinations by providing their equipment and expertise for the task; hence, they also serve to testify to the spontaneous nature of this activity.[42] The CFU fund was not the only large-scale initiative. The CCU's Croatian War Orphan Fund is estimated to have totaled 700,000 dollars, with the Croatian Relief Fund contributing another 700,000 dollars (Carter 2001: 236).

The organization of humanitarian aid, as highlighted by Sean Carter, played a dual role. While it enabled help to be given to a number of Croatians in the "old homeland," it also made a significant contribution to forging the identity of the diaspora, giving the latter a visible presence within the community at dances, dinners, and fundraising events, thereby broadening the "community of concern" for Croatian Americans. As such, people felt that they were contributing to the fight for independence in a neutral manner, without engaging in politics, while still feeling that they belonged to an expatriate community committed to a country at war—that is, a true diaspora.

During the war: military aid (1989–1996)

Humanitarian aid was, for the vast majority of Croatian Americans, the chosen means of supporting the cause, especially in the United States. However, be they former migrants, political exiles, former communists, or anti-communists, a much smaller nucleus took charge of organizing and financing the military effort in Croatia. Even today, such military aid is an extremely sensitive issue among Croatian expatriates, and recently a number of people have spoken up, demanding an explanation of what happened during this period.[43] Anthony Peraica recalls:

I remember at that time everybody started buying a fax. There was no email like now. We would communicate through telephone, fax, telex, everybody was in touch. For the fund raising, you know, we had these local radio stations most Croatian-Americans would listen to, and they would send the message: Today, at four o'clock, join us at the Church Saint this or that, at the Cultural Center here or there to support the struggle for independence. Of course we did not say "support us for buying arms." But everybody knew that, and that's what they were giving the money for: to buy weapons for the homeland war.

Although Mate Granić[44] insisted that, as far as weapons were concerned, the role of the diaspora was decisive only before the international recognition of independence, Peraica insisted that aid continued until 1995–1996, reaching a peak in 1993. CAA leaders such as Peraica were thus directly involved in financial support for the war. However, it is important to clarify that no transaction went directly via the funds of these associations. All international aid to Croatia was sent to the Croatian National Fund, with a Swiss, then an Austrian bank account whose details were secretly circulated among Croatian Americans.[45] Peraica estimated that approximately seven to ten million dollars were collected in this way between 1989 and 1995–1996 in the Chicago area alone. Nationally, it is estimated that a total of 25 to 30 million dollars were collected exclusively for the purchase of weapons.

To what extent did the diaspora contribute to financing the Croatian war effort? Here again, opinions differ. Miomir Žužul estimates the proportion of aid from the diaspora to be a "single figure percentage" of the total war effort[46] whereas, according to Peraica, the proportion is around double this figure, or between 20 and 25 percent of the total amount. The real figure probably lies between these two estimates. For obvious reasons, it is almost impossible to get precise data on this transnational flow of money. Yet what is certain is that the diaspora made a significant contribution to the supply of both funding and equipment[47] to the Croatian war effort. Thus, discussions need not be too reticent in suggesting that—without the support of certain expatriate associations, financed in turn by committed businessmen, as well as without the united effort of a large number of individual Croatian Americans—the war in the former Yugoslavia and the Republic of Croatia would have been a very different story.

The diaspora as a pressure group: the example of the United States

At the very start of the events, doubts emerged among Croatian Americans regarding the future of Croatia within Yugoslavia.[48] However, during the summer of 1990, in the face of the political brutality of Milošević, opinions were unanimous: the fighting had to stop and Croatia had to become independent. Yet as previously suggested, the international situation appeared highly unsupportive of any plans to emancipate Croatia. Beyond the international state of affairs, it was the position of the White House and the United States Department of State that seemed to be one of the biggest obstacles to independence. The greatest world power—the one with the capacity to intervene in the conflict and the potential to curb the expansionist policy of Milošević—refused to do so in the name of preserving national unity, as shown by the Human Rights Watch report of 1992:

> In contrast to the EC's activism, the Bush Administration has reacted sluggishly and ineffectively to the crisis in Yugoslavia. [...] the Bush Administration devoted too much energy in trying to preserve Yugoslav unity and the faltering government of Prime Minister Ante Marković rather than address the human rights violations by individual republican governments.
>
> (1992)

The various associations of Croatian Americans in the United States were now focused on an objective other than bilateral, humanitarian, military, or financial support for Croatia. Rather, their aim became to organize a large-scale campaign to change the position of the United States and its policy on Yugoslavia. In other words, they sought independence, diplomatic recognition from the United States and the international community, and an end to the fighting with an outcome that would guarantee territorial integrity for Croatia.

Such aims could only be achieved through action on a national scale, by active organization through one of the institutional channels of American democracy—namely, pressure groups, or to be more precise, *ethnic* pressure groups. In this sense, diaspora associations are strongly conditioned in their actions by the domestic structures. Far from drawing on the weakened condition of the nation-state, it was through its institutional channels and within a framework of nation-state thinking that these political protests were organized. The government of one nation-state, the United States, needed to be pressured into publicly recognizing the creation and existence of another nation-state, Croatia. The action of the diaspora was thus relatively far removed from discourse on cosmopolitanism or the arrival of a new "global society." In order to be effective, the rallying discourse of the diaspora evoked an essentialized, ahistorical, and "natural" nation, thereby operating within the register of a world whose natural propensity was for the nation-state (Billig 1995) and recasting the discourse of the "imagined community" (Anderson 1991).

To achieve this, a combined strategy was conceived within the headquarters of the CAA, CCU, and CFU. The Croatian diaspora needed to be "brought to the fore." American opinion needed to be shown that a large number of Croatians lived in the United States and that they supported only one position: independence. This strategy also sought to convince local, regional, and federal election candidates alike that they represented a part of the electorate whose support might be crucial (notably in Pennsylvania and Illinois), as happened with the 1991 protest previously discussed.

The second line of strategy was to apply pressure on all those institutions likely to have decision-making power in relation to the situation in Croatia, particularly the White House, the State Department, Congress, and even state governments. The nature of the American political system and the organization of lobbying along ethnic lines—modeled after the success of AIPAC and the Jewish World Congress—would subsequently drive Croatian Americans to form an ethnic lobby group. Yet even this approach would require knowing how to play by Washington's rules.

The final line of strategy was public opinion. The leaders of the CAA and other organizations were convinced that, within a comprehensive Croatian support strategy, it was vital that the Croatian cause become an "American issue" in order to—once again—be able to impact members of Congress and leaders. The situation in Yugoslavia needed to be made a campaign theme—namely, a matter of election or reelection.

The first steps in the Croatian political lobbying process occurred in the form of a test of strength that would be of further benefit to American organizations. Even after Tuđman's election, he still depended heavily on funding from abroad. His campaign had been 80 percent funded by the diaspora. His first visits to the United States[49] were funded entirely by the host associations.[50]

Thus, the CAA—and, to be more precise, Anthony Peraica and Mara Letica, the daughter of Ilija Letica—assisted Frane Golem on his arrival in Washington. Golem was newly arrived from Zagreb, with very poor English. Thus, the two CAA members took charge of finding premises to set up the Office of the Republic of Croatia. The rent, relocation, and running costs were fully covered by a rich American businessman of Croatian origin, Steve Bubalo.[51] One of the main problems, Peraica recalls, was that Golem was not "suited" to American politics:

> Whenever there was a debate or a discussion, Golem would start a long historical explanation, beginning from the king Tomislav till now. In ten minutes' time, everybody was already asleep. This is one of the reasons we contacted Jim Harff.[52]

In a word, Golem's *habitus* or "political disposition" did not suit the arena of American political practice and discourse.

Jim Harff, then President of the Ruder Finn public relations agency in Washington, was hired to lead a public relations campaign for the benefit of Croatia. In Peraica's words, Harff was brought in "to bring some sophistication"[53] to the efforts.

Harff began working for the Croatian government as early as 1991 and remained on their payroll until the Croatian-Serbian ceasefire was signed in 1992. Harff was taken on to implement all the communications technologies needed to let the Croatian message "ring out,"[54] influencing the White House, Congress, and Washington think tanks as well as Croatian American organizations. He envisioned his role as that of a translator: "We can be looked as translators between Foreign entities and the American market and culture. We create understanding."[55] In Harff's words, his activity consisted of using "appropriate phraseology" and knowing when to intervene. Ruder Finn's activities were numerous and included creating links and informal contacts with major figures and maintaining good personal contacts with the press (BBC, *Financial Times*, CNN). The company also produced regular communications and news reports aimed at those in the public eye and made decisions on how various *op-eds* were published, suggesting "the words to use, the style to use." Ruder Finn was also in charge of organizing the various visits of senators and representatives to the former Yugoslavia.

Harff had previously played a crucial role in winning over Jewish organizations. As such, it is important to consider the role of the "Jewish lobby" in the minds of Croatian leaders in the United States. According to most associations claiming to be a diaspora of one sort or another, the Jewish lobby served both as an example to follow and a power to conquer. Indeed, everybody envied the efficiency of organizations such as AIPAC and the Jewish World Congress. The most widespread view among diaspora associations was that salvation would come in winning over the Jewish lobby, both for its expertise and at the same time for its support. Jacques Merlino, former deputy editor in chief for *Antenne 2*, documented an interview with Harff regarding his pride in having been able to get the Jewish community on his side:

> Question: What achievement were you most proud of? Harff: To have managed to put Jewish opinion on our side. This was a sensitive matter, as the dossier was dangerous looked from this angle. President Tuđman was very careless in his book "Wastelands of Historical Reality." Reading this writings, one could accuse him of anti-Semitism [...]. At the beginning of August 1992, the New York Newsday came out with the affair of (Serb) concentration camps. We jumped at the opportunity immediately. We outwitted three big Jewish organizations, B'Nai Brith Anti-Defamation League, the Jewish Committee, and the American Jewish Congress. We suggested to them to publish an advertisement in the New York Times and to organize demonstrations outside the U.N. [...]. We won by targeting the Jewish audience. Almost immediately there was a clear change of language in the press, with the use of words with high emotional content, such as "ethnic cleansing," "concentration camps," etc. which evoked images of Nazi Germany and the gas chambers of Auschwitz. The emotional charge was so powerful that nobody could go against it.

Hence, it is possible to gauge the central role played by consulting firms such as Ruder Finn in the diasporic agenda: they served to translate—indeed produce— information for an audience susceptible to a precise format of information and language. Thus, associations of Croatian Americans such as the CAA were crucial, through firms such as Ruder Finn, in drawing up the political agenda of the homeland and in adapting it to the format of the hostland.

With or without Ruder Finn, the lobbying strategy was a complex matter. Initially, it consisted primarily of educating and gaining the loyalty of congressional representatives. Information was issued in the form of reports as well as through direct contact. The latter was made during various fundraising activities, cocktail parties, and receptions.[56] Another opportunity presented itself during the initial Croatian Days On The Hill—three-day meetings between members of Congress and Croatian militants, organized by the CAA from 1991. Meanwhile, the CAA also organized more than half a dozen visits to the former Yugoslavia for members of Congress in order for them to give their first-hand account of the situation upon their return.[57] For the CAA, this was also a matter of identifying strategic locations to apply political pressure, through a detailed knowledge of the workings of American institutions. The US Senate Committee on Foreign Relations and the US House of Representatives Committee on International Affairs were two committees whose actions were closely followed by the CAA and the rest of the diaspora associations.

Although the net balance of laws and amendments favored by Croatian associations was somewhat negative, this commitment shows that knowledge of the American democratic machinery was crucial if they were to have any influence at all. Here again, the key was to adapt to conventional American means of organizing political pressure; getting to know senators in order to convince them of the worth of the cause and the direct personal benefit that it would bring for them. Finally, at various congressional appearances, those members of the diaspora afforded the opportunity to present their case received a much better hearing if they were able to use a language that could "resonate" on Capitol Hill.

The first attempt was the Nickles or Nickles–Bentley Amendment.[58] Signed by President George Bush in November 1990, it was set to come into effect in May 1991. The amendment included a clause prohibiting bilateral assistance to Yugoslavia and requiring American delegates to oppose loans by international financial institutions unless the six republics held free and multiparty elections. Among the conditions imposed, the amendment also included that none of the republics could be accused of serious human rights violations. The amendment came into force on 6 May 1991, but was abandoned 20 days later by Secretary of State James Baker on the pretext that it undermined the authority of Ante Marković[59] without harming Milošević as such. The progress of the amendment was followed and supported by *Zajedničar*,[60] whose articles beseeched readers to contact their senators and representatives to secure their support when it came up for vote.

The second attempt was the Direct Aid to Democracies Act, also called the Bob Dole Act. This bill, put forward by Bob Dole, aimed to provide direct aid to the republics of the Soviet Union and Yugoslavia to foster the "development of democracy." Introduced by Dole on 14 January 1991,[61] it was blocked in the assorted committees and sub-committees of the Senate and House of Representatives. Almost every stage of its progress was followed by *Zajedničar*. Both its submission to the Subcommittee on European Affairs of the US Senate Foreign Relations Committee[62] and the hearings that ensued were editorialized while the bias of those involved was criticized. A number of appeals were also published to pressure senators into supporting the bill: "Write to your US senators and representatives and ask them to support the Direct Aid to Democracies Act pending both in the Senate and in the House."[63] During these hearings, certain members of the Croatian associations were called to testify, and a number of statements were recorded in the Congressional Record, often by senators or representatives close to these organizations.[64]

Knowing and rubbing shoulders with Congress members was thus essential in bringing the political agenda to fruition. Familiarity with the exact workings of the decision-making process and the mechanisms of the hostland democracy was also crucial. Without this knowledge, any action was doomed to failure. In this sense, it is true that the diaspora associations acted as a relay—and a vital one—in translating the language and practices of the homeland within the hostland.

Lobbying the Senate and House of Representatives could not be achieved without direct, acknowledged contact between a number of American politicians. Dole[65] was without doubt the biggest supporter of the Croatian cause. During initial protests, he participated in the visits to Croatia,[66] collaborated in the publication of supporting resolutions,[67] applied pressure on the Senate and media, and even welcomed Tudman to the United States in 1990.[68] Dole also played a decisive role in applying pressure on the Senate to recognize Croatia in 1992.[69] Yet senators and representatives supporting the Croatian cause were numerous, including Congress members Orrin Hatch,[70] William Lipinski,[71] Joe D'Amato, Tom Lantos, Joe Kolter, and Dana Rohrbacher, to name the main supporters. Outside of Congress, support from influential Croatian Americans such as Rudy Perpich, former governor of Minnesota,[72] was also of great assistance.

As November 1992 approached, Croatia found itself in a difficult situation. The Serbian rebels occupied more than a third of the territory of the republic thanks to support from the JNA. An embargo had been put in place, preventing Croatia from officially purchasing weapons to fight the JNA and the militia. International recognition had been painstakingly obtained, and the enthusiasm aroused by the arrival of United Nations forces in Zagreb had turned to disappointment[73] as they did nothing but strengthen the status quo. Finally, Bosnian-Croats were plunged into an even bloodier war, which played a significant role in the Croatian diaspora's anti-Bush vote.

One of the strengths of the diaspora associations' treatise was to present themselves as representatives of a potential electorate of 2.5 million Croatian Americans across the United States. As such, the issue of the elections was crucial. Extremely frustrated by Bush's position, which was regularly criticized and ridiculed in the pages of *Zajedničar*,[74] Croatian Americans turned to his opponents.

For the first time in its history, the *Zee* openly supported a candidate in the presidential elections: Bill Clinton.[75] However, the CAA turned first to the ultra-conservative candidate Pat Buchanan, providing him with more than 400,000 dollars for the 1992[76] primaries as well as material support. "For the New Hampshire primary we were on Buchanan's side with 500 to 600 volunteers working for him. We did everything, it was a door to door activity: there was not a single person that we didn't reach."[77] The *Zee*, for its part, regularly published articles in support of Clinton.[78]

The victory of the Democratic candidate in 1992 thus delighted diaspora associations as a whole, marking the onset of great hope for a change in American policy. Change did in fact occur, beginning in 1992. Clinton and Gore, who had explicitly acknowledged the independence of Croatia during their electoral campaigns, began a process of major consultation on the issue of the former Yugoslavia, with CFU involvement, in December 1992.[79]

What was the influence of the Croatian American vote during the campaign? Its weight is impossible to measure, if only because it is impossible to quantify the Croatian American electorate (and, in particular, its estimated 2.5 million voters). Miomir Žužul, former Croatian ambassador to the United States, maintains that such support was considerable.[80] It is nonetheless worth noting that this election demonstrates political entry into a transnational dimension implemented all the same on a national scale—that is, the attempt to recast international issues as national ones (with local reelections at stake), thereby calling into question the dichotomy between interior and foreign politics, between the *inside* and the *outside*.

Conclusion: diasporas and ethnic conflict

Generally speaking, the literature on diaspora and conflict is primarily concerned with the normative question of whether diasporas are a positive or negative factor in ethnic and civil wars (Lyons 2004; Mohamoud 2005; Smith and Stares 2007; Shain 2002). Yet, except in very few cases, no theoretical framework has been proposed to understand how, why, and under which conditions diasporas come to exist in the first place—namely, when diasporic mobilization occurs. For example, Paul Collier argues that diasporas are always a source of conflict:

> There is little mystery about this effect. Diasporas sometimes harbor rather romanticized attachments to their group of origin and may nurse grievances as a form of asserting continued belonging. They are much richer than the people in their country of origin and so can afford to finance vengeance. Above all, they do not have to suffer any of the awful consequences of renewed conflict because they are not living in the country. Hence, they are a ready market for rebel groups touting vengeance and so are a source of finance for renewed conflict.
>
> (2000: 14)

This chapter has demonstrated that almost all of these generalizing assumptions are wrong in the Croatian case. First, no single political or even "romantic" stance of the different Croatian organizations exists abroad, even if at a given historical time a convergence of opinions might have occurred. Second, a strong socio-economic divide emerged in the composition of the Croatian populations abroad; only some members of the elite of the transnational political field have important means, but they represent a single digit percentage of the group of reference. Third, many of those actively engaged did return to the country and—far from suffering from the consequences of the conflict—actively benefited from it, obtaining important positions in a newly independent state apparatus.

More importantly, this chapter has shown that these assumptions reverse the logic of the actual social processes taking place. No Croatian "diaspora" as such existed in the mid-1980s, but it did suddenly appear in 1990. Thus, the Croatian "diaspora," as such, did not contribute to the war simply because it was not a relevant unit of analysis in the social and political processes that took place. Diaspora is the category of mobilization through which a certain number of transnational actors involved in competing networks mobilized symbolic and material resources to finance a war and reach power. Moreover, the Croatian diaspora was mobilized by political actors coming specifically from the homeland; most of the social actors involved in the events of the 1990s were both in the "domestic" political field and the "diasporic" political field. This situation further underlines another weakness of the literature on diasporas and conflict as pointed out by Hägel and Peretz (2005: 468): by assuming that diasporas exist a priori—or at least are a separate entity from home states or domestic societies—these approaches preclude us from understanding the processes through which the mobilization of symbolic categories operates within a transnational political field that encompasses diasporic institutions, political parties at home, and competing political networks that are constituted across borders.

The theoretical argument developed in this book provides the basis for a more complex understanding that takes into account what occurs within the transnational political field. This chapter has shown that the Croatian diaspora as such is not a factor in the conflict; rather, on the contrary, the conflict "created" and rendered the diaspora "visible." The diaspora emerged as a result of successful war mobilization: the war created the diaspora much more than the diaspora created the war. This is primarily explained by what Bourdieu defined as a "practical *epochè*"—that is, circumstances that allow for the destabilization of the sedimented adequacy between words and things; by the dedifferentiation of the transnational political field between the "domestic" and the diasporic; and, consequently, by the development of a powerful and successful language of mobilization by a small radical group that set up the discursive boundaries of a much larger mobilization.

Notes

1 See the numerous articles quoted from *Globus* or *Nacional* referenced in this dissertation. Paul Hockenos, in his excellent *Homeland Calling* (2003), also falls into this bias toward the lack of a historical analysis of the transnational political field, focusing primarily on the most radical elements.
2 See the discussion in Chapter 1.
3 See the work of Collier as an example of bluntly uncritical statistical uses of the category of diaspora (Collier 2000; Collier *et al.* 2002).
4 Josip Manolić, idem (Glavaš, 1996). On the figure of Krajačić, see MacDonald (2002: 191–193).

5 According to his revisionist positions, the Yugoslav official history—which declared that the Ustasha regime had killed 600,000 to 700,000—largely overstated the number, which he estimated to be around 60,000.
6 It was later argued that Josip Manolić himself, while he was in the secret services, might have been responsible for Tuđman's passport.
7 Tuđman met its elected leaders several times, but the personal relationship between the Tuđman and Meštrović deteriorated when Tuđman felt that Meštrović was not putting enough effort into the promotion of his book *The National Question in Contemporary Europe*, which had been an editorial failure in the US.
8 The Official Site of the HDZ, "Povijest HDZ-a" (History of HDZ), www.hdz.hr/povijest/povijest.htm (accessed 3 July 2003).
9 Including Ivan Nogalo, Domagoj Šola, Steve Bubalo, Pero Novak, Antun Kikaš, Ilija Letica, Anthony Maglica.
10 Mainly the Toronto HNO circles: Marin Sopta, Ante Beljo, Gojko Šušak, and Fra Ljubo Krasić.
11 Interview with Mate Granić, former Croatian Minister of Foreign Affairs, Zagreb, 19 February 2003.
12 On this matter, see Daphne Winland "What is a Good Croat," in Winland (2007: 121–122).
13 GLASNIK HDZ/God II, Broj 7, Veljaca 1990, p. 16.
14 Quoted in Hudelist (2004: 510).
15 This will be further developed in the next chapter.
16 Ironically dubbed the "pizza man" by a journalist at the Croatian magazine *Globus* (Tanner 1997: 222). Born in Široki Brijeg, in Herzegovina, from an Ustasha father killed by Tito's Partisans, Šušak fled Yugoslavia in 1968 to dodge the draft. He arrived in Canada and after several years became the owner of a pizza kiosk in Ottawa. After settling down, Šušak became politically active in the Norval circle and several times hosted Tuđman during his visits to Canada. As it often happened in ideologically divided Herzegovinian families, Šušak's brother was enrolled in Široki Brijeg's UDBa, and some rumors suggested that Gojko himself might have been enrolled in the services. See "Gojko Šušak, Defense Minister of Croatia, Is Dead at 53," *New York Times*, 5 May 1998, p. 29.
17 "Interview with Gojko Šušak, Croatian Defense Minister," Personal Web page of Marko Kočić, interview conducted at the Hrvatsko Slovo, Zagreb, Croatia, 27 December 1996. URL: www.cdsp.neu.edu/info/students/marko/hrslovo/hrslovo7.html (accessed 15 July 2008).
18 Interview with Andrija Jakovčević, Croatian Ambassador to Canada (1998–2000) Zagreb, 18 February 2003.
19 The current national anthem of Croatia.
20 "From Pizza Man in Canada to Croatian Kingmaker," *New York Times*, 16 January 1994, p. 14.
21 Ibid., p. 14.
22 Interview with Anthony Peraica, former president of the CAA, Chicago, 27 June 2003.
23 Humanitarian Aid," *Zajedničar*, 7 August 1991, p. 2.
24 Interview with Anthony Peraica, former president of the CAA, Chicago, 27 June 2003.
25 "Senator Bob Dole also gave welcoming remarks and was joined by Senator Alphonse D'Amato and Congressmen Tom Lantos, Joe Kolter, Dana Rohrbacher, Pete Visclosky, Paul E. Kanjorski, David E. Bonior, Bill Paxton, Dennis Eckart and Eliot Engel. Dr. Kay King represented Congressman Dick Swett's office." In "35,000 Join Croatian Peace Rally in Washington," *Zajedničar*, 7 August 1991, p. 5.
26 "Senator Dole Lauds Croatians at Washington Rally," *Zajedničar*, 7 August 1991, p. 5.

27 "35,000 Join Croatian Peace Rally in Washington," *Zajedničar*, 7 August 1991, p. 5.
28 "Congressmen Address United Rally in Washington," *Zajedničar*, 9 October 1991, p. 15.
29 Notably under the direction of General Martin Špegelj. According to Marcus Tanner, between October and December 1990, the former Yugoslav general's efforts resulted in the cancelling of the effects of the JNA's withdrawal (Tanner 1997).
30 "La Guerre en Yougoslavie, Chronologie 1990–1995," *Balkanologie*, www.chez.com/balkanologie/chronowar.htm (accessed 9 July 2003).
31 "Taped interview with Ann Goetz, Pittsburgh 21 April 1999," quoted in Carter (2001: 213).
32 Interview with Anthony Peraica, former CAA president, Chicago, 27 June 2003.
33 "Yugoslav" may equally denote a son or daughter from a mixed Serb-Croat marriage, a Serb from Croatia, or simply somebody who identifies him- or herself with communist Yugoslavia. In 1989, however, it was impossible to use this term in a neutral manner.
34 "Seattle's Humanitarian Gesture," *Zajedničar*, 24 January 1990, p. 17.
35 Interview with Boris Maruna, President of Hrvatska Matica Iseljenika (1990–1993; 2000–), Zagreb, 19 February 1993.
36 Interview with Višnja Milas, head of the international branch of the Croatian NGO "Bedem Ljubavi," Zagreb, 20 February 2003.
37 "50 join in rally at Croatian church," *St. Louis Post Dispatch*, 12 August 1992, p. 14.
38 Humanitarian aid delivered by the ECHO programme totaled 293.80 million Euros between 1991 and 1999. "Facts and figures—EC assistance to Western Balkans," *South East Europe Online*, www.southeasteurope.org/documents/facts_figures.pdf (accessed 2 August 2003).
39 Interview with Bernard Luketich, President of the CFU, Pittsburgh, 26 June 2003.
40 "Humanitarian Fund: Health Minister Appeals For Health Aid," *Zajedničar*, 7 August 1991, p. 1.
41 "Humanitarian Aid For Croatia," *Zajedničar*, 31 July 1991, p. 2.
42 Ibid., p. 2.
43 Interview with Miomir Žužul, Croatian ambassador to the United States (1996–2000), Zagreb, 15 February 2003.
44 Interview with Mate Granić, Croatian Foreign Affairs Minister, Zagreb, 19 February 2003.
45 Interview with Anthony Peraica, former President of the CAA, Chicago, 27 June 2003.
46 Interview with Miomir Žužul, Croatian ambassador to the United States (1996–2000), Zagreb, 15 February 2003.
47 "Member of Croatian Group Charged in Arms Plot; $12 Million in Guns and Stinger Missiles Were Sought for Yugoslav Civil War, Customs Says," *Washington Post*, 13 August 1991.
48 "Croatia–Yugoslav Confederation of Independence?" *Zajedničar*, 3 October 1990, p. 17.
49 "Tuđman Meets President Bush," *Zajedničar*, 3 October 1990, p. 4.
50 "Interview with Gojko Šušak, Croatian Defense Minister," home page of Marko Kočić, interview conducted in Hrvatsko Slovo, Zagreb, Croatia, 27 December 1996; and "Interview with Anthony Peraica, former CAA President," Chicago, 27 June 2003.
51 Interview with Anthony Peraica, former President of the CAA, Chicago, 27 June 2003.
52 Ibid.
53 Interview with Anthony Peraica, 27 June 2003.
54 Interview with Jim Harff, former director of Ruder Finn Global Public Affairs, current director of Global Communicators, Washington, 20 June 2003.
55 Ibid.

56 Interview with Anthony Peraica, 27 June 2003.
57 "Croatian Embassy Update," *Zajedničar*, 29 September 1993, p. 20.
58 "Yugoslavia," *Human Rights Watch World Report 1992*, www.hrw.org/reports/1992/WR92/HSW-08.htm, consulted 18 May 2003.
59 The Prime Minister of the Federal Republic of Yugoslavia.
60 "AMAC Visits State Department," *Zajedničar*, 3 July 1991, pp. 6, 24.
61 US Senate, Congressional Record—Senate, p. S-1156.
62 "A Discordant Note," *Zajedničar*, 20 March 1991, p. 2.
63 "Defense of Yugoslavia Democracy is An American Issue," *Zajedničar*, 27 March 1991, p. 19.
64 "Congressmen Express Concern Over Yugoslav Crisis," *Zajedničar*, 17 April 1991, pp. 6, 20.
65 "Fourth Generation CFU Members," *Zajedničar*, 13 March 1991, p. 15.
66 As entered in the record of Congress by the *New York Times* (Franjo Tuđman, "All We Croatians Want is Democracy," *New York Times*, 30 June 1990), also signed by Congress members D'Amato (R-NY), Garn (R-UT), Mack (R-FL), Nickles (R-OK), Symms (R-ID), and Warner (R-VA). "All Croatians want is Democracy," *Zajedničar*, 3 October 1990, p. 4.
67 "Dole Resolution Decries Violence," *Zajedničar*, 2 October 1991, p. 15.
68 "A Croatian Perspective," *Zajedničar*, 3 October 1990, p. 4, "President Bush Welcomes President of Croatia," *US Newswire*, 27 September 1990.
69 "Proposed Senate Resolution," *Zajedničar*, 22 January 1992, p. 1.
70 "Sen. Hatch Tells Pres. Bush 'US Should Back Croatia,'" *Zajedničar*, 23 October 1991, p. 3.
71 Interview with Anthony Peraica, 27 June 2003.
72 "Gov. Perpich Moves To Croatia," *Zajedničar*, 20 February 1991, pp. 1, 7.
73 "Heaven Help Us (Because UNPROFOR Can't)," *Zajedničar*, 20 January 1993, p. 2.
74 "Any Croatian American who votes for this gang of immoral morons in the next election is a traitor to his European ancestors and the ideals of America's Founding Fathers," "Letters to the Editor/John S. Andrus," *Zajedničar*, 22 January 1992, p. 6.

75 For the first time in the history of our society, the Croatian Fraternal Union made a firm commitment to the election of the President and Vice President of the United States and committed our newspaper to organizing our members as a unified block of voters for the Clinton/Gore ticket.
("Presentation M. Luketich/National President To Clinton/Gore Transition Team," *Zajedničar*, 6 January 1993, p. 4)

76 "Along the Campaign Trail," *The National Journal*, 11 April 1992, p. 883, along with an interview with Anthony Peraica, ibid.
77 Interview with Anthony Peraica, 27 June 2003.
78 The newspaper thus writes: "We have a clear cut choice on Election Day, 1992. For the future of Croatia, Bosnia-Herzegovina, Slovenia and Macedonia, it is imperative that Bill Clinton and Al Gore are elected president and vice-president of the United States," "Make Your Vote Count," *Zajedničar*, 28 October 1992, p. 2.
79 "Clinton/Gore Listen To Croatians," *Zajedničar*, 6 January 1993, p. 2.

80 They surely had a big influence, during the vote for Clinton for example, they surely brought him a considerable amount of votes, and he knew it. I think this had an influence in his way of regarding the question in the Balkans.
(Interview with Miomir Žužul, Croatian ambassador to the United States (1996–2000), Zagreb, 15 February 2003)

References

Anderson, B. (1991) *Imagined Communities: Reflections on the Origin and Spread of Nationalism*, London: Verso.
Billig, M. (1995) *Banal Nationalism*, London: Sage.
Bourdieu, P. (1982) *Ce que parler veut dire, L'économie des signes linguistiques*, Paris: Fayard.
Bourdieu, P. (2000) *Propos sur le champ politique*, Lyon: P.U.L.
Carter, S. R. (2001) *The Geopolitics of Diaspora: Croatian Community and Identity in the United States*, PhD Thesis, Bristol: Department of Geography, Bristol University.
Collier, P. (2000) *Economic Causes of Civil Conflict and Their Implications For Policy*, Washington, DC: World Bank Working Paper.
Collier, P., Hoeffler, A. and World Bank (2000) *Greed and Grievance in Civil War*, Washington, DC: World Bank Development Research Group.
Collier, P., Hoeffler, A. and University of Oxford (2002) *Greed and Grievance in Civil War*, Oxford: University of Oxford Institute of Economics and Statistics Centre for the Study of African Economies.
Gagnon, Jr., V. P. (2004) *The Myth of Ethnic War, Serbia and Croatia in the 1990s*, Ithaca and London: Cornell University Press.
Glavaš, D. (1996) "Nismo bili agenti, nego intelektualci!" *Feral Tribune*, pp. 25–26.
Hägel, P. and Peretz, P. (2005) "States and Transnational Actors: Who's Influencing Whom? A Case Study in Jewish Diaspora Politics during the Cold War," *European Journal of International Relations*, 11(4), 467–493.
Hockenos, P. (2003) *Homeland Calling, Exile Patriotism and the Balkan Wars*, Ithaca and London: Cornell University Press.
Hudelist, D. (1999) "Banket u Hrvatskoj II: Tajna povijest vladajuće stranke," *Globus*, pp. 83–87.
Hudelist, D. (2004) *Tuđman, biografija*, Zagreb: Profil International.
Human Rights Watch (1992) "Yugoslavia," *Human Rights Watch World Report*. Available at: www.refworld.org/docid/467fca581e.html (accessed 10 March 2017).
Lovrenović, I. (2001) *Bosnia: a Cultural History*, New York: New York University Press.
Luketich, B. (1999) "Report of Shipments and Disbursements of the Croatian Fraternal Union, Croatia Humanitarian Fund 1991–1999," Prepared and Presented by CFU National President Bernard M. Luketich to Members and Delegates of the 20th CFU National Convention.
Lyons, T. (2004) *Engaging Diasporas to Promote Conflict Resolution: Transforming Hawks Into Doves*, Washington, DC: Institute for Conflict Analysis and Resolution, George Mason University.
MacDonald, D. B. (2002) *Balkan Holocausts? Serbian and Croatian Victim Centred Propaganda and the War in Yugoslavia*, Manchester: Manchester University Press.
Mandić, D. (1971) *Hrvati i Srbi dva stara različita naroda*, Muenchen; Barcelona: Knjižnica Hrvatske revije.
Mohamoud, A. A. (2005) "Diasporas: Untapped Potential for Peacebuilding in the Homelands" in Tongeren Pv and European Centre for Conflict Prevention, eds., *People Building Peace II: Successful Stories of Civil Society* (pp. xiv, 697), Boulder, CO: L. Rienner Publishers.
Okružno Javno Tužilaštvo Zagreb (1980) "Optužnica Okružnoga Javnog Tužilaštva Zagreb od 17. Studenog 1980. Protiv Dr. Franje Tuđmana" in Tuđman, F., ed., *Usudbene Povjestive* (p. 799), Zagreb: Hrvatska Sveučilišna Naklada.

Ramet, S. P. (1992) *Nationalism and Federalism in Yugoslavia, 1962–1991*, Bloomington, IN: Indiana University Press.

Ramet, S. P. (2006) *The Three Yugoslavias: State-Building and Legitimation, 1918–2004*, Bloomington, IN; Chesham: Indiana University Press; Combined Academic distributor.

Schöpflin, G. (2005) "The Rise and Fall of Yugoslavia" in McGarry, J., ed., *The Politics of Ethnic Conflict Regulation: Case Studies of Protracted Ethnic Conflicts* (172–203), London: Routledge.

Shain, Y. (1999) *Marketing the American Creed Abroad: Diasporas in the US and their Homelands*, Cambridge: Cambridge University Press.

Shain, Y. (2002) "The Role of Diasporas in Conflict Perpetuation and Resolution," *SAIS Review*, XXII(2): 115–144.

Smith, H. and Stares, P. (2007) *Diasporas in Conflict*, Tokyo; New York; Paris: United Nations University Press.

Tanner, M. (1997) *Croatia: A Nation Forged in War*, London: Yale University Press.

Tuđman, F. (1995) "Intervju dr. Franje Tuđmana Bengtu Göransonu za švedsku televiziju 1977" in Tuđman, F., ed., *Usudbene Povijestive* (pp. 346–356), Zagreb: Hrvatska Sveučilišna Naklada.

Winland, D. N. (2007) *We Are Now a Nation: Croats Between "Home" and "Homeland,"* Toronto: University of Toronto Press.

5 Diaspora as a state category

As we have seen, Socialist Yugoslavia had segmented the population abroad into three categories: the "old migration," the "Yugoslav Enemy Migration" and the "workers temporarily employed abroad." Each category corresponded to a specific kind of functional relation to the homeland: a folkloric, nostalgic relationship for the first, a policed securitized relation for the second, and an economic, social, and demographic relation for the third. Differentiated agencies managed the different categories, through the production of differentiated knowledge. The arrival of the HDZ in power, the independence of Croatia, and the beginning of the war constituted the conditions for an obliteration of these categories, and the emergence of a new all-encompassing signifier: "diaspora." The emergence of the term was grounded in material conditions: the mobilization for independence and for the war *had produced*, to a certain extent, the appearance of unity of the community, as the different diasporic organizations had all aligned—along with the government—on a few common objectives. Once in place, this reconfiguration of the symbolic divisions proved extremely powerful, and the newly established Croatian government quickly gave the "diaspora" a central position in official discourse. After the election of the HDZ, the party in power, in particular Franjo Tuđman, boasted of the "unification" of the "Homeland" and the "Emigrant" Croatia[1] a nation scattered around the world. As Ante Beljo addressed members of the HDZ: "the Croatian nation, the one in the Republic of Croatia; the one in Bosnia and Herzegovina and the one in the diaspora […] is now in the position to organize the life of all its citizens on democratic principles."[2]

This chapter explores how, in the Croatian context, the use of diasporic language by the state produces, and rationalizes, a new category of citizens to be governed. The following arguments will be made.

First, as it will appear, the understanding of "diaspora" and its relationship to the homeland draws heavily on the experiences of the past, unifying repertoires of enunciation and repertoires of action from the different Croatian and Yugoslav experiences described in Chapters 2 and 3. It also draws on the international discourses and practices of diaspora; in our particular case, mostly from the Irish and the Jewish experiences. Thus the state has developed practices in which the newly invented "diaspora," merging the previous categorizations of Croats abroad, is targeted by centralized ministries with specific programs intended to reinforce the narrative of a homogeneous community with a specific relationship to its homeland. And in the symbolic struggle over the definition of the limits and the functions of the diaspora, governments have specific advantages over diasporic institutions in transnational politics, including bureaucracies, ministries, identity cards, and citizenship registers.

However, second, the deployment of the "diaspora" as a state category—both practically and symbolically—is never a fully successful enterprise. The Croatian government encountered harsh resistance at home and abroad. While most government institutions, controlled by a small group of Norval-core members, tried to impose their views of who should represent the diaspora and what relationship it should have with the homeland, Croatian organizations abroad split along different lines, shattering the illusion of a homogeneous, unified population on the international scene.

Diasporic repertoires of enunciation

One of the first effects of the election of the Norval-supported HDZ on transnational politics was that a small group of politically marginal Canadian-Croats obtained important positions of power in the homeland. The central role of "Emigrant Croatia" in the government's discourse—as well as the crucial importance of this specific network for Franjo Tuđman's rise to power—gave them a key position within the governmental and para-governmental institutions. Indeed, especially in the first years, almost all key positions of the diaspora policies of the Republic of Croatia were held by members of the Herzegovinian "Norval" network or affiliates: Ćiro Grubišić, Ante Beljo, Gojko Šušak, Stipe Hrkać, etc. Therefore, although the diaspora policy changes between Yugoslavia and Croatia have a context of broad governmental upheaval, they are mostly to be understood as the ascent of a particular social network enacting its specific repertoire of enunciation regarding the rationalization and actualization of the link between the state and populations abroad.

As discussed in previous chapters, until the 1990s there was no unified way of thinking about Croats abroad. The control and management of populations abroad was characterized by diverse categories and policies. With the creation of the State of Croatia, these categories and policies were merged into the "*Iseljena Hrvatska*" (Emigrant Croatia), often referred to as the "diaspora." Before going into the details of the different institutions and policies dedicated to the diaspora, it is important to analyze how this new population is constituted as a legitimate object of government. This brings us back to the questions raised in Chapter 2: what is the context in which a specific rationalization emerges, what broader political economy of power is it rationalized in, and what bureaucracy and policy "solutions" are enacted to solve what is perceived to be a problem or a policy goal for the government? In this section it will be argued that the diaspora policies of the 1990s fuse the policies and rationalities previously elaborated with models from abroad in which the government constitutes a new category of population, and a new functional relationship to it.

"What does Croatia expect from its diaspora?" Vice Vukojević, an envoy of the HDZ in Latin America, asked in 1990 in the party's journal. His answer is representative of the general mix of contradictory conceptions of the diaspora that dominated the early years of the Croatian Republic:

> What does Croatia expect from the emigration? By affirming their right to decide the destiny of Croatia, their return is of utmost importance, or at least their visit to the homeland so that they can, with their experience, standards, knowledge and talent, influence the development of Croatia's mentality. To our nation abroad it is also important to remember their countries of residence, their duty to participate in all aspects of public life, because their influence on public opinion in their countries of adoption can help Croatia. In this way, Croatia would make friends who would, when the time comes, be of crucial importance to her. They are also reminded that they remain loyal citizens to their countries, and that as Croats they should be working and respectful people, in this way making Croats an example.[3]

A detailed analysis of the policy and discussion of the 1990s in Croatia presents us with three main repertoires, which draw both on Yugoslav and international blueprints. The first, dominant in the early years of Tuđman's presidency, takes its roots in the turn-of-the-century Croatian nationalists' fear of biological extinction through depopulation. The second, which echoes the claims of the "Croatian spring" from the 1970s, sees the diasporic condition as the result of flawed economic policies, and supports a massive return of citizens with skills and competences. Alongside these two positions advocating return, a third form of rationalization emerges; based on the deterritorialized nationalism analyzed in the previous chapters, it sees dispersion as a resource which can be harnessed by the state. I now examine these three positions in detail.

Diaspora as a biological extinction and the need for return

A first rationalization present in the government discourses on Emigrant Croatia uses a biological understanding of the population. Echoing the discourses of the early twentieth century, emigration is seen as a threat to the biological survival of Croatia. This vision is based on the idea that a nation can only be fully realized when physically occupying land. As Tuđman declared to the Sabor in 1990:

> Through the overall policy of the last decades, the Croatian national corpus (biće) has been brought to a status of demographic vulnerability. Considering the general moral and political climate, it is necessary to take immediate steps to prevent the further departure of our citizens in the world, as well as to increase natality.[4]

114 *Diaspora as a state category*

His position was similar in 1997:

> Taking into particular consideration the adverse demographic conditions caused by the anti-Croatian regimes in the past, we need to more decisively create the conditions for a quick and numerous return of emigrants and the temporarily employed abroad. We must be aware that the general development of Croatia depends on this demographic renewal. Thus we must give particular care to mothers and women who secure the future of their youth in our homeland.[5]

Similarly, Croatian Ambassador to the US Miomir Žužul, explained in an interview:

> We don't have enough population for an optimal development. And on the other side we have an immense potential population in the world, not only among those who emigrated, but also among their children.[6]

This narrative, based on natalist and populationist assumptions, presented a timeline in which migration was provoked by the political ("anti-Croatian regimes") will of the previous system. Therefore, with the establishment of a Croatian national government in Zagreb, the return flow should begin. This territorial, demographic understanding of the renewal of the nation through the return of the scattered population echoed the Zionist experience of the *Aliyah*—an echo which Croatian policy makers and commentators did not overlook. In fact, the Jewish/Israeli model was actively discussed by the government officials and by the press:

> Israel can be used as a successful model of management of returnees. Only in the past seven years, more than 600,000 Jews from the Soviet bloc migrated to Israel, the majority of whom have a job and a house today.
>
> (Vuksic 1997)

Similarly, the former Minister of Emigration, Zdravko Sančević, argued to promote free language classes for returnees: "not all Jews speak Hebrew, and yet they are welcome to Israel. A similar policy should be applied in Croatia."[7] Dragutin Hlad, a representative of the HDZ for Latin America, proposed to imitate the Kibbutz model: "[We] could open a certain number of camps like the Kibbutz in Israel where the youth of the Diaspora could stay for a few months and get a feel for the country."[8]

But the reference to the Jewish model could only function by replicating the totality of the narrative of a people deprived of its land, exterminated, and fighting for physical survival in a region surrounded by enemies. To this end, an interview with Ante Beljo, then director of Hrvatska Matica Iseljenika, is particularly telling:

if we were to give in to the demands of Serbs, Muslims, Italians and so on, we wouldn't have to face pressure and problems, but we would simply disappear.... As Israel, we must constantly fight for our survival, and safeguard what we achieved through so many victims [the reference here is both to the 1991–1995 war and the Bleiburg tragedy].[9]

However, the biological and demographic hopes for diasporic return are tightly knit with the hopes for the economic development created by returning Croats.

Diaspora as an actor of economic development

The second framework in which the diaspora is discussed is economic development. Drawing from the discourses on the Croatian Spring of 1971—in particular the journal *Hrvatski Tjednik* (see Šošić 1994)—emigration was understood as the result of a poor economic system. Moreover, not only was "Serboslavia" accused of privileging Serbian nationals for civil servant jobs, but the fiscal system, redistributive among republics, was accused of crippling Croatia's economy. Thus Croats were forced to look for jobs abroad. As the newly established Minister for Return and Immigration remarked in 1997:

> The Yugoslav communist system has, during its 45 years of dictatorship over all aspects of life, created bureaucratic structures through which it attempted to control the Croatian nation [...]. It was a system which suffocated economic activity, which impoverished the Croatian nation and forced it to look for a living outside of its homeland.[10]

In this framework the goal was to reverse the effects of Yugoslavia's guest-worker policy by creating the conditions for return. However, the methods were from the previous regime: by introducing the capital and professional skills acquired abroad into Croatia's economy, the government would boost Croatia's development potential. This was one of the ten priorities of the newly elected party, as Tuđman proves in the opening speech of parliament after the 1990 elections:

> Priority 8: Return and integration of the emigration. As one of its many accomplishments, [...] the HDZ has been successful in establishing unity between the homeland and Emigrant Croatia. The new Croatian government, by all means, must take the necessary steps to enable the fastest and largest return of Croats to the homeland [...]. Special attention should be given to the introduction of Croatian emigrants into all sectors of the economy. This must be our national preoccupation, because they are an immense professional, technological and financial potential which can substantially contribute to the rapid economic and democratic transformation of their homeland.[11]

116 *Diaspora as a state category*

Whereas the Jewish model was and is still usually invoked for the *political* and *national* aspects of the return policies, in terms of economic development the Irish model is preferred in public discourse. The mid-nineties were in fact the years of the "Celtic tiger" in Ireland, with GDP growth rates up to 10 percent, a development perceived to be the result of a successful return policy. As one demographer explained in 2001:

> It is a fact that the fantastic development of Ireland took place thanks to the stimulus of its diaspora. Objectively also our diaspora represents a huge potential. So we don't have to reinvent the wheel, but only follow the "Irish model." For that we need to define a policy of immigration and return for Croatia.[12]

Dispersion as a resource

Whereas the two previous discourses constituted the "diaspora" as a resource that needed to be repatriated in order to be exploited, a third discourse co-existed which instead understood the diaspora itself as a resource because it offered the possibility of delegating or privatizing one part of Croatia's foreign policy to Croatian organizations abroad.

This conception of the population abroad as a resource because of its dispersion can be traced to former Yugoslav practices. The attempted influence of organizations such as the Croatian Fraternal Union through *Matica iseljenika Hrvatske* between 1951 and 1990 contained an element of what was developed in the new rationality; the idea that a group abroad could be used as an informal ambassador to convey the ideas and policies of the home state without directly involving the home state. However, the more plausible link to explain the emergence of this discourse is the experience of politically active Croats in multicultural states such as Canada, the USA, and Australia, where ethnic lobbying is a key aspect of identity politics. As an Australian-Croat commented in the review *Hrvatska Revija* in 1995:

> I am not saying that, for the influence of some ethnic groups in multinational states such as America, Canada or Australia, official institutions such as embassies and consulates are not useful—they are in fact of great help—but civil society organizations, such as religious communities or cultural institutions […] can create a spiritual link between all the members of a national community. The Jews managed to create their unity specifically in this informal way, the only one available to them in the past, which resulted in the strong social influence of all Jewish communities in the countries in which they lived […]. It is hard to believe, despite what some incorrigible optimists argue, that third generation Croats will return to the homeland of their fathers and grandfathers, but they could be successful informal ambassadors of Croatia on Australian soil.
>
> (Tarle 1995: 495–496)

The privatization of foreign policy to Croatian organizations abroad was also conceived as a way to compensate for the absence of an established diplomatic corps. As Minister for Return and Immigration, Petrović declared in Vancouver in 1997:

> Croatia today is a member of the UN, member of the Council of Europe and a country which enjoys respect in the world and the support of powerful allies. But we should never forget that in the first days of the great Serbian aggression the homeland was alone, without any international support. The homeland had at that time only one ally, and that was Emigrant Croatia, which helped generously. I repeat, Emigrant Croatia was then the only ally.[13]

For this conceptualization, which is in direct opposition to many of the underpinnings of the two earlier ones, what is at stake is therefore how to harness, organize, and direct the influence of the population abroad so that it can best serve the interests of the government institutions such as Hrvatska Matica Iseljenika and the Croatian Information Center created by Ante Beljo:

> Through the CIC (Croatian Information Center) we want to provide both information and consolidate from the media point of view to form the Croatian emigration into a united Croatian national corpus. Because, how can we ask Croats in the world to lobby for Croatia if they do not possess timely and complete information?[14]

Here again, the Jewish/Israeli experience is taken as the central model:

> Whatever the future brings us, [...] Croats must build a strong lobby in the influential countries of the world. The small Jewish state managed to survive, thanks to its diaspora and its influential lobby. We must therefore follow this example as well, be it only for the numerous historical parallels between Israel and Croatia.
>
> (Tarle 1995: 504)

In conclusion, certainly one of the main achievements of the HDZ was to successfully abolish the "social currency" of the previously established distinctions between Croats abroad, and impose the idea of the existence of an "Emigrant Croatia"—a "diaspora" that was being reconciled with "Homeland Croatia." By operating this symbolic displacement, the HDZ formulated and legitimized a new objective for the Croatian state. That is, the "speech act" of defining the diaspora revoked the traditional distinctions between the three previous functional relations and imposed a new one. But which one exactly? As we have seen, the three narratives of diaspora were combined, drawing on the models inherited from the Yugoslav practices and looking at other historical experiences thought to be successful (whether they were accurate reconstructions is another matter), and they tried to import these models into the Croatian understanding.

118 *Diaspora as a state category*

If we now look at how these different discourses are distributed across the Croatian transnational political field, we find that unsurprisingly the most traditionally nationalist, corporatist sections of the HDZ (and parties to the right of the HDZ) supported what could be defined as sharing the "disciplinary" understanding of sovereignty found in the first two visions of the diaspora, while the more liberal parties tended to favor the third understanding of the diaspora–state relationship. The debate between former liberal minister of foreign affairs Mate Granić[15] and Miroslav Rožić, a heavy right-wing member of the Croatian Party of Rights,[16] is revealing:

> Dr Granić remarked that there exist two models of relationship with the diaspora. The first one is the so-called Israeli model which is entirely oriented towards the national question and is particularly concerned with the control of return. The second, so-called western European model (Italy, Spain, Portugal, Ireland), said Granić, is much more acceptable to Croatia, and is characterized among other aspects by good economic relations with the countries where emigrant associations are active, and in particular by a strong network of embassies and consulates. Dr Granić explained that this is why general consulates are open where strong emigrant associations are active. Granić particularly explained how the diaspora is deeply integrated in the Croatian diplomatic network.

Contrary to Granić, the representative of the Croatian Party of Rights (CPR), Miroslav Rožić, argues that the Israeli model is much more appropriate for Croatia, and that the CPR will propose in parliament another return law (*Dom i Svjiet* 2000).

The repertoires of enunciation mobilized in the transnational political field translated into concrete bureaucratic and governmental initiatives. As for the diverse discourses, below the appearance of unity, they pursued contradictory goals with limited success.

State repertoires of diasporic action

The Ministry(ies) for the Diaspora

The different ministries of the 1990s established to cater to the diaspora were founded with a clear goal in mind; to promote the return of Croats abroad for the development of the country and the repopulation of the territory. The first institution created to deal with the diaspora was the short-lived Ministry for Emigration, or Ministry for the Diaspora (*Ministarstvo za Iseljeništvo*), briefly led by Gojko Šušak in autumn 1991. Šušak was then nominated as Minister of Defense, a much more central government position, and was replaced by Zdravko Sančević, a long-time emigrant to Venezuela who had given crucial support to the HDZ abroad. While the practical outcome of the policies of this first Ministry is unclear—it disappeared during the war, up until 1997—its symbolic impact was evident. After years of opposition and exclusion from the regime, Croats abroad had their own Ministry, apparently led by two of their own.[17]

The second Ministry was set up under the Zlatko Mates government and named the Ministry for Return and Immigration (*Ministarstvo Povratka i Useljeništva*). From November 1996 to June 1999 it was led by Marijan Petrović, and then, under Jure Radić, it became the Ministry for Development, Immigration and Reconstruction (*Ministarstvo razvitka, useljeništva i obnove*) until January 2000. It included a special department for return, led by Marin Sopta. The minister's cabinet was mostly composed of former Croatian emigrants, either active politically[18] or in emigration-related cultural associations and journals.[19]

The main goal of the Ministry was to create the conditions for a Croatian *Aliyah* to begin. Several measures were taken, such as the reduction of tax for returnees, a 25 percent cap on the tax on foreign pensions, a facility for the return of capital, and special agreements for healthcare or pensions. Moreover, informative material was published, such as a guide for returnees. Some initial promises were only partially fulfilled, such as special assistance for administrative matters, an insurance plan to fund return plane tickets for poorer migrants, and the opening of a fund to provide for returnees without means of subsistence. The Ministry also planned different forms of scholarships, such as a scholarship with the Ministry of Defense for young English-speaking Croats who wanted to return.[20]

In addition to these measures, the Ministry was to collaborate with other Croatian institutions: with the diplomatic services to set up special counselors for immigration; collaboration with *Hrvatska Matica Iseljenika* and the Croatian Information Center to produce statistical information on the number and condition of the returnees and potential returnees; with the Ministry of Interior to facilitate the acquisition of Croatian citizenship.[21]

The Ministry for Return, drawing on the populationist ideology mentioned earlier, planned to use the potential flow of Croatian returnees to compensate for the rural exodus. A special agreement was to be passed with the Ministry of Interior and with the Ministry for Agriculture and Forests in order to use these returnees in rural areas.[22] This was not only an economic policy. The goal was explicitly to populate areas that Croatian citizens of Serbian ethnicity had abandoned during the last operations of the 1991–1995 war[23]:

> Dr Radić has once again remarked that not a single Croat must look for their means of subsistence anywhere outside of Croatia, for despite all its problems, Croatia has once more proved that it can provide for its citizens. If one knows that these houses are built only 30 km outside of Knin, which has been, with the help of the population from Kistanja and surroundings, which is itself the center of the great Serbian rebellion and where today the highest number of children per capita are born in Croatia, and this natality rate is among the highest in Europe, then the multiple successes of this policy of the Croatian government, in particular the Ministry for Development, and the progress of return and reconstruction are clear.[24]

Details of how many of the Ministry's proposed projects were put into practice and their effects are difficult to determine, but if one example can illustrate the activity of the Ministry it is the creation of a center for returnees. In 1998, with a letter of motivation, a curriculum vitae, a "proof of belonging" to the Croatian nation and a recommendation letter from a Croatian embassy, consulate or Catholic association, potential returnees could apply to be hosted in the center for returnees. However, the center was in fact a small building located close to the airport in the suburbs of Zagreb, which could hold 17 families at most.[25]

Despite all the positive stories of returnees published by the Ministry for Return and Immigration, out of the (often-boasted) three to five million Croats in the "diaspora," fewer than 40,000 had returned by 1997.[26] This number is to be put in the context of other figures: it is estimated that about 140,000 Croats emigrated since the end of the war from Croatia proper, and more than 200,000 from Bosnia and Herzegovina.[27]

Considering these outcomes, it is unsurprising that the Ministry was criticized from within and outside of the party. Early on, some anticipated that the return would not be as important as expected and blamed the deficiencies on the instability of the financial system and the high taxes or, as former Ambassador to the United States Miomir Žužul did, on the inherited inefficiency of the post-Yugoslav bureaucracy.[28] There are two other reasons which are not commonly included.

First is the 1991–1995 war, which obviously deterred returnees. Second is the absence of a real investment in the return policy from the Croatian government. The annual budget shows that 26,574,704 HRK (approximately €3.6 million) was allocated to the Ministry of Return in 1997, which at the time represented about 0.06 percent of the 42,780 million HRK government budget for that year. As a comparison, the budget for the Ministry of Finance represented 23.55 percent, and the budget for the Ministry of Defense represented 17.53 percent. In comparison with Israel, in 1998 the Ministry of Immigrant Absorption represented approximately €293,196,410, which is 11 times its Croatian counterpart. In relative terms, the Israeli Ministry's budget represented approximately 5 percent of the budget of the Ministry of Defense. In Croatia, in 1997, this ratio was 0.35 percent.[29]

Yet the main reason why many emigrants declined to return, and why there was an increase in the emigration rate, was the failure of the HDZ to deliver an economic development that would provide employment opportunities for any Croats at home or abroad. As the former head of *Hrvatska Matica Iseljenika* explained:

> There was essentially a bad preparation, and we have been victims of a romantic vision. When Sanader was elected, one of the first things he said was that in order to have an efficient policy of return we had to prepare the social and economic conditions for a proper return. It is true that in this regard we always had Ireland as a model. In fact, if you look at what Ireland did, like Croatia they had a lot of population abroad, and now all the Irish

all over the world are returning home. But this is because there is employment. Which is not the case of Croatia. When you can offer jobs in your country there is no need to have a policy of return, people come back by themselves.[30]

Paradoxically, therefore, it is precisely the phenomenon that the government intended to fight—the absence of a robust economic take-off—that caused the policy of planned massive returns to fail.

Hrvatska Matica Iseljenika

Other institutions approached the diaspora question differently. With the new government, the Emigrant Foundation of Croatia (*Matica iseljenika Hrvatske, M.I.H.*) was renamed the Croatian Heritage Foundation (*Hrvatska Matica Iseljenika, HMI*). Opposing the Ministries of Diaspora, *Matica*'s objective continued to be the preservation of the "homeland identity" abroad. The main difference being that *Matica* shifted from the promotion of the socialist self-management identity of the Yugoslav years to the promotion of a nationalist identity.

During its first two years *Matica* was one of the only connections between the homeland and the "diaspora" that had not been overtaken by the HDZ hardliners linked to Norval. Tuđman nominated Boris Maruna to lead the institution. Maruna had been one of the most important moderate nationalist figures of the Croatian political emigration. Close to Nova Hrvatska's Jakša Kušan, he had been general secretary of the Croatian National Congress (*Hrvatsko Narodno Vijeće*) from 1976 to 1977 and was instrumental in ousting the Otpor-led radicals (who would form the core of the Norval group a few years later). More importantly, however, he was one of the most famous figures of the emigration, and as such knew all the important actors. Despite Tudjman's appointment, Maruna refused to subordinate his work to the rule of the HDZ. While the Norval group's and Tuđman's arms, funds, and humanitarian aid transited through various institutions such as the Ministry of Defense, Maruna's networks bypassed the governmental institutions and directly connected with organizations or military units on the ground (Hockenos 2003: 83). After two years, Maruna's independence was not tolerated, and he was removed from office.

Ćiro Grubišić replaced him—the brother of Vlatko Grubišić, a Croatian-Canadian scholar whose position in the University of Waterloo was financed by rich Croatian-Canadians directly connected to Norval—but he was rapidly sent to Mostar as a Croatian consul. Ante Beljo was appointed in his place. Under Grubišić and Beljo, *Matica* grew docile under HDZ control. During the war *Matica* continued to be a central point of arrival and redistribution for weapons and humanitarian aid. In particular, with the opening of *Hrvatska Matica Iseljenika* offices in southern Herzegovina, it was suspected to be one of the covers for the arming and financing of the all-Croat army of the separatist Herzegovinian quasi-state Herceg-Bosna.[31] *Matica* was ridden with other scandals, such as the one concerning the Croatian Information Center, run by Beljo with *Matica*'s fund, which in 2000 was discovered to be a private company funneling public funds. Even when *Matica* hosted many licit projects and activities, such as the Croatian Fraternal Union-sponsored "Dora Fund," and hosted initiatives such as the "Task Force,"[32] it was accused of privileging links and initiatives with organizations favorable to the HDZ.

In time, the journal of the institution, *Matica*, became a HDZ mouthpiece, after being a Yugoslav government propaganda organ, documenting in detail the "successes" of the HDZ administration, and promoting the new official, "Croatian identity," by revisiting at length all the symbols and myths of Croatian nationalism.

Throughout the 1990s, by becoming entirely subordinated to the HDZ, *Hrvatska Matica Iseljenika* fell again into the function it had fulfilled through the years of communism: an uncritical, ignored organ of the established power. With the election of the new majority in 2000, the institution progressively depoliticized and concentrated on underfunded programs of cultural and educational exchange. It was conceived as an institution to organize Croatian lobbying and to coordinate institutions abroad, but *Matica* never fulfilled its expectations.

The Croatian World Congress

Another institution that tried to develop organizations abroad as a resource was the Croatian World Congress (*Hrvatski Svjetski Kongres, HSK*), launched in July 1993.[33] Initiated by a group of moderate emigrants, it (again) was rapidly taken over by the HDZ, under the leadership of Franjo Tuđman who appointed the Herzegovinian Franciscan friar Šimun Šito Ćorić at its head. The explicit goal was to set up a structure that could represent all the emigrant associations under one roof and reinforce their activities abroad.

Even so, the actual aim was double. First, the initiative of the CWC undoubtedly stemmed from the Croatian government's awareness, after the mobilization of 1989–1992, of the extraordinary financial and political potential of the "diaspora," as well as the sheer (claimed) numbers of the "Croatian nation abroad" as a source for political lobbying. The government therefore established the structures necessary to direct this instrument. The idea of utilizing the diaspora as a source of influence was founded on the belief among some members of the Croatian government that it was possible to use the diaspora to pursue their national interests. The second goal was defensive; by setting up an HDZ-controlled umbrella organization and controlling any alternate transnational mobilization, the political party could avoid political competition from abroad. While the second objective might have been attained, the first remained largely unfulfilled.

In fact, in most places the clumsily obvious desire to control the entire Congress and deal exclusively with organizations friendly to the HDZ created more division than unity. A local example of how the Croatian World Congress operated in British Columbia is quite telling. In an article for the *Hrvatska*

Revija, a Croatian-Canadian from Vancouver explains how the various Croatian organizations of the city decided, in 1993, to come together under the CWC-led Croatian-Canadian Congress of British Columbia. The associations worked well together until 1996, when the local HDZ branch demanded excessive representation in the voting procedure. Thus discontented by the seizure of power, half of the organizations left. Each organization continued its activities, catering only to "its" group of Croats. Instead of creating unity, after only three years of its existence the Congress had created two entrenched camps (Coric 1999: 534–535). Similar experiences, from the USA, Australia, Germany, etc., filled the homeland Croatian press and emigrant publications. As one commentator from Australia explained:

> The Croatian World Congress, it is said, was born following the model of the World Jewish Congress. But the partisan monolithism of the Congress does not reflect the pluralism of the political profile of Croats in Australia, and therefore I am afraid that such an organization does not provide much hope for the creation of a Croatian lobby.
>
> (Tarle 1995: 498)

In the United States, the only association that supported the initiative was the CAA, for obvious reasons: it was an extension of the power of the HDZ. Partly in response to the CWC, the National Federation of Croatian Americans was created, backed by the CFU. The CFU is a well-established organization in the United States, whose members are almost all the second or third generation to live in the United States. Why submit to government control and the line of the HDZ, far from the values that drive it? Indeed, the organization of the CWC was in complete opposition to the values of the CFU and other organizations such as the National Federation of Croatian Americans (NFCA), the CCU, and the AMAC. In the CFU's logic, it was not for the Croatian government to create a representative body of Croats abroad—(whose weight in Croatian domestic politics would be a dangerous unknown). Despite the achievement of being awarded a Special Consultative Status with the Ecosoc (United Nations) in 1998, the CWC remained an empty shell (Vurusic 1998: 26).[34]

Resistance and counter-conducts

As shown in the previous chapter, up until 1993 there was a relative unity of goals and objectives within diasporic organizations and between diasporic organizations and the homeland. Ironically, Zagreb's attempt to grip the "diaspora" caused this unity to shatter. While all organizations had supported the election of the HDZ and had worked to achieve Croatia's independence and sovereignty, Croatia's divisive policy in Bosnia-Herzegovina broke the consensus, and the autocratic tendency of the HDZ became apparent. In this part of the chapter, I will analyze how the homeland's attempts to control diasporic institutions failed, and how after a brief moment of unity, organizations returned to symbolic and material competition for the representation of the "diaspora" and its relationship with the homeland.

An end to the myth of unity

With the discovery of prison camps on the Croatian side (in Herzegovina), evidence of human rights violations, and war crimes, the Croatian American associations felt defenseless against the Serbian discourse which was trying to blur responsibility and share blame. This can be explained by the fact that they lost the intersection of symbolic repertoires discussed in the previous chapters. As one of Bob Dole's aides, Mira Radielović Baratta, explained in 1993 on the position of Croatian associations:

> From a domestic political standpoint, tolerating undemocratic behavior [in Croatia] hurts the credibility and the causes being supported by American Croats [...]. To defend these actions [...] limits the political effectiveness of American Croats.
> On the other hand, by acting as agents for positive change and pressing Croatian and Bosnian leaders to democratize, American Croats can increase their political "value" to the Clinton administration and the Congress.[35]

Thus the unity of Croatian American associations was shattered. The CAA, principally composed of radical political exiles, upheld the official position of the Croatian government. The direction of the CFU, which mainly represented Americans of Croatian origin, followed this position for several months,[36] prior to a radical change of course. AMAC, traditionally made up of liberal political exiles, had thus far been closer to the positions of the CAA than those of the CFU. But, in their overwhelming majority, AMAC members neither refused to support the position of the HDZ nor the political violence of Croats toward Bosnian Muslims. The CFU and AMAC thus took a public stance against Franjo Tuđman's policy in Bosnia-Herzegovina. This difference in *habitus* and thus the political claims of an outwardly homogeneous "diaspora" was brought to the fore by the words of various Croatian diplomats in the US:

> QUESTION: How would you rate the diaspora's political influence in the United States?
> MIOMIR ŽUŽUL: Well in this case it's not possible anymore to use a single word for the diasporas. There is not one political position of the diaspora, but different positions.[37]
> ANDRIJA JAKOVČEVIĆ: The issue you raise here is interesting. You see, when talking about the diaspora, it is always difficult to have one single political view, one single voice. As they are not uniformly represented and as they hardly combine or articulate their demands in a coherent way, you have to face many organizations, different in number of members and in influence, that have many particular interests, that

represent many different fields of activity and different political backgrounds, and it is very difficult to please all of them.[38]

QUESTION: A lot of countries use their immigrants for lobbying purposes. How would you describe your contacts with the Croatian diaspora since they are not inclined toward the new government in Croatia?

IVAN GREŠIĆ: It cannot be said that the whole Croatian diaspora is not supporting the new government since it has many layers and it differs in opinions about the political situation in Croatia and the decisions of the new government. I had contacts with all of the leaders within the Croatian diaspora. They are people with different political opinions.[39]

The CAA followed the HDZ's policy for various reasons. The first was surely the *habitus* of its members, the majority of whom conformed, as we have seen, to the ideal type of the radical political exile. Some of them had not renounced the legacy of Ante Pavelić, although this was never stated in public.[40] In any case, the nucleus of businessmen who had lent their support to Tuđman in 1989–1990 (revolving around campaigner Ilija Letica among others) was not against the idea of extending the Croatian borders, or indeed re-establishing the borders of 1941, especially since many of them were originally from Herzegovina. In any case, the association's leadership supported Mate Boban and his policy:

QUESTION: What was your policy toward Mate Boban and the state of Bosna-Herceg?

T. PERAICA: Well, we supported him. Without him the Serbs would have arrived in Dalmatia with no trouble at all. I remember meeting him several times in Bosnia and in the United States. He was not exactly the kind of person I appreciated, but we supported him because we thought it was useful.[41]

Short of complete marginalization, the CAA's position did hinder the lobbying initiatives in Washington "in the name of 2.5 million Croats in the US." Jim Harff, who had worked for the Croatian government and the CAA until 1992, explained the situation:

We felt that the agenda of the CAA was slightly off the mark. It did not resonate in Washington anymore. It was sometimes just formulated on the basis of an emotional agenda, not always in touch with reality. We had the impression that Tuđman himself was out of touch with reality, and we understood he was building a one-party organization. Plus you can't underestimate the ego factor in the position of the CAA.[42]

By supporting a Bosnian policy that still clashed with the majority of Croatian Americans, the CAA played a part in its own marginalization among "diaspora" associations. Hence, Edward Damich (AMAC, NFCA) explains:

The CAA was much more about agitating without a proper political aim, they were much more loquacious. We were pushing for effective lobbying but the CAA wanted to have an exclusive voice. We felt that they were ineffective and they lacked the kind of sophistication that is required on the Hill.[43]

It was this situation that prompted the founding of the NFCA.

The NFCA: an alternative "on the Hill"

The NFCA was set up in response to the direct wishes of the CFU and other Croatian American associations[44] who no longer felt represented in Washington by the CAA, which had monopolized the political pressure and lobbying tasks.

Until 1993, all associations had been collaborating. There was thus no need for any body to represent these organizations as a whole. But when these associations became divided the need for a unifying body arose; in principle, the NFCA fulfilled the goal of consolidating the political power of these organizations.

The NFCA's founding aim was to be the single umbrella organization for all "diaspora" organizations.[45] The CAA was initially incorporated in the NFCA—thanks to Tony Peraica of the CAA and Steve Rukavina (CFU, NFCA)—to preserve the unity of the "diaspora." But the progressive trend represented by Peraica was wiped out during this period of tension.

Anthony Peraica (CAA) had been one of the militants from the outset, relatively close to Rukavina (CFU, then NFCA) and Damich (CFU, then NFCA). But the CAA's founder Ilija Letica, who had also been the association's initial source of funding ($20,000–$30,000 per year), was a radical political exile who thought that the CAA should continue to support Tuđman at all costs. He laid down conditions for the merger that were unacceptable to the boards of the CFU and the NFCA, demanding among other things an exclusive contract with institutions and public figures in Washington. In Rukavina's opinion, seeking a common ground would have been easier for everyone: the NFCA would have been able to concentrate on its cultural activities and the CAA on its lobbying action. But the CAA's strategy mirrored that of the HDZ at the Croatian World Congress—total control. Thus the unwillingness to compromise on the part of the CAA's radical faction prompted the division among associations. Anthony Peraica was replaced by one of Letica's close allies, Franck Brozovich. As Rukavina explains:

I would say that there is a real lack of democracy inside the CAA, and that is maybe why it didn't really work out well. They wanted complete monopoly and we said "no."[46]

So the NFCA was founded in near-complete opposition to the post-Peraica CAA.[47] Indeed, the NFCA claimed to have a different style:

I would say that the CAA was very good at gathering crowds. The NFCA was not really good at that. The NFCA was much better at sophisticated policy making. For example we set up a clear policy of public relations. We contacted the firm Ruder Finn, and dealt with a lobbyist named Jim Harff. Our techniques were somehow different: we issued press releases whenever we thought it was adequate, we contacted Congressmen and tried to build long-term relationships with them.[48]

Therefore, the main reason for the establishment of the NFCA was the basic disparity that appeared in 1993 between the official policy of Franjo Tuđman's HDZ government in Croatia and the borders of legitimate politics in the US. The associations chose to split. The CAA, bound to the policy of the HDZ by the political conviction of its members and its main financial backers, chose the political line of the homeland. Afterwards, the majority of Croatian Americans represented by associations such as the CFU were forced to replace their political organ with a new organization. Thus the NFCA was formed with the explicit goal "to promote a greater Croatian American participation in the American democratic process and within all our Croatian American organizations."[49]

To still have "resonance"—as Jim Harff put it—on Capitol Hill, the Croatian Americans set up the NFCA, which chose to continue to represent the "interests of Croatia," even if that meant disagreeing with the policy of the government of the time. The majority of associations then agreed to join.

Despite the growing influence that they could potentially have on the White House and the State Department in the specification of foreign policy, the NFCA was much more representative of the political claims of immigrants and their children, adapted to the liberal and democratic ethos[50] of the United States, than of the hypothetical influence of the homeland (contrary to both Huntington[51] and Smith[52]). Once the political orientation and values of certain associations and those of the Croatian government diverged, the effect of the "speech act"—which offers legitimacy through the link between the "diaspora" and its homeland—came into play once again. Hence the NFCA claimed the legitimacy of knowing "what is good" for Croatia, even if this included a public stand against the Croatian government and the hardline doctrine of the HDZ.

Indeed, only those associations whose political line continued to adhere to this ethos could have any resonance in Washington, to the extent of direct opposition to associations such as the CAA which chose to take an opposing line.

Putting a liberal ethos into practice

To the great displeasure of their leaders, including Peraica and Rukavina, beginning in 1993 the associations began splintering so that they competed in terms of their activities and positions.

Tensions between associations had already begun. A typical example of the competition between associations, and in particular between the sources of their legitimacy (garnered from the *hostland* or from the *homeland*), is the controversy surrounding the nomination of the US ambassador to Croatia. The CAA, with its small numbers and recent formation, drew all of its legitimacy from its anti-communist, anti-Yugoslav stance and from its dedication to the cause of independence. This was reinforced by the unconditional support it received from Zagreb and the HDZ; as we have discussed, the two organizations were practically one. Still, the CFU was the largest, richest and oldest organization in the United States, so its legitimacy was quite different. More than representing "*Croatian*-Americans," it represented "Croatian-*Americans*."

The political weight of Bernard Luketich was very real to Zagreb. More than one consul nomination had already been blocked by the president of the CFU, which disapproved of Tuđman's choices.[53] The ambassador nomination was subject to the same treatment. To reward the Letica family for its efforts and to support the CAA, the HDZ and the CAA announced their support for Mara Letica's ambassadorship candidacy. She was appointed by the Bush administration on 7 September 1990.[54] But with the arrival of the Clinton administration as well as the CFU leadership's dissatisfaction with her, she was replaced by Peter Galbraith, who remained ambassador from 1993 to 1998. The *Zajedničar* editorial from 3 February 1993 is explicit concerning the maneuver:

> President Clinton's Secretary of State Warren M. Christopher has pledged to State Department employees that the Clinton Administration would not appoint ambassadors solely because of their political connections [...]. This is not a post to be handed out to a political appointee or one who has made a generous contribution to an election campaign. It is apparent that Mr. Christopher is following the guidelines for ambassador appointments that the CFU has advocated and has voiced to the Clinton Administration.[55]

The case of congressman Radanovich is another example of this rivalry. It is also a good example of the use of ethnic identity for winning elections. As Edward Damich explains,[56] the NFCA needed to find new supporters on Capitol Hill besides those of the CAA. So, during the 1994 elections, the leadership team of the NFCA scanned the list of candidates standing for election looking for Croatian names. When they read "Radanovich," they contacted him. He only had a vague knowledge of his ethnic origins, which could be Serbian or Croatian. He simply knew he had Yugoslav roots. With some genealogical research, he discovered his Croatian ancestry, and publicly declared his support for the Croatian cause. The NFCA then offered financial support, and they called on Croatian Americans in California to vote for him. His victory ensured that the NFCA had a strong advocate in the House of Representatives.

Another important development for the NFCA was the possibility of influencing US foreign policy in Bosnia and Croatia through hearings organized by various congressional committees. The appearance of NFCA president Edward Damich before the Foreign Affairs Commission of the House of Representatives on 11 May 1994 was a major event for the new association.[57]

It is clear that Damich's position was different from that of the Croat government at the time. He actively supported cooperation between Muslims and Croats and the preservation of a multi-ethnic Bosnia-Herzegovina by seeking to minimize the tensions between the two factions in Bosnia-Herzegovina:

> The government of Bosnia-Herzegovina is avowedly multi-ethnic and it has no designs on the territory of any other state. Atrocities committed by Muslim forces have been infrequent, isolated incidents, not state policy [...]. As with the Muslims, atrocities committed by Croatian forces have been infrequent, isolated incidents, not state policy.[58]

This was not the first time that a member of the "diaspora" was consulted by US authorities. But unlike earlier visits to Washington,[59] the only views presented here were those of Croatian American associations opposing Zagreb's positions.

Relations between the CFU and the CAA (and therefore the HDZ in Zagreb) therefore began to become strained beginning in 1993, reaching a point of no return in 1994 with the creation of the NFCA. Thus, Bernard Luketich publicly voices the sentiment that he "does not feel represented"[60] by government figures such as Gojko Šušak. This disagreement is also expressed in the symbolic acts of national rituals. When Tuđman visited, at national holidays or receptions at the Croatian embassy, the NFCA, the CFU and other associations were marginalized to the benefit of the CAA. The illusion of unity created in the special years of unitary mobilization had permanently vanished.

Conclusion

What emerges from this account is that, contrary to the theoretical approaches to the diaspora which attempt to analytically make "diasporas" a discrete, singular actor on the international scene (such as those developed by Sheffer (1986, 2003; Shain and Barth 2003; Collier *et al.* 2002; or Adamson and Demetriou 2007), united "diasporas" only exist in the mobilizing discourses of diasporic institutions or in the official categorizations of bureaucracies and state agencies. At the sociological level, the relevant units of analysis are institutions, associations, organizations, and bureaucracies which formulate competing claims on the representation of a heterogeneous set of exiles, migrants, guest workers, students or third-generation citizens who are *conceived* as homogeneous and cast as legitimately linked to a distant homeland. As empirically shown, moments of convergence of several actors, views and practices are abnormal in the conflicting dynamics of the transnational political field. The unity of the "diaspora," one of the practical effects of the "speech act," disappeared when logics of struggle and distinction prevented this unity; in our case, when the homeland government engaged in unjustifiable practices in the political fields in which diasporic organizations had embedded.

Another, paradoxical, conclusion emerges from a detailed study of the official symbolic politics of the diaspora throughout the nineties: while under

130 *Diaspora as a state category*

communism, with citizens abroad suspect and excluded, the government had deployed three distinct, well-funded policies of control and management; yet when these categories were merged into a single "Emigrant Croatia," a unification promoted as a major achievement of the party in power, the policies were not comparable to what Yugoslavia deployed. No clear policies were defined, and no real budget was dedicated to the enactment of a diaspora policy. Compared to the peak of the Yugoslav guest workers programs, wherein the government set the goal of managing more than one million Yugoslavs abroad as a "seventh republic" (in addition to overseeing political emigration and feeding folkloristic cultural content to emigrants in Buenos Aires, Ottawa, and Adelaide), the Croatian government did almost nothing for Croats abroad.

The answer is partially found in the sociology of the new elites. Many of them were directly returning from exile and felt the need to compensate for the ostracism and marginalization of the previous regime. Also a sense of thankfulness for the diaspora spread, in particular for the war effort and humanitarian aid. But the most important reasons for the diffusion of this discourse are to be found elsewhere, as shown in the next chapter.

Notes

1 Ministarstvo povratka i useljeništva, "Predsjednik Tuđman: Povratak iz iseljeništva trajni je nacionalni i gospodarski interes Republike Hrvatske," *Bilten ministarstva povratka i useljeništva*, no. 9, March 1997, pp. 1–5.
2 "Svim Ogranicama HDZ u Domovini i Iseljeništvu," *Glasnik, Hrvatski Politički Tjednik*, 28 December 1990, p. 41.
3 "Svim Ogranicama HDZ u Domovini i Iseljeništvu," *Glasnik, Hrvatski Politički Tjednik*, 28 December 1990, p. 27.
4 Franjo Tuđman, "Pristupna Riječ predsjenika dr. Franje Tuđmana," *Glasnik HDZ*, no. 11, June 1990, p. 20.
5 *Vjesnik*, 6 August 1997.
6 *Slobodna Dalmacija*, 5 October 1997.
7 Ministarstvo povratka i useljeništva, "Dr. Zdravko Sančević: Neka povratak Hrvata iz iseljeništva postane trajni proces," *Bilten ministarstva povratka i useljeništva*, no. 9, March 1997, p. 8.
8 Dragutin Hlad, "Hrvatska Dijaspora u Južnoj Americi," *Glasnik HDZ*, no. 27, 2 November 1990, p. 27.
9 Ministarstvo povratka i useljeništva, "Ministar Petrović: Hrvatskoj trebaju mladi stručnjaci," *Bilten ministarstva povratka i useljeništva*, no. 5, June 1997, p. 14.
10 Ministarstvo povratka i useljeništva (1997) "Govor Ministra Petrović Hrvatima Vancouvera," *Bilten ministarstva povratka i useljeništva*, no. 1, January 1997, p. 3.
11 Franjo Tuđman, "Pristupna Riječ predsjenika dr. Franje Tuđmana," *Glasnik HDZ*, no. 11, June 1990, p. 20.
12 Stjepan Sterc, interviewed in *Vijesnik*, 25 March 2001, p. 19.
13 Ministarstvo povratka i useljeništva (1997) "Govor Ministra Petrović Hrvatima Vancouvera," *Bilten ministarstva povratka i useljeništva*, no. 1, January 1997, p. 5.
14 D. Hudelist (2004) *Tuđman, Biografija*, Zagreb: Profil International.
15 Mate Granić was considered as the leader of the HDZ moderates. After an unsuccessful 2000 presidential election, he formed a splinter party from the HDZ, the Democratic Center, the same year.

16 The *Hrvatska Stranka Prava* (Croatian Party of Rights) is a right-wing political party located in a post-*Ustaša* tradition.
17 See www.vlada.hr/hr/naslovnica/o_vladi_rh/prethodne_vlade_rh/3_vlada_republike_ hrvatske (accessed 20 August 2009).
18 One of them, Marijan Buconjić had been convicted in the USA of assaulting a Yugoslav diplomat. See http://cases.justia.com/us-court-of-appeals/F2/581/1031/279785/.
19 Antun Babić (Australia), Domagoj Ante Petrić (Argentina), Marijan Buconjić (USA), i Nikola Vidak (Canada), Ministarstvo povratka i useljeništva "Ministar Petrović predstavio svoje pomoćnike," *Bilten ministarstva povratka i useljeništva*, no. 2, February 1997, pp. 3–6.
20 Ministarstvo povratka i useljeništva "Govor Ministra Petrović Hrvatima Vancouvera," *Bilten ministarstva povratka i useljeništva*, no. 1, January 1997, pp. 2–3.
21 Ministarstvo povratka i useljeništva "Govor Ministra Petrović Hrvatima Vancouvera," *Bilten ministarstva povratka i useljeništva*, no. 1, January 1997, pp. 3–5.
22 Ministarstvo povratka i useljeništva "Dr. Zdravko Sančević: Neka povratak Hrvata iz iseljeništva postane trajni proces," *Bilten ministarstva povratka i useljeništva*, no. 3, March 1997, pp. 7.
23 Ministarstvo povratka i useljeništva "Ministar Petrović predstavio svoje pomoćnike," *Bilten ministarstva povratka i useljeništva*, no. 2, February 1997, p. 11.
24 Ministarstvo povratka i useljeništva "Suradnja Hrvatske I SAD-a," *Bilten ministarstva povratka i useljeništva*, no. 31, February 1999, p. 7.
25 Ministarstvo povratka i useljeništva "Marijan Petrović: Politika Povratka Hrvatskih Iseljenika," *Bilten ministarstva povratka i useljeništva*, no. 12, January 1998, pp. 8–9.
26 Ministarstvo povratka i useljeništva "U Hrvatsku se vratilo 39.177 Hrvata," *Bilten ministarstva povratka i useljeništva*, no. 14, March 1998, p. 3.
27 See www.dzs.hr/Eng/Publication/2005/7–1–2_1e2005.htm (accessed 5 October 2008).
28 Ministarstvo povratka i useljeništva "Dr Miomir Žužul Hrvatski Veleposlanik u SAD: Mladi Hrvati se žele vratiti," *Bilten ministarstva povratka i useljeništva*, no. 10, November 1997, p. 18.
29 For the Croatian figures, see the online archive of the Ministry of Finance: www.mfin.hr/hr/drzavni-proracun-arhiva (accessed 22 August 2009). For the Israeli figures, see the website of the Ministry of Finance of Israel: http://ozar.mof.gov.il/bud_frame_e.htm (accessed 22 August 2009).
30 Interview with Nikola Jelinčić, head of Hrvatska Matica Iseljenika, Zagreb, 3 November 2004.
31 Interview with Nikola Jelinčić, head of Hrvatska Matica Iseljenika, Zagreb, 3 November 2004. This question is extensively discussed in Chapter 7.
32 www.matis.hr/eng/projekti_opsirnije.php?id=11.
33 "Croat Diaspora Meet In Zagreb—Part I," *Zajedničar*, 13 October 1993, p. 8.
34 See also: www.crocc.org/english/about.asp?subcat=general (accessed 22 August 2009).
35 Mira Radielović Baratta, "The American Croats: How to be more effective in Washington," *Journal of Croatian Studies*, vol. 40, 1999, pp. 43–44.
36 "Uskrsna Čestitka Mate Bobana," *Zajedničar*, 14 April 1993, p. 16; " Muslim Aggression Against HVO, Chronology of Events," *Zajedničar*, 28 April 1993, p. 21.
37 Interview with Miomir Žužul, Croatian ambassador to the United States (1996–2000), Zagreb, 15 February 2003.
38 Interview with Andrija Jakovčević, Croatian ambassador to Canada (1998–2000), Zagreb, 18 February 2003.
39 Interview with Ivan Grdešić, current ambassador to the United States, *Večernji List*, 1 September 2001.
40 In an appendix on methodology, Sean Carter expresses his feelings on visiting the "Croatian diaspora" in Chicago as follows: "It is impossible to ignore the Ustasha factor among this group—although probably very few of these people were members

132 *Diaspora as a state category*

of the fascist organization, among this community the Ustasha are seen in a fairly positive light—as those who liberated Croatia from the first Yugoslavia, even if they did use the Axis powers to help them," in Carter, Sean Raymond *The Geo-Politics of Diaspora:Croatian Community and Identity in the United States,* unpublished thesis, University of Bristol, October 2001, p. 296.

41 Interview with Anthony Peraica, former President of the CAA, Chicago, 27 June 2003.
42 Interview with Jim Harff, former director of Ruder Finn Global Public Affairs, current director of Global Communicators, Washington, 20 June 2003.
43 Interview with Edward Damich, former president of the NFCA, Washington, 17 June 2003.
44 American Croatian Relief Project, American Initiative for Croatia (AIC), AMA Croatica, Capital, AMA Croatica, Mid-Atlantic Chapter, AMA Croatica, Midwest Chapter AMA Croatica, Rudjer-Bosković, Croatian American Club-San Pedro, Croatian American Goodwill Association, Croatian American Political Club, Croatian Catholic Union (CCU), Croatian Council (Kansas City), Croatian Council (New York), Croatian Cultural Society (Omaha), Croatian Cultural Society (Minnesota), Croatian Fraternal Union (CFU), CFU Lodge #1836, CFU Lodge #1976, Croatian Philatelic Society, Croatian Relief Project (Kansas City), Croatian National Association, Eastern Virginia Croatian Club, Federation of Croatian Societies (Milwaukee), St. Joseph's Croatian Catholic Church, Truth About Croatia, Inc. In NFCA, Assembly of Delegates Conference, 2–23 January 1994, St. Louis, Missouri (brochure).
45 "The 2.5 Million Americans of Croatian descent will soon have a new voice in Washington, the National Federation of Croatian Americans (NFCA)." With nearly 600 Croatian American organizations, the Croatian American community has long felt the need for a national umbrella organization to facilitate communication and to coordinate its educational and political activities." In "Croatian Americans Establish Federation," *Zajedničar*, 9 February 1994, pp. 1, 7.
46 Interview with Steve Rukavina, former president of the NFCA, current Vice-President, Washington, 19 June 2003.
47 Interview with Anthony Peraica, former president of the CAA, Chicago, 27 June 2003.
48 Interview with Edward Damich, former president of the NFCA, Washington, 17 June 2003.
49 NFCA, Assembly of Delegates Conference, January 22–23 1994, St. Louis, Missouri (brochure), p. 2.
50 Y. Shain (1998) *Marketing the American Creed Abroad: Diasporas in the US and their Homelands*, Cambridge University Press: Cambridge, p. 51.
51 Samuel Huntington, "The Erosion Of American National Interests" in *Foreign Affairs*, 76(5), September–October 1997.
52 Tony Smith, *Foreign Attachments*, London: Harvard University Press, 2000.
53 "Unofficial Diplomat," *Pittsburgh Post-Gazette*, 14 May 2000.
54 "Nomination of United States Ambassadors to Bosnia-Herzegovina, Croatia, and Slovenia," *Public Papers of the Presidents*, 17 September 1992.
55 "On The Right Track," *Zajedničar*, 3 February 1993, p. 2.
56 Interview with Edward Damich, former president of the NFCA, Washington, 17 June 2003.
57 "Testimony May 11, 1994 Edward J. Damich President National Federation of Croatian Americans House Foreign Affairs US Policy Toward Bosnia and Balkans," *Federal Document Clearing House Congressional Testimony*, 11 May 1994.
58 Ibid.
59 "AMAC Visits State Department," *Zajedničar*, 3 July 1991, pp. 6, 24.
60 Interview with Bernard Luketich, president of the CFU, Pittsburgh, 26 June 2003.

References

Adamson, F. and Demetriou, M. (2007) "Remapping the Boundaries of 'State' and 'National Identity': Incorporating Diasporas into IR Theorizing," *European Journal of International Relations*, 13(4), pp. 489–526.

Collier, P., Hoeffler, A. and University of Oxford (2002) *Greed and Grievance in Civil War*, Oxford: University of Oxford Institute of Economics and Statistics Centre for the Study of African Economies.

Coric, D. (1999) "Raskol u Hrvatskom kanadskom kongresu," *Hrvatska Revija*, 49, pp. 534–536.

Dom i Svjiet (2000) "Kidaju li se namjerno veze između domovinske i iseljene Hrvatske?" *Dom i Svjiet*.

Hockenos, P. (2003) *Homeland Calling, Exile Patriotism and the Balkan Wars*, Ithaca and London: Cornell University Press.

Shain, Y. and Barth, A. (2003) "Diasporas and International Relations Theory," *International Organization*, 57(3), pp. 449–479.

Sheffer, G. (1986) *Modern Diasporas in International Politics*, London: Croom Helm.

Sheffer, G. (2003) *Diaspora Politics: At Home Abroad*, Cambridge, UK; New York: Cambridge University Press.

Šošić, H. (1994) "Hrvatski tjednik i 1971. godina," *Kolo Matice hrvatske*, 152(4), pp. 1163–1190.

Tarle, M. (1995) "Hrvati u Australiji i povratak u domovinu: hrvatski lobby u Australiji," *Hrvatska Revija*, 4, pp. 494–504.

Vuksic, B. (1997) "Zidovi su pobijedili pustinju," *Obzor*, pp. 58–59.

Vurusic, V. (1998) "Vecina hrvatskih emigranata ne bi voljela da opozicija pobjedi na izborima, ali se ja ne bojim ako SDP dođe na vlast!" *Globus*, pp. 24–28.

6 Diasporic citizenship, territory, and the politics of belonging

What were the motivations behind the overwhelming use of the public discourse about diaspora if so few government funds were devoted to developing a serious policy of return, to developing the activities of *Matica Hrvatska Iseljenika* or to developing an efficient Croatian World Congress? In the two following chapters, I will argue that the answer is to be found not in the institutions explicitly devoted to the diaspora, but in the foundations of the modern Croatian state.

This chapter primarily deals with the question of citizenship and the politics of belonging. Croatian citizenship laws were used to enact the post-territorial nationalism elaborated by the HDZ—a nationalism that, by taking Croatian ethnicity as its cornerstone, intended to homogenize the national population through the exclusion of non-Croats and to include all ethnic Croats in a single national group, regardless of their place of residence.

As discussed earlier, when the literature on "diasporas" and "transnational communities" emerged in the 1990s, many saw these new objects of enquiry as challengers or successors to the nation-state (Cohen 1996; Glick Schiller *et al.* 1992; Tölölyan 1996). The prevalence of multiple allegiances and overlapping identities illustrated the unbundling of territory and identifications on a global scale (Appadurai 1991). Contrary to the long tradition of the sociology of immigration, migrants were not to be understood in relation to their successful or failed "assimilation" or "integration" in the host society, but as new forms of "transnational communities" emerging across territorial borders and questioning the traditional Westphalian model of territorialized communities (Portes 1995; Guarnizo and Smith 1998). By the end of the 1990s the initial enthusiasm gave way to genuine debates on the modalities through which diasporas and transnational communities encountered and reformed the aspects of governmental control (Koopmans and Statham 1999, 2001).

The field of citizenship studies—which overlaps the field of diaspora and of transnationalism studies—has been structured along similar lines: on the one hand "post-nationalists" and "cosmopolitanists" have reflected upon the ways in which migrants have pushed the boundaries of national citizenship, particularly with the help of international human rights norms (Benhabib 2006; Jacobson 1996; Soysal 1994; Soysal 1996). Others remained skeptical of this change and instead understood citizenship as both a modality of government and exclusion as well as a locus of political struggle (Hindess 2004; Isin 2002; Isin and Net-Library Inc. 1999; Nyers 2003). Seyla Benhabib's work is a good example of the first stance. Benhabib's central diagnosis is that the "transnationalization" of migration has made new forms of local, postnational citizenship possible because in "today's world the civil and social rights of migrants, aliens and denizens are increasingly protected by international human rights documents" (Benhabib 2007: 19).[1]

Even those suspicious of the possibility of "postnational" citizenship have shared similar faith in migrants' ability to bring about more inclusive forms of belonging. Engin Isin argues that the object of his book *Being Political*

> was to write histories of citizenship from the point of view of its alterities in the sense of recovering those solidaristic, agonistic and alienating moments of reversal and transvaluation, where strangers and outsiders constituted themselves as citizens or insiders and in so doing altered the ways of being political [...]. Being political provokes acts of speaking against injustice and vocalizing grievances as equal beings.
>
> (2002: 277)

Thus for Isin, just as Benhabib, the "diaspora" or the "transnational community" is the historical subject through which change will take place. To be sure, the reasons for this convergence are probably located in what Jef Huysmans has remarked to be

> the name "migrant['s]" essential capacity to raise or become involved in what could be called a problematique of contested political community [...]. Therefore it should not be surprising that migration has been a key phenomenon—together with war and class differences—in relation to which political community and citizenship has traditionally been defined.
>
> (2000: 151)

Yet by focusing on the question of "immigration" and trends of the "South" coming to the "North" or the "West," the current literature on citizenship has overlooked the heuristic power which the question of migration as "emigration" can provide in thinking about the new politics of belonging brought about by processes of globalization. Except for a few exceptions, most authors have acknowledged the phenomenon of transnationalism, but they have essentially understood it as one more process in a move toward cosmopolitan norms (with a few exceptions: Joppke 2003; Baubock 2005). As Benhabib put it,

> Increasingly, Mexico and central American governments such as El Salvador and Guatemala are permitting those who are born to citizen parents in foreign countries to retain voting rights at home and even to run for office; the practice of recognizing dual citizenship is becoming widespread.

In South Asia, particularly among economic elites who carry three or more passports and navigate three or more national economies, the institution of "flexible citizenship" (Ong) is taking hold.

(2007: 20)

What has been overlooked is that diasporic politics very often represent exactly what they seem to oppose; modalities of exclusion based on "ethnicity," language or culture. This is particularly clear when "sending states" engage in "diaspora policies." In this chapter I argue that, contrary to the dominant discourse in the literature about the relationship between "diasporic" formations or transnational communities and citizenship (as any other form of social boundary making), the diasporic discourse is founded on a specific form of exclusion. Croatia's post-communist citizenship policies outline what I define as forms of post-territorial belonging; ethnicity is dissociated from territory as a modality of inclusion/exclusion and new forms of bounding the nation are imagined. By studying legislative practices (in the constitution and in the citizenship law of 1991) I first analyze the deployment of the discourse of diaspora as a way to legitimize the exclusion of non-ethnic Croat populations from civic and political citizenship. Next, I address the question of post-war minority return and integration.

Post-territorial understandings of Croatian citizenship

One of the pillars of the transnational political arena, occupied by homeland institutions, hostland institutions, and diasporic institutions, we have seen, is the very definition of the boundaries of who is inside and who is outside. Yet all actors are not equal in this competition. Governments have at their disposal techniques of inclusion and exclusion which carry much stronger symbolic and material effects. In the first section of this chapter, I discuss the effects of homeland states' citizenship policies in defining an official diaspora, and the intrinsic logic of exclusion that is carried in the passage from a territorial to a post-territorial understanding of belonging.

The citizenship law in former Yugoslavia

Paradoxically, in the passage from Yugoslav to Croatian citizenship the major change did not occur along the division between "Renanian" (*jus soli*) and "Herderian" (*jus sanguinis*) conceptions of citizenship, but at the level of the referent geography of the nation—that is, from a territorial to a post-territorial conception. As was common to communist states,[2] Yugoslavia's conception of citizenship was closely knit with the ethnic understandings of the nation. From the start, Yugoslav citizenship was defined by descent (Ragazzi and Štiks 2009; Medvedović 1998: 27–29; Tepić and Bašić 1969: xxxvi). Thus the citizenship of the Federal People's Republic of Yugoslavia (FPRY)—which would become the Socialist Federal Republic of Yugoslavia (SFRY) on 5 July 1956[3]—was first defined by belonging to a particular nation (*narod*), which itself belonged to the federation. Nations themselves were *territorialized* as constitutive peoples of one of the six republics inside the federation. Consequently, Yugoslav citizens enjoyed a parallel, dual citizenship: one of the federation, and one of the republics. While initially there were some distinctions of status between citizens and non-citizens of the republics, the 1974 constitution provided that "a citizen of a republic on the territory of another republic has the same rights and obligations as the citizens of that republic."[4] Citizens of Yugoslavia rarely bothered to change citizenship when they moved within the federation (Ragazzi and Štiks 2009). So while every citizen officially declared a (voluntary) "ethnic" affiliation,[5] every republic was the republic of one or more particular constitutive nations, and every citizen had a republic citizenship, it was rather irrelevant while one remained inside the borders of Yugoslavia (Štiks 2006).

As discussed in the previous chapters, the main line of exclusion established by the Yugoslav communist party after 1946 was ideological, not ethnic. The government was worried about the "enemies of the state," and the processes of securitization of "enemy" groups mostly consisted of a territorial solution: it was about "rooting out" the "internal enemy," banning it, and surveilling it abroad. The Yugoslav federation passed, among others, the law on deprivation of citizenship—the *Act on the Deprivation of Citizenship for Officers and Non-Commissioned Officers of the Former Yugoslav Army Who do not Want to Return to the Homeland, and for the Members of Military Forces Who Have Served the Enemy and Have Defected Abroad.*[6] Furthermore, the law on citizenship was revised to exclude all citizens of German ethnicity residing abroad from Yugoslav citizenship on the basis of their "disloyal conduct toward the national and state interests of the peoples of FPRY."[7] With the reforms of 1965, although Yugoslavs were entitled to a passport and travel, Yugoslavia itself retained a territorialized, disciplinary control—with some limited forms of liberal free movement from the 1960s.

Including Croats

With the Croatian Declaration of Independence of 25 June 1991, a new citizenship act was introduced,[8] changing the link between the "nation" and "territory." The act was conceived on the basis of two principles: legal continuity with citizenship of the Socialist Republic of Croatia, and Croatian ethnicity (Omejec 1998: 99).

By law, all possessors of the former Croatian republic citizenship became citizens of the new state, making all other residents *aliens* overnight, regardless of the duration of their residency in Croatia. Their naturalization was then regulated by article 8 of the Croatian Citizenship Act, which requires five years of registered residence in Croatia, provided that the following conditions were met: no foreign citizenship or proof of release from a previous citizenship if admitted to Croatian citizenship; *proficiency* in the Croatian language and *Latin* script;

conduct that reflects an attachment to the customs and legal system of the Republic of Croatia; and, finally, acceptance of *the Croatian culture*.[9] These supplementary criteria rendered the territorial element in the attribution of citizenship irrelevant.

Croatian ethnic origin was usually determined through any official document released by SFRY or the authorities of the republic in which one declared oneself as an ethnic Croat, but sometimes peculiar documents such as Catholic Church certificates were also accepted by the state authorities (among Southern Slavs, being a Roman Catholic has been considered the strongest proof of someone"s "Croatianness," if born south of Slovenia).[10]

The act facilitated the naturalization of emigrants and their descendants who accepted the Croatian legal system, customs and culture, even if they did not match the criteria defined in article 8. Article 12 provided that:

> A foreign citizen whose admission to Croatian citizenship would be of interest for the Republic of Croatia, can acquire Croatian citizenship by naturalization although he or she does not meet the prerequisites from Article 8, paragraph 1, points 1–4 of this Law.
>
> Croatian citizenship can be acquired by the spouse of the person from paragraph 1 of this Article who has acquired Croatian citizenship although he or she does not meet the prerequisites from Article 8, paragraph 1, point 1–4 of this Law.
>
> The authorized Ministry shall issue an opinion on the existence of an interest in the admission to Croatian citizenship of a foreigner from paragraph 1 of this Article.

Moreover, it allowed ethnic Croats without previous or current residence in Croatia to obtain Croatian nationality by declaration through article 16:

> A member of the Croatian people who does not have a place of residence in the Republic of Croatia can acquire Croatian citizenship if he or she meets the prerequisites from Article 8, paragraph 1, point 5 of this Law and if he or she issues a written statement that he or she considers himself or herself to be a Croatian citizen.
>
> The statement from paragraph 1 of this Article shall be given before the competent authority or before the diplomatic or consular office of the Republic of Croatia abroad.

This affected not only the historical "diaspora" in the US, Canada, and Argentina, but also Croats from neighboring Bosnia and Herzegovina. Despite being one of the "constitutive peoples" of the Republic of Bosnia and Herzegovina, they were considered potential Croatian citizens in "diaspora" and included in the legislative provisions. Indeed, article 16 facilitated the naturalization of ethnic Croats living in the "near abroad" (former Yugoslav republics), especially for those in Bosnia and Herzegovina, while article 11 facilitated the naturalization of republic Croatian ethnic emigrants and their descendants, even if they did not satisfy the conditions stated in article 8 regarding proficiency in the Croatian language:

> An emigrant, as well as his or her descendants, may acquire Croatian citizenship by naturalization although they do not meet the prerequisites from Article 8, paragraph 1, points 1–4 of this Act.
>
> The foreign citizen who is married to an emigrant who has acquired Croatian citizenship according to the provisions of paragraph 1 of this Article can acquire Croatian citizenship although he or she does not meet the prerequisites from Article 8 paragraph 1, points 1–4 of this Act.
>
> Pursuant to paragraph 1 of this Article, an emigrant is a person who has emigrated from Croatia with the intention to live permanently abroad.

It is difficult to know how many Croats abroad received citizenship, as enquiries to obtain statistical information were unfruitful.[11] After several letters addressed to the Croatian Ministry of Interior, the following response was received in June 2008:

> In the period between 2002 and 2007, 53,095 requests for acquisition of Croatian citizenship were favourably resolved, and 11,321 requests were denied. During the same period, the requests for acquisition of Croatian citizenship submitted by 7,057 persons were suspended or rejected.
>
> We would like to underline that we are communicating the above-cited data with a reserve, and that we cannot be held responsible for their accuracy. We do not possess the technical equipment necessary to generate exact statistical data. In the above-mentioned period, there were no unified parameters for the statistical treatment of data related to the acquisition of Croatian citizenship. As for the period between 1991 and 2001 we are unable to communicate the required data. During this period, no statistical data was produced in relation to the resolved requests for acquisition of Croatian citizenship, because there was no adequate informational system for this database.
>
> (Ragazzi and Štiks 2009)

It is difficult to assess the reliability of this statement. On the one hand, the first years of Croatian independence were marked by war and administrative reorganization. This gives credit to the Ministry's claims. On the other hand, the highly politicized question of Croatian citizenship, as well as the "ethnic engineering" aspect of the citizenship policies are obviously something that the Croatian government did not want to see quantified, so the statement that between 1991 and 2001 there was "no adequate informational system for this database" seems suspicious. The fact that another author (Omejec 1998) was able to obtain some data for that period and that these data were quoted in a UNCHR report (1997), confirms that some statistical data must be available:

In the period from October 8, 1991, to June 30, 1995, the Ministry of Internal Affairs of RC [Republic of Croatia] resolved 557,379 requests for determination of Croatian citizenship according to art. 30 para. 1 LCC [Law on Croatian Citizenship]. According to the analysis, these cases mostly involved citizens of the former SFRY with a residence in SRC [Socialist Republic of Croatia] who were not registered in the citizens' registry of SRC or were registered after February 29, 1978 yet did not have a citizenship recorded in the "republican citizenship" section, and their citizenship was disputable. There is no data regarding how many of the 557,379 requests submitted on the grounds of art. 30 para. 1 LCC were denied. In the same period (October 8, 1991–June 3, 1995) the MIA of RC resolved 394,910 requests for subsequent registration on the grounds of art. 30 para. 2 LCC. These cases mostly involved ethnically-Croatian individuals who were not citizens of SRC, but who had a residence on its territory and submitted a statement that they considered themselves to be Croats. Therefore, in the period from October 8, 1991, to June 30, 1995, 952,331 procedures for determination of Croatian citizenship were executed on the basis of art. 30 LCC (Omejec 1998: 116).[12]

(Ragazzi and Štiks 2009)

Excluding Serbs

While the new act included previously ostracized Croats abroad, it had suddenly excluded from citizenship former Croatian citizens who had lived all their lives in Croatia: ethnic Serbs.[13] The new citizenship act put those with less than five years of registered residence and those who were unable to prove that they had been released from foreign citizenship (i.e., previous republic citizenship)[14] in a particularly difficult position. In a context in which Croatia was at war with the Yugoslav federation (which comprised initially the Republics of Serbia, Montenegro, Macedonia, and Bosnia and Herzegovina and then progressively shrunk to Serbia and Montenegro) it was virtually impossible to satisfy this condition. Only aliens born in the territory, spouses, emigrants and those whose citizenship was of interest to Croatia did not have to prove release from their previous citizenship under the naturalization procedure. Moreover, all applicants for naturalization had to prove that they accepted "the Croatian legal system" and "customs" and "culture." Furthermore, between 1991 and 1993, the Ministry of Interior's decisions on applications were discretionary, since the Ministry was not obliged to state its reasons for refusing a request. In 1993 the Constitutional Court ordered the Ministry to begin explaining its decisions.[15]

The ethnic, post-territorial features of the 1991 Citizenship Act were confirmed in the transitional provisions, determining the initial citizenry of Croatia and including a special mode of acquiring citizenship for ethnic Croats who were registered but did not possess Croatian republic-level citizenship. They could acquire Croatian citizenship by submitting a written statement to the police that they considered themselves Croatian citizens. Once the police had confirmed that the applicant fulfilled the above requirements, the applicant was entered into the citizenship registry (see art. 30, para. 2).[16] In 1993, the Croatian Constitutional Court defended article 30 against the petition filed by the Social Democratic Union, which demanded its annulment on the basis of the discrimination against non-Croats. The Court stated that the Croatian Citizenship Act respected international law on statelessness and that it did not threaten to "leave a person without citizenship" since all SFRY citizens had to have a republic-level citizenship. Furthermore, the Court stated that the Act itself did not explicitly revoke anyone's citizenship (UNHCR 1997: 17).

Since legal continuity with previous citizenship in the Socialist Republic of Croatia was the determining factor for the establishment of the initial citizenry of the newly independent state, the Republic Registrar's Office was supposed to issue Croatian citizenship certificates. However, problems arose if the person was registered but his or her republic citizenship was not Croatian (if, for instance, the father's republic citizenship was sometimes used to determine the republic citizenship of a child), or if no republic citizenship was officially recorded. The former cases were considered aliens and had to apply for naturalization, whereas the latter were sent to police agencies to have their citizenship determined or were allowed to register as Croatian citizens—according to art. 30, para. 2—if they were able to prove Croat ethnic origins (UNHCR 1997). If they were not able to provide the necessary proof or were simply of a different ethnicity, they remained aliens under the law.

For Serbs who had remained in Croatia, the exclusion was not only symbolic; it had a direct impact on everyday life. They could lose their jobs under the Act on Employment of Aliens, which regulated work for the new non-citizens, requiring them to obtain a work permit. Work permits could be issued to foreigners only if they held specific qualifications that were needed in the country and were taking on positions which could not be filled by Croatian citizens. Thus, ethnic discrimination in the workplace could be justified at a massive scale through the new citizenship act (Human Rights Watch 1995: 15).

The citizenship status of Croatia's Serb minority in the Krajina region was even more problematic.[17] After the Croatian Serb militia, with the help of the Yugoslav federal army, took control of almost one-third of Croatia's territory, mostly in the Krajina region (but also in Central and Eastern Slavonia) in 1991, the citizenship status of the ethnic Serb population living in these regions remained unresolved for almost a decade. Croatian Serb refugees who fled or were forced to leave Krajina during and after the Croatian military takeover in 1995 found themselves in Serbia or Bosnia-Herzegovina (in the Serb entity) and were in a particularly difficult situation.

All those who held Croatian republic citizenship from before the war (in SFRY) legally should have been recognized as Croatian citizens, but could not obtain the necessary proof of previously holding Croatian republic citizenship, and thus could not obtain a certificate of Croatian citizenship (Domovnica) nor claim any of the rights due to a Croatian citizen. Others, who had lived in Croatia for several decades before the war and who held residence in Croatia but were unaware that they did not hold republic citizenship, could not regulate their status in Croatia before 2000—regardless of having obtained all of their other rights during their lifetime in Croatia, including pension, reconstruction, qualifications and degrees, etc.—when the Ministry of the Interior provided a legal venue. This was accessible to only a few Serb returnees who were in Croatia at the time (Serbian Democratic Forum 2013). Unlike Croats who did not live in Croatia before 1991, Serbs who had had residence in Croatia before the war were subjected to a discriminatory regime which did not differentiate between returnees and aliens who desired to reside in Croatia, for instance, for the sake of employment. Subsequent laws failed to successfully address the matter of the citizenship and status of Serb returnees to Croatia, opening for them only the regime accessible to *regular* aliens, whether it was obtaining the right to temporary or permanent residence, or access to citizenship. Only recently, in 2015, have amendments to the Croatian Citizenship Act opened up citizenship to any person registered in the citizenship registries as a citizen of the former republic between 1 March 1978 and 8 October 1991 who has been issued a public identification document which attests to the fact.[18] This amendment limited the discretionary powers of the competent authorities where it came to recognizing citizenship status which was held pursuant to applicable citizenship laws before the existence of post-SFRY Croatian citizenship.

Clearly a fundamental shift in the conception of citizenship occurred: not a passage from a "civic" to an "ethnic" conception (it was always de facto "ethnic"), but the passage from territorial residence to ethnicity as the main criterion of inclusion or exclusion from citizenship. In its very mechanism, the law provided for the exclusion of the territorially present non-Croatian and for the inclusion of ethnic Croats, no matter where they lived. The effect of the citizenship law is also clear: it watered down the importance of Serbs in the ethnic balance, by excluding as many as possible, and by including Croats from abroad. However, this presupposed broader changes in the understanding of the *place* of citizenship, from a territorial understanding of the "nation" to a post-territorial "community" located anywhere in the world.

Representation and belonging

The most evident manner in which the shifting of the balance from Serbs to Croats occurred was at the level of political representation. But the exclusion of Serbs was also carried out through the disciplinary practice of excluding people, by directly and indirectly preventing them from coming—as a direct counterpart to the advocated policy of the return of Croats.

Reshuffling representation and belonging

The constitution of 1990 guaranteed the right to vote to all Croatian citizens regardless of residential status.[19] Although the HDZ had advocated for a diaspora ballot since 1990, it was only on 18 September 1995 that the Croatian parliament was presented with a new election act which included, for the first time, the right to vote for Croats residing outside of the borders of Croatia.[20] It is believed that the act was an initiative of HDZ hardliners, and in particular the "Herzegovinian Lobby" (Gojko Šušak, Ivica Pašalić). The act set up a fixed number of representatives for the parliament, elected in a separate electoral unit and on a separated electoral list. By the introduction of this new legislation, the electoral corpus of Croatia was increased by about 10 percent, and the "diaspora" was thus awarded 12 seats in the Sabor (Salay et al. 1996: iii). The list of candidates, however, had not been decided by the "diaspora," but was representative of HDZ's long-time supporters and crucial active members: Ante Beljo, Zdravka Bušić, Ratko Ferenčić, Ivan Nogalo and Zdravko Sančević (Bajruši 2007).

The 2010 amendments to the Constitution[21] changed the number of diaspora representatives, fixing it to three, which Kasapović deems arbitrary, "a result of a compromise researched behind closed doors" in a political trade-off between the government and the opposition (Kasapović 2010, 2012). The Constitutional Act saw changes in 2010 as well, whereby all national minorities in Croatia, except Serbs, were awarded a double right to vote, a minority representative vote, and a general one.[22] The electoral base was thus, as Kasapović notes, divided into Croat majority voters, Serbian minority voters with one vote, and the other minority voters with two votes, legalizing inequality among voters (Kasapović 2010). The amendment to the Constitutional Act was successfully challenged before the Constitutional Court which held the proposed change unconstitutional and abolished the amended rule.[23]

The anticipated 1995 elections were to be organized in advance to capitalize on the victory of the operations Flash (*Bljesak*) and Storm (*Oluja*), which led the way to the forced reintegration of the separatist provinces of Krajina and Eastern Slavonia. Observers commented that the granting of voting rights to the "HDZ-sympathetic" diaspora was a move to further consolidate the party's power in parliament. The move did benefit Tuđman's party as 398,839 voters were registered abroad and although the turnout was rather low (109,389, i.e., 27.4 percent), all 12 seats went to the HDZ (Kasapović 1996: 270).

However, the diaspora vote was contested on several fronts. First, technically the mandate on the "diaspora" list represented fewer people than the average seat; a representative of the "diaspora" stood for 8,981 votes, instead of the 30,217 as was the case for the other representatives, which is to say three times as many. Moreover, the effect on the electoral outcome was quite important, as with the diaspora votes the HDZ obtained a large majority of 59.1 percent instead of the 54.8 percent which they would have got without it (Mecanović 1999).

The legitimacy of the vote was also contested for more fundamental reasons: how can people who do not pay taxes vote? How can people who do not live the consequences of their choices vote? As Mirjana Kasapović put it, the diaspora's right to vote posed central questions for the democracy:

> Who has the right to vote and to be elected in this country? All the bearers of a Croatian passport, from Vinjan Donji to Alaska? All ethnic Croats with

a passport? Only the real Croatian emigration, i.e., citizens of the Republic of Croatia who emigrated for political or economic reasons and for whom it is easy to prove a former stay in the country? Only the ones who completed military service and pay taxes in Croatia?

(1999)

In 1999, after heated debates, the electoral system was changed.[24] From a fixed number of seats, the new act proposed proportional representation based on voter turnout. This again guaranteed the HDZ six seats out of six in the 2000 elections (Zdenka Babić-Petričević, Milan Kovač, Ljubo Ćesić Rojs, Ante Beljo, Zdravka Bušić and Krunoslav Kordić). This again had an important political impact. Although the HDZ lost overall, the SDP–HSLS coalition (led by Ivica Račan and Stipe Mesić) obtained 47 percent of the votes instead of the 50.7 percent majority they would have won without the diaspora seats. Moreover, the extra seats made the HDZ first in the parliament in terms of single-party representation.

The diaspora constituency continued to make and break candidates. In the presidential campaign of 2005, despite the low turnout (19 percent) the diaspora vote both prevented the election of Stipe Mesić (HNS) in the first round and allowed the HDZ candidate Jadranka Kosor to dispute the second round instead of Boris Mikšić, who would have qualified instead. The political importance of the vote was even higher in 2007, when it provided the HDZ with the necessary extra seats to form a government (Izbori 2005, 2007).

It therefore appears clear that Croatia's "diasporic" citizenship policy is deeply embedded in a process of inclusion of ethnic Croats. Yet, the other side of the coin of this post-territorial citizenship policy, far from the cosmopolitan, postnational ideals that some authors would advocate for, is the forcible exclusion of non-Croats present on the territory from citizenship. And the close entanglement of these two features was directly addressed in the debates linked to the question of the right to vote and to be represented in parliament. As one member of the Sabor, elected on the diaspora ticket explained:

> I am mostly saddened by the discussions which examine the number [i.e., reduction] of representatives from the diaspora. We have been forced out of the homeland because of the circumstances, not only me, but thousands of Croats. We helped to create the free Croatia in many ways, and today we have only twelve members of parliament [...]. On the other hand, no one mentions the members of parliament representing the national minorities, the majority of which, if they haven't taken part in it themselves, have at least advocated for the aggression [i.e., the war] against the Republic of Croatia.[25]

This common argument was in stark contrast to the reality. In fact, since the independence of Croatia, the HDZ's policies had reduced the importance of minority representation.

The 1992 act on the rights of national minorities,[26] was enacted under pressure from the European Community, granting 13 out of 138 seats to the minorities in the Croatian Sabor. Since the law allowed only minorities representing more than 8 percent of the population to be represented, all 13 seats were taken by Serbs. The representation of minorities was calculated on the basis of the 1981 Yugoslav census.[27] Yet in 1995 the new act erased the reference to the 1981 census stating that minority representation was postponed until a new census was completed, a technicality to prevent minorities from being represented[28] (Burrai 2008: 13). Moreover, voter participation was tightened and openly discriminated against non-ethnic Croats. While registration was extended to 300,000 out-of-country ethnic Croat voters, 200,000 primarily ethnic Serb voters (5 percent of the potential electorate) who had fled the country were excluded from the ballot (OSCE 1997: 3). The new act of 1999 had further restricted minority representation, and Serbs only obtained one representative in the Sabor.

In the 2000 parliamentary election, the attribution of minority seats had "diluted" the representation of the Serb population by allowing other minorities to be represented. One seat was allocated for Serbs, Italians, Hungarians, Czechs, and Slovaks together with "others" (Austrians, Germans, Ukrainians, Ruthenians, and Jews) (OSCE 2000: 3). The electoral procedure further discriminated between the internally displaced "expellees" and "displaced persons":

> A large number of polling stations were established for "expelled" persons who are generally ethnic-Croats, whereas only two polling stations were set up for "displaced persons," generally ethnic-Serbs. This segregation of internally displaced voters between two categories and the disproportionate number of polling stations provided to each category, in effect, discriminate between voters of Croat and Serb ethnic origin.
> (OSCE/ODHIR 2000: 6–7)

However, this progressive reduction of minority representation was reversed with the end of the Tuđman era and the election of Stipe Mesić and the installation of the left-wing Račan-led government. In 2000 a new Constitutional Act on National Minorities was passed, increasing the representation of minorities in the Sabor. For the 2003 and 2007 parliamentary elections and the 2005 presidential election, although the HDZ regained power, the provisions remained unchanged.

In sum, the reintegration of Serbs into the body politic was linked to legal issues of citizenship and representation, and the more pernicious reversal of a diffused policy of physically eliminating the minority from Croatia's territory.

Disciplinary practices: from constitutive people to unwanted bodies

During his transformation from convinced communist general to nationalist historical revisionist, Tuđman expressed the need to ethnically homogenize Croatia. On several occasions he had formulated the possibility of a "peaceful" and "democratic" exchange of populations with Serbia. Once in power, the HDZ's policy intended to reduce the percentage of Serbs living in Croatia to a minimum.

To understand the political impact of the HDZ's policy we must briefly study the previous system of collective rights in the SFRY. As Valentina Burrai explains, the Yugoslav system had an elaborate hierarchical recognition of collective rights: Yugoslav nations in their republic (*Narodi Jugoslavije*),[29] the national minorities or "nationalities" (*narodnosti*), the Yugoslav nations outside their own republics, and the ethnic groups. "Nations" were entitled to a republic. Nationalities were essentially minorities of neighboring countries. Yet the symbolic difference in hierarchical status between *nations* and *nationalities* was such that even when numerically a minority in another republic, a "nation" could only be considered as such. "For this reason, Serbs in Croatia were not considered a national minority, but rather a nation, which was always mentioned along with the Croat one in all symbolic sections of the constitution" (Burrai 2008: 7–8). At the bottom, "ethnic groups" (*etničke grupe*) were groups without a republic or a homeland outside of Yugoslavia, such as the Roma or the Vlachs. The Croatian Constitution of 1974 therefore defined the Socialist Republic "as a national state of the Croatian people, *state of the Serbian people in Croatia* [emphasis added] and state of nationalities living on its territory" (Art. 1).

In December 1990, the new Croatian Constitution proclaimed "the Republic of Croatia as the national state of the Croatian people and the state of members of other nations and minorities who are its citizens," fundamentally revoking the principle of equality between Croats and Serbs, and relegating the latter to a new position they had never occupied in Croatia. It is no surprise, therefore, that Croatian Serbs boycotted the referendum for independence on 19 May 1991, wherein citizens were asked to recognize "the Republic of Croatia as a sovereign and independent state that guarantees *the Serbs and members of other nationalities in Croatia* cultural autonomy and all rights of a citizen,"[30] and even held their own to express their desire to remain within Yugoslavia. The protest notwithstanding, on 25 June 1991 Croatian independence was declared on the basis of that referendum.

With the independence declared, recognition became the most important goal of the newly-created breakaway state, as discussed in Chapter 4. Under pressure from the European Commission which was attempting to defuse the emerging conflict, a law was passed to recognize minority rights.[31] Ironically, "while the government needed to re-establish control over Slavonia and Krajina to assert its sovereignty within the borders of Croatia, at the same time it had to limit the extent of such control within the borders if it wanted its sovereignty to be recognized effectively internationally" (Burrai 2008: 18). Yet the territories were already beyond Zagreb's control, and after the end of the war, in 1995, the act was almost entirely sapped of its effect.[32] With the end of the war, it became evident that the same laws on citizenship and political representation that had included Croats abroad were disenfranchising and excluding non-Croats who were still living in or who wanted to return to the territory.

Although the Croatian government had indeed encouraged the "return" of Croats abroad, it made no effort to honour the promises made in international agreements for the return of Serbs. Upon the fall of the Croatian Serb separatist regions of Krajina and Eastern Slavonia, an estimated 300,000 to 350,000 ethnic Serbs fled from Croatia (Human Rights Watch 2006: 1). By 2006, only about 120,000 of those had officially returned to Croatia, around a third. In reality, it is thought that only 60 percent of this figure represent actual returns, the rest are individuals who declared their return (for various reasons, including obtaining pensions, collecting rent from their houses, etc.) but de facto live outside of Croatia, either in Bosnia-Herzegovina or in Serbia. In short, the Serbian population was estimated at 12 percent before the war, and in the 2001 census it was only 4.5 percent (Human Rights Watch 2006: 1).[33]

In 1997, a return policy (primarily for Croatian Serbs who had escaped during the war) was implemented in the section of Slavonia still temporarily occupied by international forces (UNTAES). Besides being enshrined in international law,[34] the principle of return was explicitly agreed upon by Croatia in the Dayton Peace Accords. In theory, all displaced persons (Croatian Serbs) were authorized to stay in the houses they occupied at the time, before they could return to their original houses (usually occupied by Croats, often themselves refugees from Bosnia-Herzegovina). But after UN withdrawal, thousands of Croats returned and claimed their possessions. As Blitz noted:

> Of the 90,000 people who had been displaced from the Danube region prior to 1995, only a handful of Serb returns were facilitated by the two-way return mechanism. The majority of Serbs displaced from the Danube region left for third countries as a consequence of harassment and psychological pressure.
> (2005: 367–368)

New legislation was passed under international pressure to revise its policy, yet the "Mandatory instructions" and the "Programme for Return and Housing Care of Expelled Persons, Refugees, and Displaced Persons" continued to describe Serbs as persons who had "voluntarily abandoned the Republic of Croatia" (Blitz 2005: 367–368).

In addition to obstructing the return of Serbian minorities, local government authorities (often controlled by the HDZ) actively discouraged the departure of temporary Croatian refugees from their new homes. Officially, local authorities claimed that Croats had the intention of freeing the occupied homes to return to their places of origin, but that they were unable to. This prevented the return of Serbs and Muslims to their temporarily occupied houses. Yet, as Harvey argues:

> there was little evidence that the HDZ genuinely supported the return of Croats to their pre-war homes; rather, incentives were offered in many cases to people to remain in their place of refuge, or to resettle in areas that had previously been inhabited by a majority of another ethnicity.
> (2006: 97)

The reluctant policy of return for ethnic Serbs is of course to be put in direct relation with the enthusiastic policy of "return" (even though as second or third-generation Croats in Canada, US or Argentina, they had never "left") of ethnic Croats abroad. Here, the double logic of inclusion of ethnic Croats and exclusion of ethnic Serbs appears with clarity: the same movement of "return" is handled by two different policies and administrations and with two radically different objectives in mind.

Similarly, the HDZ adopted a housing and reconstruction policy that actively discriminated against ethnic minorities while favoring Croats, especially those willing to resettle from abroad. The housing problem was a central question. During the war, refugees from one "cleansed" camp begun to occupy houses left by "cleansed" populations of the other camp, at the rhythm of the victories and defeats of the armies. An estimated 195,000 homes were destroyed during the war, and while the government conducted a policy of reconstruction (with the support of international donors), in the attribution of the houses it discriminated between ethnic Croats and minorities (Blitz 2005: 368).

Another issue related to housing was (and remains) the question of tenancy rights to socially owned properties. Under the SFRY, many resided in houses belonging to a state-owned company or a public administration. With the switch from a socialist to a free-market economy, property was privatized. With the Act on Temporary Take-Over and Administration of Specified Property (LTTP) of 1995,[35] Croats were redefined as "settlers" and were privileged in the adjudication over private and state-owned property. The act revoked any rights for citizens absent for more than three months, and coincided with the outbreak of the war. Thus the provision targeted the Serbs who had fled during the war. Only in 2002 has a law been passed to provide alternatives to those excluded, but no action has been taken in this direction (Harvey 2006: 93; International Crisis Group 2002; Blitz 2005: 368). Moreover, many court hearings were conducted in the absence of the Serbian owners or beneficiaries, which further dispossessed an estimated 23,700 in 2003 alone (Human Rights Watch 2003: 34).

The judicial system blocked Serbian return and reintegration in respect of more than property rights. During the years following the Dayton Peace Accords, the (often unfounded) indictment of "war crimes" under the 1996 amnesty law was used both against individual returnees and as a technique to deter further returns in specific areas. About 1,500 Croatian Serbs were indicted after the war—and many were arrested—even after they had been "cleared" for return by the Croatian authorities. Simultaneously, Croats wanted for war crimes by the International Criminal Tribunal for Yugoslavia (ICTY) were protected by the state (Harvey 2006: 93; Blitz 2005: 372; Human Rights Watch 2004).

Following the 2001 "Knin Conclusions," the new left-wing majority marked a change, by passing a new Constitutional Act on National Minorities[36] (Blitz 2005: 368) to introduce improvements of the representation of minorities in the Sabor and other provisions, as well as the Act on Areas of Special State Concern[37] that reduced the discrepancy between Croats and minorities in issues of tenancy rights.

Diasporic citizenship, territory, belonging 149

More recent reports indicating discriminatory standards and practice where it comes to housing for Serbs in Croatia show that Serbian returnees who held tenancy rights in Croatia faced a tougher regime than the one set up for the housing of other individuals who held tenancy rights, such as members of the Croatian military, members of the Croatian Defence Council from Bosnia and Herzegovina, and Croats who were provided housing pursuant to the Act on the lease of flats in freed territories[38] (Serbian Democratic Forum 2012). Furthermore, the relevant laws excluded returnees who were Serbs—as well as those who were Croats or any other minority who had fled from the Republic of Serbia, and returnees located in the areas of special care of the state—from access to the right to housing in state-owned family houses and flats donated by the state (Serbian Democratic Forum 2012).

Conclusion

This account leads to several conclusions. The first is that the policies of inclusion of the diaspora in civic, cultural, and political citizenship were not only concurrent with but also tied to the exclusion of non-Croat minorities from the independent Republic of Croatia; the very same laws that included the former excluded the latter. Therefore, the diasporic practices of citizenship and belonging are techniques of managing alterity and difference. Far from being the progressive logic promised by postnational theorists, diasporic citizenship promotes othering and exclusion. Christian Joppke understands diaspora citizenship policies in the framework of the de-ethnicization and re-ethnicization of citizenship:

> On the side of emigration, international migration tips the balance [...] toward re-ethnicized citizenship, in the sense of providing incentives for states to retain links with their members abroad, particularly across generations. Failing to do so would not just violate the national vocation of the state, according to which the state is an intergenerational community with "a common ancestry and a common destiny" (Zolberg 1999, p. 84); there are also material interests in terms of remittances and influence abroad that move the state in this direction.
>
> (2003: 430)

Christian Joppke has a point in his debate with the post-nationalists; nevertheless, he disregards the idea that diasporic citizenship becomes the managing of new, deterritorialized conceptions of the nation. Diasporic citizenship is the main feature of a *new* form of *transnational* nationalism (Kastoryano 2006). This chapter clearly illustrates how the diasporic question marks the uneasy coexistence between two competing modalities of nationalism. On the one hand the politics of citizenship and belonging are rooted in an old-fashioned, Zionist-like desire to create the conditions for return, for the occupation of the land and the "filling-up" of the territory through physical bodies, resulting in the forced departure and prevention of return of the unwanted—a nationalist logic in the most territorialized, disciplinary, bounded sense. Yet on the other hand, in the case of citizenship and political representation, we find a logic of symbolic inclusion of those abroad not attached to their return, in which their dispersion is celebrated, they are not considered illegitimate and they deserve representation (as was the official discourse of Israel until the 1990s)—the fundamentally political redefinition of the location of the nation, of the location of the group to be recognized, *despite territorial borders* instead of *within* territorial borders.

This brings us to another consideration about the location of the nation. Diaspora politics, in terms of the history of citizenship, seem to follow the same path as the progressive extensions of citizenship rights from only a privileged few to larger sections of the population. It could be argued that in the same fashion as political parties instrumentally pushed for the opening of the vote to certain constituencies (the poor, women, younger voters), the HDZ has pushed for the extension of the right to vote and to be elected to the diaspora for circumstantial reasons. Yet what are the longer-term effects of these policies, in particular for understandings of the location of politics and the location of the population who elect its representatives? If the contestation of ethnic transnational practices of citizenship does not focus on their *transnational* nature (as the left-wing parties have traditionally done, calling for a re-territorialization of the criteria of belonging) but on their *ethnic* aspect, then a progressive transnationalization of the boundaries of belonging and political representation may develop. Before pursuing this line of reflection in the final conclusion, we need to consider one more troubling effect of the diasporic speech act.

Notes

1 Benhabib accepts that

> the changes in modalities of political belonging have been accompanied by other, more ominous, forms of exclusion, namely, the liminality of the condition of asylum seekers, who have not benefited from the spread of cosmopolitan norms and the criminalization of migrants.
>
> (2007: 20–21)

She also recognizes that this state of affairs has led some authors to dismiss the cosmopolitan narrative altogether in favor of more pessimistic views such as Empire (Hard and Negri) or the state of exception (Agamben). Finally, she acknowledges that some authors might find "more radical political potentials of the present moment" (Balibar 2004; Benhabib 2007: 20–21). Yet for her, what appears clearly is that despite the differences in interpretation, it is a fact that the transformation of sovereignty goes along with a spread of cosmopolitan norms (Benhabib 2007: 21).
2 As Brubaker (1996) has shown.
3 *Official Gazette of Democratic Federal Yugoslavia* 64/1945. The law was confirmed and amended on 5 July 1946 (see *Official Gazette of the Federal People's Republic of Yugoslavia (FPRY)* 54/1946). The law was further amended and revised in 1947 (see *Official Gazette of the FPRY* 104/1947) and twice in 1948 (see *Official Gazette of the FPRY* 88 and 105/1948).
4 Art. 249 of the 1974 constitution of Yugoslavia.
5 Unlike the USSR it was not printed on identification documents, but was present in other administrative registers.

Diasporic citizenship, territory, belonging 151

6 *Official Gazette of the FPRY* 86/1948 and 22/1962.
7 *Official Gazette of the FPRY* 105/1948.
8 *Official Gazette of the Republic of Croatia* 53/1991; modifications and amendments in *Official Gazette of the Republic of Croatia* 28/92.
9 A foreign citizen who files a petition for acquiring Croatian citizenship shall acquire Croatian citizenship by naturalization if he or she meets the following prerequisites:
   1. that he or she has reached the age of 18 years and that his or her legal capacity has not been taken away;
   2. that he or she has had his or her foreign citizenship revoked or that he or she submits proof that he or she will get a revocation if he or she would be admitted to Croatian citizenship;
   3. that before the filing of the petition he or she had a registered place of residence for a period of not less than five years constantly on the territory of the Republic of Croatia;
   4. that he or she is proficient in the Croatian language and Latin script;
   5. that a conclusion can be derived from his or her conduct that he or she is attached to the legal system and customs persisting in the Republic of Croatia and that he or she accepts the Croatian culture. It shall be deemed that the prerequisites from point 2 paragraph 1 of this Article have been met, if the petition was filed by a stateless person or by a person who, according to the Law of the country whose citizen he or she is, will lose it by naturalization [...].
10 If a person did not declare himself or herself an ethnic Croat in official documents such as birth or marriage certificates, or if a person had declared ethnicity as Yugoslav and/or was born in a so-called "mixed marriage," the state authorities (the Ministry of the Interior) established a person's membership of the Croatian people by using Catholic Church certificates (if available) and even passed judgment on the "Croatianness" of a person's family name. This was certainly a somewhat delicate matter since a large percentage of "Croatian" family names are shared by Serbs and other South Slavic groups.
11 Part of this research was carried out with Igor Štiks; for the full article see Ragazzi and Štiks 2009.
12 The UNCHR report quotes the same data, but adds that "a total of 412,137 requests were submitted to the Ministry of Internal Affairs between 8 October 1991 and 31 December 1995 under article 30 paragraph 2." This slightly changed the total number of processed requests through art. 30, paras. 1 and 2, available in Omejec (1998) and fixed it at 969,553 at the end of 1995 (UNHCR 1997: 16). Indeed, Jasna Omejec is quoted as a co-author of the national report on Croatia published in UNHCR. Although published in 1998, her own article was obviously written before the UNCHR report published in 1997.
13 *Official Gazette of the Republic of Croatia* 53/91; modifications and amendments in *Official Gazette of the Republic of Croatia* 28/92. These amendments were mainly corrections of inconsistencies in the law, or legal clarifications of its provisions, written and adopted hastily in the context of Croatia's declaration of independence from SFRY and its open conflict with Belgrade. Some changes were obviously made after complaints were received from the ground about the implementation of the law. An important amendment was that the renunciation of foreign citizenship was eased (see note 24).
14 The 1992 amendments, however, facilitated access to Croatian citizenship for those who are for various reasons unable to obtain release from their previous citizenship. Following these amendments, applicants have to state that they will renounce their previous citizenship, if granted Croatian citizenship.

15 *Official Gazette of the Republic of Croatia* 113/1993.
16 The 1991 act additionally required ten years of residence for this group, which was not in accordance with art. 8 and art. 16 and was therefore corrected in the amendments adopted only seven months later on 8 May 1992. Applicants merely had to prove that they were registered as residents (see *Official Gazette of the Republic of Croatia* 28/1992).
17 A significant number of the Croatian Serbs continued to live in territory controlled by the Croatian authorities. They managed to regulate their status either smoothly (i.e., as holders of the former Croatian republican citizenship they were automatically registered into the new registries of citizens), or in some cases, with considerable difficulties. Numerous reports testify to cases of violations of their right to Croatian citizenship in the 1990s. See, for instance, reports on the issue published in Dika *et al.* 1998 and also the report on Croatia in Imeri 2006.
18 *Official Gazette* 110/2015.
19 Article 45 of the constitution, before the 2010 amendments, read: All Croatian citizens of the Republic of Croatia who have reached the age of eighteen years shall have universal and equal suffrage. This right shall be exercised through direct elections by secret ballot. In elections for the Croatian Parliament and for the President of the Republic, the Republic of Croatia shall ensure suffrage to its citizens *who are abroad* at the time of the elections, so that they may vote in the countries in which they are or in any other way specified by law (Croatia 1998 [1991]).
20 *Official Gazette of the Republic of Croatia* 68/1995 (*Odluka o proglašenju Zakona o izmjenama i dopunama Zakona o izborima zastupnika u Sabor Republike Hrvatske*).
21 *Official Gazette* 76/2010. In Article 45 after the 2010 amendments, the relevant section reads: All Croatian citizens of the Republic of Croatia who have reached the age of eighteen years shall have universal and equal suffrage in elections for Croatian parliament, President of the Republic of Croatia and the European parliament, as well as in any referendum, in accordance with relevant laws. In elections for the Croatian parliament, voters who do not have residence in the Republic of Croatia may elect three representatives, in accordance with the law [...].
22 *Ustavni zakon o izmjenama i dopunama Ustavnog zakona o pravima nacionalnih manjina*, *Official Gazette* 80/2010. Article 19 of the consolidated Constitutional Act read: [...] (2) National minorities which on the day of entry into force of this Constitutional Act participate with more than 1.5 percent in the total population of the Republic of Croatia are guaranteed at least three representative seats for such national minority in the Croatian parliament, and have universal and equal suffrage on minority party lists or lists proposed by the voters of said national minority, in accordance with the law on election of representatives to the Croatian parliament. (3) National minorities which in the total population of the Republic of Croatia participate with less than 1.5 percent are, along with general voting rights, entitled to a special vote to elect five representatives of national minorities, in a special constituency, whereby obtained rights of the national minority cannot be decreased, in accordance with the law on election of representatives to the Croatian parliament.
23 Decision of the Constitutional Court of the Republic of Croatia, no. U-I-3597/2010 *et al.*, of 29 July 2011, *Official Gazette* 93/2010. The constitutional challenge was lodged by three civil society organizations, Serbian Democratic Forum, Croatian Helsinki Committee, and GONG, the Socialist Party of Croatia, and by one individual citizen.
24 *Official Gazette of the Republic of Croatia* 116/1999.
25 *Ministarstvo povratka i useljeništva*. "Zastupnički portret: Ivan Nogalo," *Bilten Ministarstva povratka i useljeništva*, no. 27, April 1998, p. 9.
26 Constitutional Act on Human Rights and Freedoms and on the Rights of Ethnic and National Communities or Minorities [*Ustavni zakon o ljudskim pravima i slobodama i o pravima etničkih i nacionalnih zajednica ili manjina u Republici Hrvatskoj*,

Official Gazette of the Republic of Croatia 65/1991, and amendments published in *Official Gazette of the Republic of Croatia* 27/1992], hereinafter Constitutional Act (UZEM).
27 *Official Gazette of the Republic of Croatia* 34/1992, Arts. 21–51, amended text.
28 Art. 10, "*Zakon o izborima zastupnika u Sabor Republike Hrvatske*" [Act on the Election of the Representatives to the Sabor of the Republic of Croatia], *Official Gazette of the Republic of Croatia* 22/1992; Art. 16 "*Zakon o izborima zastupnika u hrvatski državni Sabor*" [Act on the Election of the Representatives to the Croatian State Sabor], *Official Gazette of the Republic of Croatia* 116/1999.
29 These were: Serbs, Croats, Slovenes, Macedonians, Montenegrins, and Muslims.
30 *Official Gazette of the Republic of Croatia* 21/1991.
31 *Ustavni zakon o ljudskim pravima i slobodama i o pravima etničkih i nacionalnih zajednica ili manjina u Republici Hrvatskoj* [Constitutional Act on Human Rights and Freedoms and on the Rights of Ethnic and National Communities or Minorities], *Official Gazette of the Republic of Croatia* 65/1991, and amendments *Official Gazette of the Republic of Croatia* 27/1992.
32 See *Ustavni Zakon o privremenom neprimjenjivanju pojedinih odredbi Ustavnog zakona o ljudskim pravima i slobodama i o pravima etničkih zajednica ili manjina u Republici Hrvatskoj* [Constitutional Act on the temporary suspension of some provisions of the Constitutional Act], *Official Gazette of the Republic of Croatia* 68/1995.
33 Official census data available at www.dzs.hr/ (accessed 24 August 2009).
34 The right to return is explicitly contained in the International Covenant on Civil and Political Rights (ICCPR), G.A. res. 2200A (XXI), 21 U.N. GAOR Supp. (No. 16) at 52, U.N. Doc. A/6316 (1966), entered into force 23 March 1976, article 12. Croatia became a party to the ICCPR in 1991 (Human Rights Watch 2006: 2).
35 *Official Gazette of the Republic of Croatia* 73/1995, 7/1996, and 100/1997.
36 *Official Gazette of the Republic of Croatia* 155/2002.
37 *Official Gazette of the Republic of Croatia* 26/2003.
38 *Zakon o davanju u najam stanova na oslobođenom teritoriju, Official Gazette* 73/1995.

References

Appadurai, A. (1991) "Global Ethnoscapes: Notes and Queries for a Transnational Anthropology" in Fox, R., ed., *Recapturing Anthropology: Working in the Present* (pp. 191–210), Santa Fe, NM: School of American Research Press.
Bajruši, R. (2007) "Svi grijesi Zdenke Babić—Petričević," *Nacional*, 21 June 2007.
Balibar, E. (2004) *We, the People of Europe?: Reflections on Transnational Citizenship*, English trans. James Swenson, Princeton, NJ: Princeton University Press.
Bauböck, R. (2005) "Expansive Citizenship – Voting beyond Territory and Membership," *PS: Political Science & Politics*, 38(5).
Benhabib, S. (2006) *Another Cosmopolitanism*, New York: Oxford University Press.
Benhabib, S. (2007) "Twilight of Sovereignty or the Emergence of Cosmopolitan Norms? Rethinking Citizenship in Volatile Times," *Citizenship Studies*, 11(1), pp. 19–36.
Blitz, B. K. (2005) "Refugee Returns, Civic Differentiation, and Minority Rights in Croatia, 1991–2004," *Journal of Refugee Studies*, 18(3), pp. 362–386.
Brubaker, R. (1996) *Nationalism Reframed: Nationhood and the National Question in the New Europe*, Cambridge, UK; New York: Cambridge University Press.
Burrai, V. (2008) "Kin-state Politics and Equal Treatment in Croatia," *ASN Annual Convention*, New York.

Cohen, R. (1996) "Diasporas and the Nation-State: From Victims to Challengers," *International Affairs*, 72(3), pp. 507–520.

Croatia (1998 [1991]) *The Constitution of the Republic of Croatia*, Zagreb: Narodne Novine.

Dika, M. A., Helton, C., and Omejec, J. (1998) "The Citizenship Status of Citizens of the Former SFR Yugoslavia after its Dissolution," *Croatian Critical Law Review*, 3(1–2), pp. 1–259.

Glick Schiller, N., Basch, L. G., and Szanton Blanc, C. (1992) *Towards a Transnational Perspective on Migration: Race, Class, Ethnicity, and Nationalism Reconsidered. Annals of the New York Academy of Sciences*, New York: New York Academy of Sciences.

Guarnizo, L. and Smith, M. P. (1998) *Transnationalism from Below* (pp. 3–34), New Brunswick, NJ: Transaction Publishers.

Harvey, J. (2006) "Return Dynamics in Bosnia and Croatia: A Comparative Analysis," *International Migration*, 44(3), pp. 89–144.

Hindess, B. (2004) "Citizenship for All," *Citizenship Studies*, 8(3), pp. 11.

Human Rights Watch (1995) *Civil and Political Rights in Croatia*, New York: Human Rights Watch.

Human Rights Watch (2003) *Broken Promises: Impediments to Refugee Return to Croatia*, New York: Human Rights Watch.

Human Rights Watch (2004) *ICTY Justice at Risk: War Crimes Trials in Croatia, Bosnia and Herzegovina, and Serbia and Montenegro*, New York: Human Rights Watch.

Human Rights Watch (2006) *Croatia: A Decade of Disappointment Continuing Obstacles to the Reintegration of Serb Returnees*, 18(7), September 2006. Available at: www.hrw.org/report/2006/09/04/croatia-decade-disappointment/continuing-obstacles-reintegration-serb-returnees (accessed 13 March 2017).

Huysmans, J. (2000) "Contested Community: Migration and the Question of the Political in the EU" in Kelstrup, M. and Williams, M. C., eds., *International Relations Theory and the Politics of European Integration: Power, Security, and Community* (pp. xii, 304), London; New York: Routledge.

Imeri, Sh. (2006) *Rule of Law in the Countries of the Former SFR Yugoslavia and Albania: Between Theory and Practice*, Gostivar: Association for Democratic Initiatives.

International Crisis Group (2002) *A Half-Hearted Welcome: Refugee Returns to Croatia*, Zagreb/Brussels: International Crisis Group.

Isin, E. F. (2002) *Being Political: Genealogies of Citizenship*, Minneapolis: University of Minnesota Press.

Isin, E. F. and NetLibrary Inc. (1999) *Citizenship and Identity*, London; Thousand Oaks, CA: Sage.

Izbori (2005) *Arhiva*. Available at: www.izbori.hr/2005Pred/ (accessed 12 May 2008).

Izbori (2007) *Rezultati*. Available at: www.izbori.hr/izbori/izbori07.nsf/FI?OpenForm (accessed 12 May 2008).

Jacobson, D. (1996) *Rights Across Borders: Immigration and the Decline of Citizenship*, Baltimore: Johns Hopkins University Press.

Joppke, C. (2003) "Citizenship between De- and Re-Ethnicization," *European Journal of Sociology*, 44(3), p. 30.

Kasapović, M. (1996) "1995 Parliamentary Elections in Croatia," *Electoral Studies*, 15(2), p. 6.

Kasapović, M. (1999) "Znaju li uopće koliko glasova košta jedan mandat?" *Globus*, no. 440, pp. 10–11.

Kasapović, M. (2010) "Tko i kako predstavlja 'dijasporu'," *Političke analize*, 1(3), pp. 15–17.

Kasapović, M. (2012) "Voting Rights, Electoral Systems, and Political Representation of Diaspora in Croatia," *East European Politics and Societies and Cultures*, 26(4), pp. 777–791.

Kastoryano, R. (2006) "Vers un nationalisme transnational. Redéfinir la nation, le nationalisme et le territoire," *Revue Française de Science Politique*, 56(4), pp. 533–555.

Koopmans, R. and Statham, P. (1999) "Challenging the Liberal Nation-State? Postnationalism, Multiculturalism, and the Collective Claims-Making of Migrants and Ethnic Minorities in Britain and Germany," *The American Journal of Sociology*, 105(3), pp. 652–696.

Koopmans, R. and Statham, P. (2001) *How National Citizenship Shapes Transnationalism: A Comparative Analysis of Migrant Claims-Making in Germany, Great Britain and the Netherlands*, Working paper on Transnational Communities, Oxford: University of Oxford Transnational Communities Programme.

Mecanović, I. (1999) "Izbori i Dijaspora," *Pravni Vjesnik*, 14(1), pp. 7–18.

Medvedović, D. (1998) "Federal and Republican Citizenship in the Former SFR Yugoslavia at the Time of its Dissolution," *Croatian Critical Law Review*, 3(1–2), pp. 21–56.

Nyers, P. (2003) "Abject Cosmopolitanism: The Politics of Protection in the Anti-Deportation Movement," *Third World Quarterly—Journal of Emerging Areas*, 24(6), p. 25.

Omejec, J. (1998) "Initial Citizenry of the Republic of Croatia at the Time of the Dissolution of Legal Ties with the SFRY, and Acquisition and Termination of Croatian Citizenship," *Croatian Critical Law Review*, 3(3), pp. 99–127.

OSCE (1997) *Statement, Presidential Election in the Republic of Croatia, 15 June 1997*. Available at: www.osce.org/item/1536.html (accessed 12 May 2008).

OSCE (2000) *Election of Representatives to the State Parliament—2–3 January 2000, International Election Observation Mission Preliminary Statement*. Available at: www.oscepa.org/documents/all-documents/election-observation/election-observation-statements/croatia/statements-7/1402-2000-parliamentary-4/file (accessed 11 March 2017).

OSCE/ODHIR (2000) *Republic of Croatia Extraordinary Presidential Elections 24 January & 7 February 2000, OSCE/ODHIR Election Observation Mission Final Report*. Available at: www.osce.org/odihr/elections/croatia/115536 (accessed 11 March 2017).

Portes, A. (1995) "Transnational Communities: Their Emergence and Significance in the Contemporary World System," *19th Annual Conference of the Political Economy of the World-System*, North-South Center at the University of Miami.

Ragazzi, F. and Štiks, I. (2009) "Croatian Citizenship: From Ethnic Engineering to Inclusiveness" in Bauböck, R., Sievers, W., and Perchinig, B., eds., *A Call to Kinship? Citizenship and Migration in the New Member and Accession States of the EU*, Amsterdam: University of Amsterdam Press.

Salay, C., Duich, K. and International Foundation for Electoral Systems (1996) *Republic of Croatia: 1995 Election Observation Report*, Washington, DC: International Foundation for Election Systems.

Serbian Democratic Forum (2012) *Different, Unequal and Discriminatory Standards and Practice in Access to the Right to Housing in the Republic of Croatia [Različiti, nejedinstveni i diskriminacijski standardi i praksa u ostvarivanju prava na stambeno zbrinjavanje u Republici Hrvatskoj]*. Available at sdf.hr/publikacije/Stambeno_zbrinjavnje_u_RH_diskriminacija_2012.doc (accessed 12 May 2008).

Serbian Democratic Forum (2013) *Support for the Rule of Law with Respect to the Status and Access to Rights of Minorities [Podrška vladavini prava u pogledu položaja i ostvarivanja prava manjinskih zajednica]*. Available at http://sdf.hr/publikacije/podrska_vladavini_prava.pdf (accessed 12 May 2008).

Soysal, Y. N. (1994) *Limits of Citizenship: Migrants and Postnational Membership in Europe*, Chicago, IL: University of Chicago Press.

Soysal, Y. N. (1996) *Changing Parameters of Citizenship and Claims-Making: Organized Islam*, Badia Fiesolana: European University Institute, European Forum.

Štiks, I. (2006) "Nationality and Citizenship in the Former Yugoslavia: From Disintegration to the European Integration," *South East European and Black Sea Studies*, 6(4), pp. 483–500.

Tepić, Đ. and Bašić, I. (1969) *Zbirka propisa o državljanstvu [The Collection of the Citizenship Regulations]*, Zagreb: Narodne novine.

Tölölyan K (1996) Rethinking Diaspora(s): Stateless Power in the Transnational Moment. *Diaspora*, 5(1), pp. 3–36.

UNHCR RBfE (1997) *Citizenship and Prevention of Statelessness Linked to the Disintegration of the Socialist Federal Republic of Yugoslavia, European Series*, 3(1), Geneva: UNHCR.

7 Croatia and Bosnia-Herzegovina
Diaspora, territory, annexation

In addition to the ethnic cleansing of Croatian citizenship reviewed in the previous chapter, the diaspora speech act justified another practice: the de facto annexation of Herceg-Bosna, the short-lived all-Croatian state created during the 1992–1995 war. The policy of the HDZ with respect to Herceg-Bosna, until the Dayton accords, had been a traditional nationalist plan of territorial annexation. With the failure of the military operations to create an ethnically homogeneous state which could claim independence and eventually be (re)joined with Croatia, the Croatian government recategorized what was to become an integral part of the Croatian nation as its "diaspora," taking advantage of the blurry boundaries of the concept. In doing so, the Zagreb-based HDZ first managed to include in the diaspora about 800,000 citizens who should have been simply one of the "constitutive peoples" of a neighboring country, Bosnia-Herzegovina, thus infringing the Dayton accords. Second, to carry out a policy, if not *de jure* then certainly de facto, of the annexation of the region thereby established what could be defined as practices of *post-territorial annexation*.

In various indictments against members and leaders of the entity of "Herceg-Bosna"[1] (the all-Croat separatist political entity formed during the war in Bosnia and Herzegovina[2]) ICTY[3] judges often tried to prove the commonly known but undocumented connection between the Croatian government in Zagreb and the Bosnian-Croat separatist groups in BiH. They intended to show that the Republic of Croatia was not only a victim of Serbian/Yugoslav aggression, but that it was also an aggressor in the conflict in BiH (particularly in regard to the Muslim population).

As this chapter will thoroughly discuss, enough evidence has now been collected to show that Franjo Tuđman, Gojko Šušak and others in the leadership of the HDZ from 1991 played a double game; an official recognition of the international borders of Bosnia and Herzegovina as an independent state on the one hand, and political, military and financial support to the Bosnian-Croat separatists for the unification of South Bosnia (Herzegovina) and Croatia on the other, with the intention of recreating the historical borders of the short-lived "Banovina Hrvatska," an administrative division of the Kingdom of Yugoslavia between 1939 and 1941.[4]

For contemporary Western scholars, thoughts of annexation, irredentism, and territorial expansion come with accents of nineteenth and early twentieth century history, when such enterprises were legitimate. It is difficult to determine precisely why and how ideas such as "annexation" and "irredentism" have ceased to be legitimate policies and practices of international relations. Memories of World War II, the new codification of international law, fifty years of apparent territorial "freeze" during the Cold War, and the relative peace in Western Europe between the main actors of WWI and WWII surely played an important role. More importantly, however, it seems that the major economic, social, and political evolution in Europe and the United States in the past fifty years has made territorial sovereignty a secondary concern. Political actors relying on "territorial nationalism"—political discourse and practice that insists upon the adequacy between a nation, a territory, and a sovereign—had used three main arguments; the access to the land for agriculture, the access to natural resources for industry, and the concerns for the transportation of goods such as access to the sea were, regardless of their validity, leitmotivs of expansionism. The move to a service-based economy and the dominance of deterritorialized financial markets has rendered these concerns marginal.[5]

Expansionisms were socially and politically motivated by the alleged territorial needs of the population, from the most brutal ideas of "*Lebensraum*" (Germany) to ideas of the "natural borders" (rivers and mountains in France). These discourses, despite the traditional divide between the "ethnic" (Herderian) and the "civic" (Renanian or Mazzinian), shared some assumptions about the necessary bundling of identities (nations), borders (territory), and orders (the state).[6] From the "primordialist" positions assuming a pre-modern ethnic essence of nations (Smith 1979) to the "modernists" positing "nations" as the product of modern capitalism (Anderson 1991; Gellner 1983), scholars of nationalism agree that the nationalist enterprises were about defending, expanding, recovering or imagining the *territory* of the nation (Kastoryano 2006). A certain number of important historical trends such as the processes of decolonization, the large wave of migration to Europe of the 1960s and 1970s, the rise of the "identity movements" of the 1970s and 1980s, and the passage from a mass consumption and standardized society to a society encouraging the expression of individualized, localized "niche" identities, have rendered the political arguments of sovereign nationalist expansionism obsolete.

As discussed earlier, the Cold War and the progressive elimination of borders within the European Union has led some scholars to announce the birth of a postnational world, in which postnational citizenship would become the dominant form of political existence, rendering the balance between national belonging and territorial control obsolete. However, in this chapter I argue that "territorial nationalism" has not disappeared, but has adapted. The *territorial* aspect of nationalism have been discredited and rendered illegitimate by both international law and practical norms (Zacher 2001; Osiander 2001), but nationalist entrepreneurs have imagined new forms of political identification and mobilization with new modalities of legitimation, and the discourse of "diaspora" has gained a central position in these enterprises.

This chapter will precisely document how nationalist discourses and practices evolve from a territorial expression to a transnational, diasporic expression, through a study of the practices of the nationalist Croatian party HDZ in Bosnia and Herzegovina. Why do nationalist entrepreneurs reframe their irredentism in diasporic language? How are tools of "inner sovereignty" used to justify transnational practices? What are the effects of these practices? In the first section I consider the competing territorial conceptions of Croatia and BiH in play before and during the war. In the second section I analyze the HDZ and its pursuit of a double strategy of official recognition and covert undermining of BiH integrity, motivated by the vision of a "Greater Croatia." In the third section I show how the failure of the territorial annexation is circumvented by using "diaspora politics" to pursue the same objective.

Nationalist geographies of Croatia and Bosnia-Herzegovina

Although the free elections in 1990 gave the majority of the National Assembly to the HDZ on an ambiguously independent platform, the voters certainly had not voted for the territorial division and eventual annexation of Bosnia and Herzegovina to the Republic of Croatia. Yet this was the policy of the Tuđman government from 1991. Before specifically dealing with these policies, it is important to map the territorial conceptions which formed the political goals of the belligerents in Croatia and BiH, with particular attention to Franjo Tuđman and the HDZ's hardliners.[7]

Tuđman and the HDZ: an irredentist ideology

Bosnia and Herzegovina was always central in the symbolic tradition of Croatian nationalism. With the creation of Yugoslavia post-World War II, and the outlining of the borders of modern Croatia, many contested the "artificial" separation of the Croatian nation into two administrative entities, although the federative nature of the state allowed all Croats to be still under one roof, despite their division into republics. Indeed, the federative project was precisely aimed at balancing the need for the territorial continuity of the state and the dispersion of nations across the territory (Bianchini 1996). However, Tuđman's ideas had evolved toward dismissing BiH as an artificial construction. First, based on the ideas of Starčević and other late nineteenth century nationalist thinkers, Tuđman formulated the idea that there was no such thing as a Muslim identity or ethnicity, estimating that 80 percent of Muslims were actually Croats (Tuđman 1996: 104). The Muslim "ethnicity," according to Tuđman, was purely a Communist invention (it was recognized by SFRY only in 1968), and an aberration. As he declared in an interview to Vjesnik in 1990:

> We believe that Muslims are a constituent part of the Croatian national corpus even if the historical conditions are such that it is now rewarding for Muslims to declare themselves as a nation. But the historical developments are open.
>
> (25 February 1990)

Consequently—and this was a crucial point in Tuđman's agreement with the Herzegovinian Croats at the Norval Center—the AVNOJ[8] borders of 1945, which had shaped the territorial borders of contemporary Serbia, Bosnia-Herzegovina, and Croatia within the Yugoslav federation were considered artificial, unfair to Croatia and historically absurd. Instead, Tuđman often argued that Croatia should have much larger, historical borders, marked by the Danube, the Sava and the Drina rivers. These had been the historical borders of the Independent State of Croatia (NDH) from 1941 to 1944. Only later on did he admit that the borders of Croatia could actually be the borders of another entity, the short-lived administrative unit of Banovina Hrvatska, the result of a deal between the Croatian leader Maček and the Serbian leader Cvetković in 1939 to tame nationalist tensions inside the Kingdom of Yugoslavia (Tuđman 1996: 103–104).

As Sabrina Ramet explains, this ideological framework has its own coherence. In order to support the hegemonic claims of Croatian nationalism over the entire BiH, and more particularly the claim that Bosnia's borders should be open to renegotiation whereas Croatia's borders were to be respected, the thesis of the inexistence of Muslim identity (and the inability to think of a nation as a "civic" conception rather than in Herderian, essentialist terms) was resolved by the denegation of the Muslim right to territory. Only the harsh resistance of the Muslim-dominated Army of Bosnia and Herzegovina (ARBiH) and the Dayton accords would prove Tuđman wrong.[9]

Bosnia and Herzegovina: territory, community, and "civic citizenship"

In BiH, the past two hundred years have been marked by the alternation between the predominance of a communitarian equilibrium and the centrifugal forces of territorial nationalism imposed from Belgrade and Zagreb. As Xavier Bougarel shows, from the middle of the eighteenth century the Millet system in the Ottoman empire had reinforced the organization of the BiH society on communitarian lines, increasing the relevance of religious institutions. A traditional practice of good neighborhooding (*komšiluk*) had made it possible to codify tolerant relationships, but it had also reinforced the communitarian divides (Bougarel 1996: 88). The emergence of Serbian and Croatian territorial nationalism during the Austro-Hungarian occupation motivated the Muslims to demand cultural and religious autonomy. This was tamed during the first Yugoslavia, and while Croats and Serbs increasingly looked to Zagreb and Belgrade, Muslim elites, in decline, were pushed toward a form of "national indeterminism" and "tactical Yugoslavism." This led to a crisis in the traditional social and political organizations, and outrage in Muslim organizations (Bougarel 1996: 91). It is no surprise, therefore, that after the brutal violence of 1941–1945—the *Ustaša* massacres of Serbs, Četnik massacres of Muslims and reprisals—the Partizans won the support of the population both for their guarantee of physical security and the promotion of Yugoslavism, as well as "champion[ing] the rural population's demands for agrarian reform, and to reproduce a communitarian structure on this basis," which is the way BiH was governed after 1945. Throughout the Yugoslav regime, with religion minimized in public and social life and a lifestyle "modernization," a progressive feeling of "Bosnian-ness" transcended the communitarian divide in the ethnically diverse large cities and rural areas (Bougarel 1996: 91).

The everyday political representation of the Croats of Bosnia-Herzegovina, in this context, was essentially divided into two. Whereas in ethnically mixed areas of Bosnia Croats usually identified with Bosnia-Herzegovina as a multinational republic, in southern Herzegovina, which was much more homogeneous, nationalist, separatist views—some of them reminiscent of the years of the NDH—had a much higher currency.

The failed territorial annexation of Herzegovina (1991–1995)

When the war started in 1991, the Tuđman government saw, along with the hardline faction of the HDZ, the historical and political conditions for the modification of the AVNOJ borders of 1945. Yet they were constrained by two elements; the strength of the Milošević-led Yugoslav People's Army (*Jugoslovenska Narodna Armija—JNA*) on the one side, and the international community on the other. This is what pushed the government into a double policy. First, with Serbian hardliners around Milošević, they believed Tuđman could broker a deal for the expansion of the Croatian and Serbian borders, at the expense of the Muslim population of BiH. With regards to the international community, they believed they could officially recognize BiH while presenting Croatian separatism as independent from Croatia's intervention, which would therefore be legitimate.

Independence, war, and the establishment of the HZ-HB (1991–1992)

The first multiparty elections that took place in BiH (18 November and 9 December 1990) brought three nationalist political parties to power. Alija Izetbegović of the Party of Democratic Action (*Stranka Demokratske Akcije*, SDA) as President, Momčilo Krajišnik of the Serbian Democratic Party (*Srpska Demokratska Stranka*, SDS) as President of Parliament, and Jure Pelivan of the Croatian Democratic Union of Bosnia and Herzegovina (*Hrvatska Demokratska Zajednica Bosne i Hercegovine*, HDZ-BiH) as Prime Minister. Collaboration between the nationalists quickly deteriorated. On 15 October 1991, the parliament voted on a resolution for BiH independence and 73 Serbian delegates walked out in protest. Again, the 29 February 1992 referendum on independence was boycotted by the Serbian leaders, despite a 63.4 percent turnout voting 99.7 percent for independence (Ramet 2006: 416). Nonetheless, independence was declared on 3 March 1992. The Serbian representatives withdrew from Sarajevo's parliament and established an Assembly of Serbs in Bosnia on 24 October 1991. On 9 January 1992, the formation of the Serbian republic of Bosnia and

Herzegovina in union with the Yugoslav federation was declared. Hostilities between the SDS-led factions and the rest of the BiH organizations began within a few days.

In reaction to the Serbian position—but secretly with the support and at the suggestion of Zagreb's HDZ—the Croats from southern BiH mobilized territorially. On 18 November 1991, 30 municipalities declared the formation of the Community of Herceg-Bosna (*Zajednica Herceg-Bosne*, HZ-HB), as a community of self-defense. The military and executive Croatian Defence Council (*Hrvatsko Vijeće Obrane*, HVO) was set up on 8 April 1992, with the military component established on 15 May 1992. The Serbian entity had done the same three days prior with the establishment of the Army of the Republika Srpska (*Vojska Republike Srpske*, VRS).

The establishment of a single party, mononational quasi-state (1992–1993)

From the beginning of the conflict in BiH, the HDZ-led Republic of Croatia continued the double strategy of publicly supporting the Sarajevo government[10] while providing military, financial, and political support to the HZ-HB and ensuring that the hardliners' vision of a territorial Banovina Hrvatska took form. Two obstacles prevented the annexationist goals of the HZ-HB. First, the leader of the HDZ of Bosnia and Herzegovina (HDZ-BiH), Stjepan Kljuić,[11] was reluctant to directly follow Zagreb so advocated for a broader autonomy for Croats within the Republic of BiH and opposed unification with Croatia. He was replaced by the servile Mate Boban in February 1992. Second, within Croatia's political scene some leaders, such as ultra-nationalist Dobroslav Paraga, were involved with paramilitary units that supported the Bosnian army formed in 1992,[12] the Croatian Defence Forces (*Hrvatske Obrambene Snage*, HOS). The paramilitary units were fighting for a unified BiH with the NDH map including a Muslim and Croatian BiH, not the one of Croatian-only "Banovina Hrvatska." Tuđman made sure that the HOS stayed clear of HVO through threats and, sometimes, the physical elimination of its members. Once these obstacles were removed, Mate Boban and the leadership of the HZ-HB could proclaim the formation of the Community. As a constitutional jurist, Ciril Ribičić, notes, the Community of Herceg-Bosna was a single-party, mononational territorial quasi-state.

Single-party. According to its "Foundational decree" (*Narodni List* 1992b) the Croatian Democratic Union of Bosnia and Herzegovina (HDZ-BiH) is the constitutive political party of the entity, excluding other political formations. The HDZ-BiH was initially a local branch of Zagreb's HDZ, but in 1992 it officially became part of its bureau (Ribičić 2001: 92).[13]

Mononational. In the preamble of the foundational decree, the HZ-HB defined itself as emerging from the "will of the Croats of BiH" in order to "defend the Croatian ethnic and historical territories and the Croatian nation of BiH" (*Narodni List* 1992b). Whereas all former Yugoslav republics who had declared their independence had—at least formally—guaranteed some degree of recognition and protection to minorities, the 1992 document contained no mention of Muslims or Serbs (Ribičić 2001: 43). Likewise, the army of the HZ-HB, the Croatian Defence Council (HVO), was formed only to protect the "Croatian nation." But the civic and political obligations of the non-Croats in the 30 municipalities did not differ from the Croats', thus de facto creating second-class citizens (*Narodni List* 1992a, in Ribičić 2001: 48).

Territorial. While the document mentioned the "Croats of BiH" and the necessity to protect the territories of the Croatian nation, the existence of the entity was declared on the territorial basis of 30 municipalities, with Mostar as its capital (Ribičić 2001: 36).[14] This fact shows the contradiction in the HZ-HB project; while it defined itself as emerging from the will of the Croats in BiH, it only referred to a territorially defined portion of them—the ones living in the future territories of the Banovina Hrvatska—ignoring the Croatian populations established in other parts of BiH. "From this point of view the creation of the HZ-HB has been more in the interest of the Republic of Croatia in regards to its border rather than in the interest of all Croats who lived in [BiH], particularly in its central and northern parts" (Ribičić 2001: 39).[15]

Quasi-state. Since its creation on 18 November 1991, the community's legal activity was ignorant of any BiH rulings or legislation. It established its own judicial system, and tolerated the laws of BiH only inasmuch as they did not contradict the laws of HZ-HB. This was reciprocal, since the government of BiH had declared the community illegitimate and illegal within the first days.

Officially, the Republic of Croatia never recognized the entity's independence nor autonomy. Much of the Croatian Sabor was not aware of the double policy of Tuđman's HDZ. The government officially supported the multi-ethnic BiH and its AVNOJ borders, but the government's unofficial activities were much bleaker:

> There are only a few steps from [the legal provisions of HZ-HB] to the creation and enforcement of a policy of ethnic homogenization of HZ-HB, through assimilation, ethnic cleansing of communities and immigration of Croats from other parts of BiH.
>
> (Ribičić 2001: 46)

The HVO–ARBiH war until Dayton (1993–1995)

When the legitimate government in Sarajevo officially declared war against the Belgrade-supported VRS on 20 May 1991, more than half of the republic's territory was occupied by the Serb forces. Initially, the HVO and the Army of the Republic of Bosnia and Herzegovina (*Armija Republike Bosne i Hercegovine*, ARBiH) fought together, but their alliance deteriorated. To the surprise of most of the Croatian and Bosnian populations who were unaware of HDZ's policy, conflict soon erupted between the Army of BiH and HZ-HB's paramilitary formation, the HVO.

Several reasons explain the conflict between the HVO and the ARBiH. Charles Shrader, in his military history of the "Muslim–Croat" conflict, apportioned responsibility for the conflict to the ARBiH, invoking the ARBiH's military superiority and intention to seize strategic weapons and positions (Shrader 2003: 65). Sabrina Ramet is more cautious about who bore the responsibility.[16] However, two factors stand out in explaining the conflict: the Tuđman–Milošević agreement of Karađorđevo and the Vance–Owen Plan of 1993.

As is now publicly known, Franjo Tuđman and Slobodan Milošević secretly met on several occasions to coordinate the dismantlement of Bosnia on 26 March 1991 at Karađorđevo, and on 15 April 1991 at Tikveš (Duchesneau-Bernier 2006: 243). Tuđman believed that he could negotiate territorial arrangements without going to war. The discussions between Tuđman and Milošević were nearly replicated in public in Graz during the 6 May 1992 encounter between the Bosno-Croat leader Mate Boban and the Bosnian-Serb leader Radovan Karadžić (International Crisis Group 1998: 2–3). The Muslims were entirely marginalized, and refused the "peace plan" from that meeting.

Several elements clearly connect the government of Croatia to the HVO–ARBiH conflict. First, the presence of Croatian Army counselors and special agents is thoroughly documented (Ramet 2006: 436). Moreover, from June to October 1992 there were regular Croatian Army (HV) units in the field to support HVO units, plus a major weapons supplier: "It is quite clear that the HVO in central Bosnia benefited directly from the logistical support provided by Croatia and may have benefited indirectly from the intervention of HV units in southern Bosnia-Herzegovina" (Shrader 2003: 49). However, this is not true of other parts of BiH (central or western BiH), confirming Ribičić's conclusion that the Croatian intervention in BiH was about the territory of HZ-BH, not about defending all Croats.[17] This was done without the official sanction of the Croatian Sabor or of any other institution (Duchesneau-Bernier 2006: 225; Ramet 2006: 436).

The HVO–ARBiH conflict escalated with the proposal of the Vance–Owen peace plan. The plan confirmed to all involved that ethnic homogenization of BiH ("ethnic cleansing") would ultimately be recognized by the "international community" as the basis for negotiations. Because of the international community's inability to fully understand the conflict they accepted the very proposals that were at the root of the conflict—for a necessary territorial homogeneous ethnic distribution of the population (what David Campbell defined as the West's "Ontopology"[18]). Indeed, the 1993 Vance–Owen Plan was the first to suggest that the territory should be divided based on ethnic homogeneity. According to the plan, the HVO and the ARBiH should mutually submit to each other in the municipalities in which they had the majority. For the Croats, the order allegedly arrived directly from Zagreb. Although the plan was ultimately refused by Izetbegović, the HVO redoubled its effort to militarily occupy the territories anticipated in the map (Hoare 1997: 132).

In April 1993, the conflict mounted when Zagreb ordered the HV and the HVO to cooperate with the Bosnian-Serb army (VRS). By January 1994, it is estimated that about 30,000 HV soldiers were fighting against the ARBiH. After international pressure on both sides (from US brokers Charles Redman and Peter Galbraith) the Washington Agreement marking the peace between the HVO and the ARBiH was signed on 18 March 1994, creating the Federation of Bosnia and Herzegovina, composed of ten autonomous cantons. One year later, after the massacre at Srebrenica, the shelling of Sarajevo, the subsequent NATO bombardments of Serbian positions and the end of the Sarajevo siege, the "General Framework Agreement for Peace in Bosnia and Herzegovina," also known as the Dayton agreement, was signed in on 14 December 1995.

Diaspora politics as deterritorialized annexation (1995–1999)

With the Dayton peace agreements, the plans for the territorial expansion of Croatia's territory as imagined by the "Herzegovinian Lobby" were considerably compromised. Yet the HDZ in Croatia did not abandon the idea of incorporating the Croats of BiH into the Croatian Republic. Faced with the impossibility of having direct relations with Herceg-Bosna, the discourse shifted to diaspora politics. Overnight, when it became clear that they could not be considered part of the Croatian nation, Croats from Herceg-Bosna simultaneously became the constitutive peoples of Bosnia-Herzegovina and the largest section of Croatia's "diaspora."

The official Croatia–BiH relations (1995–1999)

The war in Bosnia and Herzegovina temporarily ended the double game of Franjo Tuđman and the most radical wing of the HDZ, the so-called "Herzegovinian Lobby."

Tuđman's determination to act only according to the international community's dictates ultimately kept his partitionist project in check. Faced with worldwide condemnation and threats of sanctions, he ultimately agreed to the formation of a Muslim-Croat federation (Hoare 1997: 136). First, the Republic of Croatia signed all international agreements concerning the sovereignty of BiH. Along with the president of BiH, Alija Izetbegović, and the president of the Federal Republic of Yugoslavia (FRY), Slobodan Milošević, on 14 December 1995 Tuđman signed the Dayton peace agreements. Article 1 explicitly states:

> the Parties shall fully respect the sovereign equality of one another, shall settle disputes by peaceful means, and shall refrain from any action, by threat or use of force or otherwise, against the territorial integrity or political independence of Bosnia and Herzegovina or any other State.[19]

Also, article 5 made specific mention of the mutual respect for constitutions.

Second, the Republic of Croatia established a diplomatic link with the Croatian cantons according to the officially recognized legal protocol. Following the provisions of BiH's constitution,[20] entities within the Republic of BiH were allowed to establish direct links with foreign states. In this context, on 22 November 1998 the Republic of Croatia and the Federation of Bosnia and Herzegovina (including the Muslim-Croatian federation but excluding the Republika Srpska) established an agreement for special relations.[21]

The agreement was to be temporary and concerned 14 domains, including economics, investments and infrastructures, property titles, social policy, and tourism. The agreement also created a Cooperation Council between Croatia and the federation, which never became active. Two annexes complemented the agreement, one promoting cooperation in science and technology, the second tourism. Both annexes were signed on 15 June 1999. Negotiations concerning the possibility of establishing agreements of reciprocity in the field of pensions, cultural cooperation, the protection for natural catastrophes, energy, and social protection began in July 1999, but these discussions never materialized in an agreement, and were abandoned by the Croatian government after 1999 in favor of inter-state relations over state–entity relations.

Yet even this internationally acceptable bilateral cooperation between the Republic of Croatia and the Muslim-Croat federation of BiH had come under fire from two different sectors; from Zagreb, after the overturn of ten years of HDZ rule in the elections of 1999 (Duchesneau-Bernier 2006: 230); from Sarajevo, with the appointment of Wolfgang Petritsch, the new head of OHR determined to end the de facto continuation of Herceg-Bosna's practices.

"Diaspora politics" as the continuation of annexationist politics

Indeed, the abandonment of the *official* pursuit of Herceg-Bosna in the second half of the 1990s did not hide the HDZ's overt and covert promotion of the dream of the "Banovina Hrvatska" through the political inclusion of Bosnian-Croats, through voting rights in advantageous electoral units, and finally the broader interference of Croatia in BiH through secret funding.

The first aspect of the deterritorialized annexation of Herceg-Bosna was the inclusion of Bosnian-Croats in the "diaspora" constituency. After the new citizenship laws were passed, roughly 90 percent of those who acquired Croatian citizenship outside of the territory were the Croats from BiH. When the territorial inclusion in the Republic of Croatia was removed from Herceg-Bosna, Croats from BiH came to populate massively the 11th electoral district. In 1995, 80 percent to 90 percent of the electorate occupied a single location, BiH (Kasapović 2001: 24). For the presidential elections of 1997, out of about 377,700 registered voters living outside the country, 330,000 were BiH citizens (8.5 percent of the total electorate), while the overall potential electorate was about 4,060,300. The majority of the 158 polling places in 46 foreign countries were placed in southern Herzegovina (OSCE 1997: 6). Likewise, for the 2 and 3 January 2000 parliamentary (Sabor) elections, about 315,000 out of 360,000 voters were from BiH (OSCE 2000: 14). Out-of-country voting was held over two days in diplomatic representations of Croatia in 79 countries; in BiH voting occurred at 15 locations (with 29 polling stations) following an agreement between the authorities of BiH and Croatia (OSCE 2000: 3). The 2000, 2003, and 2007 elections showed similar numbers (OSCE/ODHIR 2000: 17; OSCE/ODHIR 2004: 9; OSCE/ODHIR 2009: 11). Only the 2007 parliamentary elections showed an increase in the number of voters from Germany (38,234) and Serbia (23,717) (OSCE/ODHIR 2009: 11).

However, what is particularly striking about the "diaspora" constituency in BiH is that the elections were held outside of diplomatic premises, such as in schools, churches, or sports facilities. This led to many irregularities, as several national and international organizations observed (OSCE 2000: 3). But it confirms the impression that sections of the territory of BiH seemed to be under the rule of Croatia.

Another striking feature of the "diaspora" electoral unit is the consistent domination of the HDZ. In October 1995, the HDZ obtained 90.02 percent of the vote in the 11th district, while national results were 59.06 percent; in the 2000 parliamentary elections, it was 85.89 percent against 30.46 percent nationally.[22] The same year, HDZ's candidate for the presidential election, Mate Granić, obtained 67.65 percent of the 11th district and lost the elections with 22.47 percent nationally.[23] In the 2003 parliamentary elections, the HDZ won 57.64 percent of the 11th district and 43.42 percent nationally,[24] and in 2005 the presidential candidate Jadranka Kosor dominated with 85.26 percent against Stipe Mesić but only gained 20.31 percent nationally, and Mesić won the elections. For the 2007 Sabor elections, the HDZ again dominated diaspora voters with 81.92 percent against 31.04 percent nationally.[25] This predominance of the HDZ in the diaspora constituency reaffirmed the stereotype that Croats abroad are essentially nationalists who are nostalgic for the NDH. The fact that the majority of those diaspora votes were from Herzegovina was blurred by the various meanings of the word "diaspora," and the instrumental use made of it.

Yet the reasons for the domination of the HDZ in the diaspora electoral district—which represented the electoral district for BiH (and in particular Herzegovina)—were to be found in the fact that the state of Herceg-Bosna continued to live de facto until 2001.

In the post-Dayton years, the policy of the HDZ-BiH (directly dependent upon the HDZ in Croatia) had in fact continued, in covert ways, the project of the separation of Herzegovina and the incorporation of the territory in Croatia. In order to pursue this goal, it had pushed for the ethnic homogenization of Herzegovina, discouraging Muslims from occupying Croat areas but also discouraging internally displaced refugees temporarily living in Herzegovina from scattering into other parts of the Bosnian territory and blocking their return outside of Herzegovina (International Crisis Group 2001: 3).[26] Institutionally, this had translated in the refusal neither to merge institutions nor to collaborate with non-Croatian institutions in the mixed canton no. 7 of Neretva (Mostar). As a classic case of mono-party, vote-catching politics, in southern Herzegovina the HDZ was the state and the state was the HDZ. Or to put it in the words of the International Crisis Group report:

Even though many moderate Croats oppose HDZ policies, the fact of the matter is that the HDZ pays the salaries of all bureaucrats, judges, police officers and other civil servants, while providing political patronage through its control over the yet-to-be privatized state-owned economy. A major source of revenue for the institutions of Herceg-Bosna comes from smuggling operations that exploit Bosnia and Herzegovina's porous borders with Croatia.

(International Crisis Group 2001: 8)

From the early days of the war up until 2001, the HDZ-BiH had in fact directly ruled the country, duplicating all state institutions and, under the cover of being the "diaspora," constituted de facto an annexed territory of Croatia. The majority, if not all, of the aspects of Croatian Herzegovinian political and institutional life were ruled by the HDZ-BiH, and therefore by the HDZ in Zagreb: the national budget, the army, the police, the schooling and academic system.

In terms of national finances, Croats in BiH were fully included in Zagreb's annual national budget. The funding had arrived informally up to 1997 and was made official from 1998 with the bilateral agreement between the Republic of Croatia and the Muslim-Croat federation in 1998. Officially, "the money was sent for the salaries of the Croat component in the Bosnia-Herzegovina Federation Army through Hercegovačka Banka in Mostar,"[27] but in practice there was no distinction between funds for the parallel state and funds for the party. The bank's board of trustees included former HZ-HB president Ante Jelavić and Croatian Member of Parliament Ljubo Ćesić Rojs (elected on the "diaspora" ticket). According to a 2000 International Crisis Group report, Hercegovačka Banka "operate[d] as the central bank of Herceg-Bosna. [But] Hercegovačka Banka [was] not designed just as a financial subject, rather as the financial logistics of the HDZ-BiH" (International Crisis Group 2000: 35). The HDZ-dominated parallel state could continue to exist with this funding, so in the Herzegovinian cantons there practically existed two states with two separate budgets (International Crisis Group 2000: 49).

The funds from the Republic of Croatia arrived either from the secret funds of the Ministry of Defence, then controlled by Gojko Šušak, or from the Ministry of Finance. The exact sum is difficult to measure, but estimates show a huge figure. According to the sensationalistic magazine *Nacional*, from 1992 to 1999 the Ministry of Defence transferred over 5.8 billion Kuna (about €773 million—10 percent of Croatia's total budget in 2000[28]) to Herzegovina institutions, while about twice that is thought to have been sent from the Ministry of Finance (Šoštarić 2003). In a 2003 interview, Andrija Hebrang, several times minister during the Tuđman years, argued that "[from 1998 on] the [yearly] amount of 1.148bn Kunas [€153 million] was halved and everything was channelled lawfully, through the government and parliament."[29] To add to the massive financial presence of Croatia in this region, the Kuna, Croatia's official currency, was and still is commonly used in everyday life transactions. Here are some examples of the institutions financed by these channels.

HVO and Bosno-Croatian Army. During and after the war, the logistical center of Grude was particularly important to the army through the secret financial channels (International Crisis Group 1998). In the 1990s it was speculated that as much as 20 billion Kuna (€2.6 billion) went directly from Croatia's Ministry of Defence to the HVO, for all expenses from uniforms to salaries.[30] This was denied by government officials who estimated the figure to be 20 times less (around 1.2 billion Kuna). In 1999, 680 million Kunas (€90.6 million) were transferred to BiH "on the basis of the Agreement on special relations between the Republic of Croatia and the Federation BiH," representing about 6 percent of the overall budget of the Ministry of Finance of Croatia (Ministarstvo Financije Republike Hrvatske 1999). In 2000 the transfer was reduced to 300 million Kuna (€40 million), but an additional 121.8 million Kunas (US$16.1 million) were transferred to BiH from the Ministry for the Veterans of the Patriotic War[31] as "means for the victims of the war in the Federation of BiH."[32]

Police forces and the judicial system were also separated until the early 2000s, financed on separate budgets, and each patrolling and processing cases exclusively within its own ethnic district. Each depended on a separate command structure and a separate Ministry of Interior (International Crisis Group 2000: 46). As one journalist of *Oslobođene* (Sarajevo's leading newspaper) noted in 2000: "Mostar may be the only city in Europe in which police officers do not use the same radio frequency."[33]

Schooling. Schooling and university were similarly separated at the canton level.[34] Although many students from Mostar studied in Zagreb, Croatia financed part of the campus of the Mostar university, with about 300 million Kunas (€40 million) (Bajruši 2007).

Healthcare. During the war, the territories occupied by Croatian forces did not have important hospitals. Thirteen military hospitals were created with funds from Zagreb. Buildings were converted into hospitals across the territory such as a Franciscan church in Nova Bila, a Catholic chapel in Orašje, a school in Žepče, a tobacco factory in Grude, a hotel in Neum, and a computer company in Rama. In 2000, 4.1 million Kunas (€546,000) were transferred to build the Nova Bila hospital (Horton 1999: 2223), and approximately €15 million were spent to finish the construction of the hospital in Mostar (Bajruši 2007).

At the end of the 1990s, the state–diaspora relationship had all the characteristics of a de facto annexation, leading Croatian political science professor Mirijana Kasapović to this grim conclusion:

> The Croatian ethnic community in Bosnia and Herzegovina is a separate vote-catching group which has been during the war, and still is today, politically and financially dependent on the government of the Croatian state. The HVO—the so-called "Croatian component" of the armed forces of Bosnia and Herzegovina, the administrations in the communes and cantons with a Croatian majority, the schooling, pension and health care system, all these services are directly financed by the budget of the Republic of Croatia. This is "paid back" by the absolute electoral support of the Croats of Bosnia and Herzegovina to the HDZ.
>
> (2001: 23–24)

Practices of resistance: from contesting to reclaiming transnational belonging

Yet the practices of *transnational exclusion* have not gone uncontested. The resistance to the diaspora politics of the 1990s has taken two directions: some social actors contested the legitimacy of transnational practices of belonging—therefore articulating the claim that governmental policies should stick to the strict, Westphalian, territorial borders; others, instead, have accepted the transnational as the legitimate sphere of belonging, formulating claims against the ethnic homogeneity of the diaspora.

The first stance was taken, throughout the HDZ reign, by civil society organizations such as the Serbian Democratic Forum, GONG, and the opposition party SDP. After 2000, it had the chance to bring about significant changes in Croatian state practices. The deaths of Tuđman and Gojko Šušak in 1998 and 1999, the election of a left-wing president and government in 2000, as well as the marginalization of the conservative faction of the HDZ in favor of more liberal elements, created a radically different climate. In 2001, an International Crisis Group report argued that:

> Much of the HDZ's strength is derived from its control of illegal revenue from various public and private companies. To shut off this revenue the international community should use its powers of audit and criminal investigation.
>
> (2001: 10)

This is what the OHR, with the help of the SFOR, did in that year. The Hercegovačka Banka was put under investigation during the mandate of OHR representative Petritsch, and was the object of a thorough report in 2002. Evidence from this report is currently used by the Hague tribunal to indict the former presidency of the HZ-HB, and to prove the direct involvement of the Republic of Croatia in the conflict in Bosnia-Herzegovina.

The then newly elected president Mesić set a different tone for Croatia–Diaspora relations:

> [W]e are also making it known that the involvement [of Croatia] in the internal affairs of BiH is coming to an end ... in every sense there is still the big problem of the continued existence of the remnants of Herceg-Bosna, and Croatia cannot and should not finance these. It is clear that all of these must be incorporated into the Federation and into BiH. There cannot be this Chamber of Commerce and that Chamber of Commerce, one for this part of the state and one for the other. The remnants of Herceg-Bosna, with which some still offer the false picture or illusion that Bosnia and Herzegovina will be divided, cannot survive.
>
> (Interview with Stipe Mesić, "Ostaci 'Herceg-Bosne' ne mogu opstati," *Oslobođenje*, 22 March 2000, in International Crisis Group 2000: 29)

In October 2005, Ante Jelavić of the HDZ-BiH was sent to prison for embezzlement of the funds sent by Croatia to BiH through the bank HINA.[35] Miroslav Prce, former Bosnian federation Defence Minister was sentenced to five years.[36] In this sense, all these events marked a devalorization of the concept of diaspora, and a strong push to refocus state prerogatives on the territorial borders of Croatia. Yet other forms of resistance progressively appeared.

While the claims presented above essentially demanded the abolition of the transnational as a legitimate space for politics, two different claims contributed to its reinforcement.

The first claim came from Croatian organizations abroad who felt disempowered and tricked by the diaspora politics of the 1990s. Some organizations, from Canada or the USA, contested the modalities of selection of the representatives of the diaspora in the Sabor, claiming that, first, it shouldn't be the HDZ's headquarters in Zagreb that designated the candidate but Croats abroad and, second, that Croats from Herzegovina had no right to be counted as part of the "diaspora." In sum, the domination of Herzegovinians in the political and electoral process was seen as a usurpation of the right of the "real" diaspora to be elected and represented in Croatian political institutions.

Even more interesting, perhaps, was the move of some ethnic Serb Croats, refugees in Serbia and Montenegro, who claimed the right to be also included in the Croatian "diaspora"—and in particular the right to vote and be elected (OSCE 2005: 3).

The interesting aspect of this claim is that contrary to the claims of the opposition parties, or the civil society organizations that saw in transnational practices the very root cause of exclusionary politics, transnational politics of belonging are not contested as such, only their exclusionary nature. While on the one hand it reinforces the transnational as a symbolic and practical space for politics, it shows that it can be a terrain for political struggle and plural politics. If this trend continues—in which members of minority groups (here Serbs) formulate claims of belonging to "diasporas" that are precisely created to exclude them—then what we might be witnessing is the progressive legitimation of transnational identity politics, and a further devalorization of the territory as a frame of reference.

Conclusion: diaspora, governmentality, and the transnational political field

If we set aside the different aspects of the grey economy (which in our case does not present features that make it particularly interesting from a theoretical point of view), what do the Croatian state practices tell us about the concept of diaspora, the government of diasporas, and the transnational political field?

First, the practices of the Croatian state pose a serious problem to mainstream theorization of the "diaspora." Historically and socially, indeed, a scholar following the definition of "diaspora" as a social group answering to a certain number of categories could only determine that historically and sociologically

Croats in Bosnia and Herzegovina do not fit the criteria: they are not a "real" diaspora, but are a kin-state minority. But what does it mean for the State of Croatia to define them as such, and absolutely not as a kin-state minority? This question falls out of the theoretical concerns of such an approach.

As we have shown, it has become a powerful discourse to justify different practices of power. In the previous chapter, two practices of power have been analyzed; the ethnic homogenization of a nation redefined as territorial and a vote-catching strategy to secure seats in parliament. A third set of practices which we have documented empirically in this chapter is the pursuit of annexationist politics "by other means." Indeed, here, the discourse of diaspora allowed the Croatian government to walk a thin line by recasting the population of a neighboring country as part of its national population: in many ways, as has been extensively documented by international organizations, Croatia's citizenship and electoral policies are in contradiction with the letter of the Dayton accords, which specifies that Croats are a "constitutive people" of the State of Bosnia and Herzegovina. Had the Croatian government defined Croats in Bosnia-Herzegovina as a part of the nation of the Republic of Croatia, the contradiction with the international agreements would have been blatant. Nowhere does international law accept that an entire nation belongs to two different states—multinational or not. But by playing on the ambiguities of the discourse of diaspora, and through citizenship policies, it is precisely what Tudjman managed to accomplish: the inclusion, in all possible ways, of Croats from BiH in the Republic of Croatia's institutions, while respecting its international agreements. Indicative of the result of this position is an OSCE report of 1997 stating that "This practice of enfranchising ethnic Croats [...] *may* also be in contravention of the spirit and letter of the Dayton (OSCE 1997: 6, emphasis added)." It is therefore no surprise that the political and legal construction could only be attacked on technicalities, such as the number of votes per seat, or the enlistment procedures. In this sense again, "diaspora" as a state category functions as a powerful performative utterance which allows the redefinition of the functional relationship of a specific population and the state. It makes it possible to legitimize state practices that would otherwise not be accepted.

Yet the regime of justification does not say much about the actual practices of power that are deployed. What is apparent through the study of the Croatian Diaspora relation in Bosnia and Herzegovina is that in addition to the legitimation strategy the diasporic discourse allows for the blurring of the divisions between what is "inside" and what is "outside" a state. What took place between roughly 1990 and 2000—and to a lesser degree after that date—is in fact the government of an entire province abroad—or an example of what could be defined as post-territorial annexation. The three monopolies of power discussed in the first chapter were in fact exported outside of the legitimate borders of the state: the monopoly of violence (through the control of the army and police) the monopoly over the distribution of resources (through a complete control of the economy, even if underground), and finally the monopoly over "symbolic violence," namely the production and reproduction of a state identity and narrative through schools and universities. Other everyday symbolic elements—what Michael Billig would define as "banal nationalism," such as the use of the Croatian currency or the location of polling stations in typical "domestic" locations (and not in diplomatic premises), reinforce this impression that these parts of Bosnia and Herzegovina were de facto in Croatia. It therefore seems that while the discourse on the establishment of a Great Croatia (or a Banovina Hrvatska) shifted from outright *annexation* to *inclusion of the diaspora*, the *practices* of government remained essentially the same until a series of concordant events such as the change in Croatia's government, international pressure, and the SFOR intervention eventually put an end to these state practices.

Notes

1 Hereafter: HZ-HB (Hrvatska Zajednica Herceg-Bosne).
2 Hereafter: BiH.
3 International Criminal Tribunal for Former Yugoslavia.
4 On this aspect, see Ramet 2006: 413–469; Ribičić 2001; Duchesneau-Bernier 2006.
5 See the developments on "economic nationalism" in Helleiner and Pickel (2005), in particular the introduction.
6 For a development on the framework of identities/borders/orders, see Albert *et al.* 2001.
7 It is important to note that like every "national movement" the HDZ in the late 1980s and early 1990s was composed of a heterogeneous mixture of political positions, represented by different political actors who had partially intersecting, often conflicting, stakes in the political game. The free elections of 1990 represented a moment in which these positions coalesced behind the figure of Franjo Tuđman, but the ideological positions of the HDZ did not only originate from one man, regardless of his influence. For the sake of this book, the writings and speeches of Franjo Tuđman should rather be understood as a uniquely relevant place to analyze the *doxa* of this broader group of political actors who came to power in 1990.
8 Antifašističko V(ij)eće Narodnog Oslobođenja Jugoslavije, standing for "Anti-Fascist Council of National Liberation of Yugoslavia," the executive organ of the Communist party during and after World War II in Yugoslavia. The council set the borders and administrative separations of Yugoslavia in 1945–1946.
9 For example, this change can be seen in the constitutional shifts between 1990 and 1997. In 1990, the constitution stated that

> The Croatian Republic is founded as the national state of the Croatian people and as the state of the following peoples and minorities: Serbs, Muslims, Slovenians, Czechs, Slovaks, Italians, Hungarians, Jews and others. Their equality with citizens of Croatian ethnicity and the exercise of their minority rights is guaranteed in accordance with the democratic norms of the Organization of the United Nations and the norms of the free world.The constitutional changes of 1997 mark the elimination of Muslims and Slovenians, but the entrance of Germans, Austrians, Ukrainians, and Russians.
>
> (See Sokol and Smerdel 2006)

10 Croatia officially recognized the territorial borders of its new neighbor one month after the declaration of independence, on 7 March 1992 (Duchesneau-Bernier 2006: 224).

11 Stjepan Kljuić from September 1991 to February 1992 united BiH. HZ was a question of autonomy. Boban replaced him in February 1992.
12 The Army of Bosnia and Herzegovina (ARBiH) was formed on 20 May 1992 by a presidential decree. It was mainly organized on the basis of the JNA structures and incorporated another group of units inherited from Yugoslavia's fear of Stalin, the Territorial Defences. This was a similar process to what the Croatian regular army had done in 1991 (Duchesneau-Bernier 2006: 224).
13 See Duchesneau-Bernier 2006: 247.
14 The 30 municipalities are: Jajce, Kreševo, Busovača, Vitez, Novi Travnik, Travnik, Kiseljak, Fojnica, Skender Vakuf, Kakanj, Vareš, Kotor Varoš, Tomislavgrad, Livno, Kupres, Bugojno, Gornji Vakuf, Prozor, Konjić, Jablanica, Posušje, Mostar, Široki Brijeg, Grude, Ljubuški, Čitluk, Čapljina, Neum, Stolac, Trebinje (Article 2 of *Narodni List* 1992b).
15 Also HVO DB, 249, 15 May 1992.
16 She cites the arrival of "*mujaheddin*" fighters, not eager to collaborate with the Croats, the role of the media on both sides in distorting reality and creating an atmosphere of animosity, the rapid change in the structure of municipalities, and the fact that some ARBiH commanders (such as Sead Delić) had been previously involved in the fighting in Croatia, usually on the Yugoslav (Serbian) side (Ramet 2006: 434–435). Duchesneau-Bernier adds to this the fact that the government of BiH had never adopted a clear position on the Slovenian and Croatian wars (Duchesneau-Bernier 2006: 247).
17 the actual presence of HV combatants in central Bosnia remains unproved. Despite persistent rumours, the accusations of Bosnia-Herzegovina's Muslim-led government and of Muslim witnesses before the ICTY, a great deal of speculation on the part of UNPROFOR and ECMM observers, and a straightforward statement by the UN Security Council, there is, in fact, no convincing public evidence that the Croatian Army ever intervened in the Muslim–Croat conflict in *central* Bosnia.

(Shrader 2003: 50)

18 See Campbell's chapter, "Ontopology: Representing the violence in Bosnia" (Campbell 1998: 33–82).
19 OHR 1995, article 1.
20 Article 3, line 2 of the constitution. See Duchesneau-Bernier 2006: 229.
21 See www.mvpei.hr/CustomPages/Static/HRV//templates/_frt_bilateralni_odnosi_po_drzavama_en.asp?id=62.
22 www.izbori.hr/2000Sabor/IJ11.PDF.
23 www.izbori.hr/2000Pred/Pred1Krug.htm.
24 www.izbori.hr/2003Sabor/index.htm.
25 www.izbori.hr/izbori/izbori07.nsf/FI?OpenForm.
26 In this sense, the goal was the same as the disciplinary rationality analyzed in Chapter 5: "Fill" the territory with as many ethnic Croats as possible, and avoid dispersion (although the parallel entity of Herceg-Bosna was electorally described as part of the "diaspora").
27 OBN TV, Sarajevo, in Bosnian/Croatian/Serbian 2000 gmt, 18 December 2003.
28 The overall budget for the Republic of Croatia in 2000 was 54,938,056,100 HRK, the equivalent of US$11,678,511,989.29.
29 OBN TV, Sarajevo, in Bosnian/Croatian/Serbian 2000 gmt, 18 December 2003.
30 Croatian Radio, Zagreb, in Croatian 1300 gmt, 17 April 2003.
31 Ministarstvo Branitelja iz Domovinskog Rata.
32 Ministarstvo Financija Republike Hrvatske, 2000.
33 Sporo Ujedinjenje Policije, *Oslobođenje*, 10 February 2000, p. 10, quoted in International Crisis Group 2000: 46.

34 "Education in Bosnia and Herzegovina: Governance, Finance and Administration," *Report by the Council of Europe for the World Bank*, 10 November 1999. Quoted in International Crisis Group (2000: 50).
35 News agency, Zagreb, in English 15:09 GMT, 6 October 2005.
36 News agency, Zagreb, in English 18:22 GMT, 14 October 2004.

References

Albert, M., Jacobson, D., Lapid, Y., *et al.* (2001) *Identities, Borders, Orders: Rethinking International Relations Theory*, Minneapolis, MN; London: University of Minnesota Press.
Anderson, B. (1991) *Imagined Communities: Reflections on the Origin and Spread of Nationalism*, London: Verso.
Bajruši, R. (2007) "Svi grijesi Zdenke Babić—Petričević," *Nacional*, 21 June 2007.
Bianchini, S. (1996) *Sarajevo, Le Radici dell'Odio—Identità e Destino dei Popoli Balcanici*, Roma: Edizioni Associate.
Bougarel, X. (1996) "Bosnia and Hercegovina—State and Communitarianism" in Dyker, D. A. and Vejvoda, I., eds., *Yugoslavia and After* (pp. 87–115), London and New York: Longman.
Campbell, D. (1998) *National Deconstruction: Violence, Identity, and Justice in Bosnia*, Minneapolis, MN: University of Minnesota Press.
Duchesneau-Bernier, J. (2006) "Les relations bilatérales entre la Croatie et la Bosnie" in Lukic, R., ed., *La Politique étrangère de la Croatie, de son indépendance à nos jours 1991–2006* (pp. 219–262), Québec: Les Presses de l'Université de Laval.
Gellner, E. (1983) *Nations and Nationalism*, Oxford: Blackwell.
Helleiner, E. and Pickel, A. (2005) *Economic Nationalism in a Globalizing World*, Ithaca, NY: Cornell University Press.
Hoare, A. (1997) "The Croatian Project to Partition Bosnia-Hercegovina, 1990–1994," *East European Quarterly*, 31(1), p. 121.
Horton R. (1999) "Croatia and Bosnia: the Imprints of War—II. Restoration," *The Lancet*, 353(9171), pp. 2223–2228.
International Crisis Group (1998) *Changing Course?: Implications of the Divide in Bosnian Croat Politics*, Zagreb/Brussels: International Crisis Group.
International Crisis Group (2000) *Reunifying Mostar, Opportunities for Progress*, Sarajevo/Washington/Brussels: International Crisis Group.
International Crisis Group (2001) *Turning Strife to Advantage: A Blueprint to Integrate the Croats in Bosnia-Herzegovina*, Sarajevo/Brussels: International Crisis Group.
Kasapović, M. (2001) *Hrvatska politika 1990—2000: izbori, stranke i parlament u Hrvatskoj*, Zagreb: Fakultet politickih znanosti Sveucilista.
Kastoryano, R. (2006) "Vers un nationalisme transnational. Redéfinir la nation, le nationalisme et le territoire," *Revue française de science politique*, 56(4), pp. 533–555.
Ministarstvo Financija Republika Hrvatske (1999) *Pozicije Plana 1999*, Zagreb.
Ministarstvo Financija Republika Hrvatske (2000) *Pozicije Plana 2000*, Zagreb.
Narodni List (1992a) "Odluka o Formiranju Hrvatskog Vijeća Obrane, 1/1992," *Narodni List HZ H-B*.
Narodni List (1992b) "Odluka o Uspostavi Hrvatske Zajednice Herceg-Bosna, 1/1992," *Narodni List HZ H-B*.
OHR (1995) *The General Framework Agreement for Peace in Bosnia and Hercegovina*. Available at: www.ohr.int/?page_id=1252 (accessed 12 May 2008).

OSCE (1997) *Statement, Presidential Election in the Republic of Croatia, 15 June 1997*. Available at: www.osce.org/item/1536.html (accessed 12 May 2008).

OSCE (2000) *Election of Representatives to the State Parliament—2–3 January 2000. International Election Observation Mission Preliminary Statement*, Zagreb: OSCE.

OSCE (2005) *Background Report: Victory for President Mesić, Renewed Debate on Electoral Reform*, Zagreb: OSCE.

OSCE/ODHIR (2000) *Republic of Croatia Extraordinary Presidential Elections 24 January & 7 February 2000. OSCE/ODHIR Election Observation Mission Final Report*, Warsaw: OSCE.

OSCE/ODHIR (2004) *Republic of Croatia Parliamentary Elections—23 November 2003. OSCE/ODHIR Election Observation Mission Report*. Available at: www.osce.org/item/2102.html (accessed 12 May 2008).

OSCE/ODHIR (2009) *Republic of Croatia, Parliamentary Elections 25 November 2007*, Warsaw: OSCE/ODIHR Limited Election Observation Mission Report.

Osiander, A. (2001) "Sovereignty, International Relations and the Westphalian Myth," *International Organization*, 55(2), pp. 251–287.

Ramet, S. P. (2006) *The Three Yugoslavias: State-Building and Legitimation, 1918–2004*, Bloomington, IN, Chesham: Indiana University Press; Combined Academic Distributor.

Ribičić, C. (2001) *Geneza Jedna Zablude*, Zagreb, Sarajevo, Idrija: Naklada Jesenski i Turk, Sejtarija, Zalozba Bogataj.

Shrader, C. R. (2003) *The Muslim-Croat Civil War in Central Bosnia: A Military History, 1992–1994*, College Station: Texas A & M University Press.

Smith, A. D. (1979) *Nationalism in the Twentieth Century*, Oxford: Martin Robertson.

Sokol, S. and Smerdel, B. (2006) *Ustavno Pravo*, Zagreb: Pravni fakultet.

Šoštarić, E. (2003) MORH je Herceg Bosni uplatio 5.893.852.236,59 kuna, *Nacional*, 29 April 2003.

Tuđman, F. (1996) *Nacionalno Pitanje u Suvremenoj Europi*, Zagreb: Nakladni Zavod Matice Hrvatske.

Zacher, M. (2001) The Territorial Integrity Norm: International Boundaries and the Use of Force, *International Organization*, 55(2), pp. 215–250.

8 Conclusion

Theorizing the government of diasporas[1]

In this book, I have dealt with a diverse set of empirical sources, ranging from historical archives to laws, electoral results, qualitative interviews, newspapers, and magazine and internet articles. However, my primary objective has been theoretical. This naturally leads to an important question: how can we generalize from a single case? Going against a certain tradition in political science and international relations, I have avoided adopting a comparative approach, which would typically derive theoretical conclusions from a choice of representative cases.

Instead, I make my case using the words of French historian Louis Dumont. In his 1966 groundbreaking analysis of the Indian caste system, Dumont argued that the detailed study of one society is in fact already a comparative approach—that is, a comparison between the observer's values and practices and the values and practices of the studied society. Indeed, a single case study might be the only way to draw appropriate universal conclusions.

> The universal can be reached as such only through specific categories, each time different, of each type of society. What is the sense of going to India, if not to contribute to the discovery of how and why the Indian civilization, through its own particularity, represents a form of the universal? Eventually, it is the one who considers carefully, with utmost humility, the smallest particularity [who] leaves the route of the universal open. It is the one who is ready to dedicate all the necessary time to the study of all aspects of Indian culture who has the chance, under certain conditions, of transcending it and eventually finding some truth that he can use.
>
> (Dumont 1966: 16)

In putting together the various chapters of this book, I have been driven by a dissatisfaction with the existing theorization on the notion of diaspora as well as the results of these epistemological underpinnings on diaspora studies. By relying on an a priori definition of diaspora as a sociological concept in addition to attributing agency to an essentialized group, many studies on diaspora are marred by hasty generalizations and uncritically reproduce diasporic or state institutions' discourses. However, my starting point has been to take the emergence and spread of the discourse on diaspora in one particular case to analyze the ways in which it emerged, diffused, and functioned as a practical device of politics. At this point, I will return to some of the key arguments derived from my study.

The notion of diaspora

The concepts of race, class, and nation have been subjected to several treatments of deconstruction—to the point that today it seems hard to find a scholar of nationalism defining him- or herself as a primordialist. Yet the concept of diaspora has slipped through the net of critical scholarship in certain disciplines (for a notable exception, see Brubaker 2005). Such work in anthropology and sociology has led to debates around diaspora having a slight taste of *dépassé* (the seminal articles of Clifford and Gilroy date from 1994, and most discussions occurred over the course of the 1990s). Still, diaspora seems to have been uncritically adopted in political science and international relations, two disciplines prone to generalizations and essentializations for the sake of the parsimony of variables or easy translation into policy briefs.

I have argued that these two latter disciplines cannot afford to overlook the conceptual foundations of their analysis of diaspora politics. Therefore, it is necessary to engage in a theoretical discussion on the relationship between language and political practice. Is political discourse secondary, as positivists (be they Marxists or Realists) assert, or is it the starting point of political practice? In this book, I have argued that discourse is central in shaping the social reality of political actors; nowhere else but in language can the "brute facts" (as John Searle would define them) be understood, put in context, framed, and set up in narratives that attribute causality and call for solutions. As has been shown in detail for Croatia, whether governments define a group of emigrants as political émigrés, temporary workers abroad, or part of the "emigrant Croatia," groups and individuals are caught up in completely different sets of relations of power, subjected to completely different policies, ruled by different laws, and may collaborate or resist these practices in different ways.

Diaspora, performativity, and the transnational political field

This has at least two implications: first, no single definition exists. Rather, there are many definitions of diaspora—in fact, as many definitions as there are social actors who formulate claims about diaspora. It has already been noted (Tölölyan) that scholars claiming to impose a definition of diaspora are only actors among others. They might have a specific capital with regard to other actors (academic authority); their texts and articles might even have a direct influence on some governments,[2] but they do not have a monopoly over the discourse itself.

This understanding raises several questions, but first calls for the elaboration of theoretical tools to "seize" the diasporic processes. Methodologically, which claims should we scholars consider? Epistemologically, if we take language as the starting point of the analysis, are we to presuppose that everything only happens in language, as Derrideans would claim?[3] More centrally, if we must reject the concept, what remains? Here I relied on Bourdieu's framework of fields: the performativity of the diasporic discourse is always to be put in relation to the different positions of power of the social actors within a transnational field. Bourdieu defines social fields using two metaphors; as fields of (magnetic) forces in which a particular worldview is shared by social actors involved in the field, thereby leading to a common understanding of the stakes of the field, and as fields of struggle, referring to social spaces in which social actors are in competition for the monopoly of the representation, the borders, and what the field ought to be doing. In this sense, according to Bourdieu, society—or the social space—comprises a multiplicity of different social fields (the artistic field, the economic field, the religious field, the political field, etc.) organized into hierarchical relationships, where some are more powerful than others. By positing the existence of fields, Bourdieu explained social behavior "by [the agents'] position in the structure of the power relationship characteristic of the field in a precise moment" (Bourdieu 2000: 61). As a result, the question of the field's borders becomes an empirical question. An agent is inside the field if his actions have an effect on the power relations within the field (Bourdieu 2000: 53).

Yet Bourdieu never fully escaped the methodological nationalism (Wimmer and Schiller 2002) in which his theory was embedded, and he never conceptualized the possibility of transnational social fields, even going so far as to engage in serious "acts of misrecognition" about the nature of transnational politics.[4] For this reason, it seems that authors in the field of migration and transnationalism studies have borrowed his concepts, but dismissed his theoretical approach. For example, Nina Glick Schiller, who explicitly uses the concept of fields, acknowledged the work of Bourdieu but abandoned his nationalist framework. Yet outside the field of migration and diaspora studies, authors have successfully used Bourdieu's concept of fields, adapting it to the transnational realm (Bigo 2008; Dezalay and Garth 2001; Georgakakis 2002). The main displacement that these authors have brought about has been to remove the state from its privileged status of "capital converter" between fields and include it in the analysis as the bureaucratic field—namely, one field among others.

But what does an understanding in terms of fields add to the current literature on diaspora or transnationalism studies? Previous conceptualizations in transnational social fields have already been used (Faist 2000; Levitt and Schiller 2004; Pries 2001; Itzigsohn and Saucedo 2002; Portes *et al.* 1999). Meanwhile, my approach is distinct in that it allows for several factors.

First, analyzing the specificity of distinct transnational social fields. What is more often overlooked in the existing theorization (particularly by Glick Schiller) is that transnational social spaces constitute multiple distinct social fields, not only one social field. In this sense, what is often referred to as a diaspora or transnational community is in fact subdivided into a multiplicity of socio-professional fields, or microcosms, each ruled by its particular rules of the game—what Bourdieu called *illusio*. These multiple fields are organized in terms of domination, with the political field usually in a position of domination over the other fields (economic, artistic, intellectual).

Second, setting a category of analysis distinct from the categories of practice allows us to do away with essentializing the concepts of community—namely, transnational communities—that tend to mask the heterogeneity of the political dynamics occurring within a transnational political field. In this sense, a diaspora is not a social actor; it does not "do things." Therefore, the methodological advantage is that the limits of the analysis are broader than what self-appointed diasporic political leaders, hostland, or homeland bureaucratic institutions define as the relevant political field. Social processes and actors are considered as soon as they produce effects in the political field (even when they deny the political nature of their activities or their interventions); consequently, the analysis does not take the principles of division of the dominant actors of the field as the principles of scholarly analysis (Bourdieu 2000: 53).

Third, understanding the performative power of categories of practice. Social actors represent themselves as being and/or carrying out activities in diaspora, in exile, or in emigration. In other words, the diaspora or exile are symbolic referents, categories of practice that refer to a bounded social space involving actors in common dynamics located in the homeland, in different hostlands, and within diasporic institutions. However, the specificity of the political field over other fields stems from the fact that social agents are in a struggle not only for ideas, but for very specific ideas that are the production and establishment of the legitimate principles of vision and division of the social world.[5] As a result, "politics is a struggle for ideas but for a kind of ideas that is very particular, i.e., strong ideas (*idées-forces*) who empower by working as mobilization strength" (Bourdieu 2000: 63). Political discourse is in fact performative. It more often than not creates the reality it describes. Therefore, "changing the principles of categorization is not only an intellectual act, it is also a political act because principles of categorization produce a class, which can then be mobilized" (Bourdieu 2000: 67).

Fourth, analyzing political behavior as structured by overlapping sovereignties. Far from being a stateless condition, the transnational social space is a space structured by multiple overlapping forms of authority and power, in which both homeland and hostland governments and bureaucratic institutions have a disproportionate power over diasporic institutions in structuring the field, particularly in demarcating and enforcing a division between the inside (domestic) and the outside (foreign) of the field. If transnational actors' political positions and political behavior are to be analyzed in relation to their ideological claims, it is mostly in relation to their position toward other actors—namely, other diasporic, homeland, and hostland institutions. As Bourdieu put it,

> to say that there is a political field is to remember that people that are in it can do or say things that are determined not by their direct relationship of those whom they represent, but with other members of the field.
>
> (2000: 57)

Conclusion: governing diasporas in IR 181

The social uses of the language of diaspora are therefore intimately linked with the material practices attached to it, as empirically evident in practices of the Croatian authorities in Bosnia-Herzegovina. Most scholars in Croatia and most diasporic institutions in the USA, Canada, and Australia have argued that the Croats of Bosnia-Herzegovina were not part of what they understood to be the diaspora, yet their inclusion in the citizenry and their representation in parliament became an unchallengeable fact.

The second implication is that many definitions exist not only of what a diaspora is, but also what a diaspora ought to do. Indeed, categorizations, as specific speech acts, are always a description of both what you are and what you should be. Nikolas Rose's logic outlined in his analysis of the spread of the discourse of community supports this idea:

> Like so many other similar loci of allegiance—class, civil society, ethnicity—arguments about community employ a Janus-faced logic [...]. Each assertion of community refers itself to something that already exists and has a claim on us: our common fate as gay men, as women of color, as people with AIDS, as members of an ethnic group [...]. Within such a style of thought, community exists and is to be achieved, yet the achievement is nothing more than the birth-to-presence of a form of being which pre-exists.
> (1996: 334)

In the case of the Croatian diaspora, we clearly witnessed the divergent views on the role and function of the diaspora after 1993, when the brief moment of agreement and action between the diasporic institutions and the Croatian government (toward financing the HDZ's campaign, supporting the war effort, etc.) vanished. The divergence occurred between the government and diasporic institutions and among the diasporic institutions themselves.

Doing away with determinism and essentialism

From these examples it appears that at least two positions concerning the political behavior of diasporas often found in the literature are simply not tenable. The first could be labeled as determinist; the second, as essentialist. The former attribute one particular type of political behavior to diasporas because of the structural conditions in which social agents are located: diasporas provoke conflicts (Collier); diasporas defuse conflicts and diffuse democracy (Shain); diasporas are good for development; diasporas are bad for development; diasporas are the historical subject of progress, political change, and postnationalism; and diasporas are intrinsically ethno-national and exclusionary. These stances all assume that the political behavior and effect of diaspora politics can be derived from their condition. For example, for Anderson, the product of the interaction of one exiled/immigrant culture with the majority culture of the immigration country pushes the members of the immigrant group to harden their identities, creating serious but unaccountable politics. No taxes are paid in the country where these politics have an impact, and long-distant nationalists are not accountable to the judiciary system and do not vote because they remain citizens of another country:

> But, well and safely positioned in the First World, he can send money and guns, circulate propaganda, and build intercontinental computer information circuits, all of which can have incalculable consequences in the zone of their ultimate destinations. They are deeply rooted in a consciousness that his exile is self-chosen and that the nationalism he claims on e-mail is also the ground on which an embattled ethnic identity is to be fashioned in the ethnicized nation-state that he remains determined to inhabit. That same metropole that marginalizes and stigmatizes him simultaneously enables him to play, in a flash, on the other side of the planet, national hero.
> (Anderson 1998: 62)

Just like Collier's position discussed in Chapter 4, the problem of this stance lies in the homogeneity attributed to social agents. It denies the agency of social agents in exile by assuming the inevitability of nationalist politics while denying the heterogeneity of political formations abroad as well as the dynamics and changes that occur over time within and between political formations. Finally, it is oblivious to the importance of external factors in empowering one group over another within the constellation of political associations and groups abroad. As I have shown in this book, it is neither the structural conditions of socialization nor the social background of migrants per se that explain political behavior; rather, it is the interaction of the two. As extensively discussed in Chapter 2, the dynamic relations within the transnational political field between the *habitus* actors and the structure of the field explain the different political positions.

The second position that no longer holds is the one that could be defined as essentialist, as it makes diasporas unitary actors, which is a supposedly useful category of analysis. Mainstream constructivism in international relations (IR) has been particularly prone to this shortcoming. While accepting the constructed nature of diasporas, it nevertheless conceptualizes them as discrete entities—individual actors who may influence or benefit from interactions with equally essentialized states (Shain and Barth 2003: 451).[6] For King and Melvin, for example, "basic categories of analysis employed in the study of dispersed ethnic groups—'homelands' and 'diasporas'—are not given and static." Yet these authors sidestep the question of precisely how diasporas are constituted through the symbolic politics of the sending state and, thus, fall into the classic problem of "groupism."[7] The existence of diasporas on the one hand and nation states on the other therefore remains unchallenged (King and Melvin 1999: 106–108). Adamson's approach (Adamson and Demetriou 2007) is vulnerable to a similar criticism; although Adamson goes further than King and Melvin by acknowledging that "states as institutional structures are still at the center of current processes of spatial reconfiguration, and that the symbolic importance of both 'national identity' and 'territory' are not necessarily fading, but are rather being

Conclusion: governing diasporas in IR   183

reappropriated and rearticulated through a variety of transnational practices and politics" (Adamson and Demetriou 2007: 490), she dismisses critical scholarship's "conceptual focus on non-state identities" for being "often paired to a political project located within the field of IR, rather than an IR project that seeks to understand the real world of international politics" (Adamson and Demetriou 2007: 495). Instead, she proposes returning to what Brubaker abandoned; the use of diaspora as a "category of analysis" (Brubaker 2005).[8]

The effects of the diasporic speech act

If we abandon the use of diaspora as a subject and rather take it as the result of a specific speech act, then the question becomes why do social actors engage in the re-labeling of minorities, ethnic groups, migrants, and political exiles into diasporas? I have argued that this could be explained by three attractive effects of the speech act of diaspora: the illusion of homogeneity (which is uncritically assumed by essentialist approaches to diaspora); the illusion of a natural link between a group and a remote homeland (justifying transnational practices of power); and the legitimacy of certain spokespersons to speak in the name of the diaspora. These three effects are generally pursued by all social actors engaging in the competition for the monopoly of what a diaspora is and what it ought to do.

However, the central argument of this book has been more specific. When governments mobilize the diasporic language, the diasporic speech act allows them to engage in transnational practices of power that would otherwise be considered illegitimate. By "playing the system" of minority rights and multicultural rights—discourses that are becoming increasingly legitimate at the international level—homeland governments are in fact able to justify a certain number of practices of power targeting their populations abroad and, in doing so, exporting claims and practices traditionally founded on domestic claims of sovereignty. Empirical research has highlighted three instances in the Croatian case in which the performative utterance of diaspora has justified these practices. First, by re-categorizing previously excluded populations of Croats abroad and widely distributing citizenship to Croats abroad, the HDZ-led Croatian government pursued its goal of ethnic homogenization through the ethnic cleansing of citizenship. Second, this subsequently enabled the ruling HDZ to secure a large portion of seats in parliament. Finally, it allowed the de facto annexation of Herzegovina to Croatia at least up to the early 2000s. By blurring the distinctions between the different categories of Croats abroad (long-term, assimilated emigrants; recently emigrated Croats; and Croats from Bosnia-Herzegovina who never left their territory), the diaspora constituency has been used to represent and justify these post-territorial annexationist practices.

From governing territories to governing populations

In the specific case of Yugoslavia/Croatia/Bosnia-Herzegovina, the evolution of government rationalizations is explained by a sociology of the bureaucratic agencies and the political elites that have a stake in this specific issue. Through the ascent of the Norval network and the HDZ hardliners, competition in conceptualizations of the geography of the nation, the invention of the "Emigrant Croatia," and the heterogeneous set of practices aimed at constituting a legitimate domestic abroad have been central in deploying the new diaspora policies.

As I have shown in this book, these changes in the rationalizations and practices of power are rooted in a longer history of governmental management of populations abroad, each originating from a specific set of interpretations of the social and political phenomena and dealing with specific ministries through the deployment of specific practices of power. Similarly, the policies of the 1990s created a precedent for the political struggles to come by shaping new spaces of political contestation. As discussed in Chapter 2, Yugoslav governmental practices had already started to legitimize transnational conceptions of the political field, yet the discourse always referred to a strict territorial understanding of the legitimate politics and state policies. In this sense, guest worker programs could only provide temporary employment for workers abroad, thereby making return policies so important during the 1970s and 1980s. However, the HDZ policies of the 1990s justified transnational governmental practices through the discourse of diaspora, outlining the concepts of the nation, citizenship, and the legitimate space of sovereignty as disconnected from the territory. Thus, governmental practices toward their diasporas are not just one of several policies. By formulating claims of sovereignty outside the borders that legitimize it, they manifest a shift in the rationality of the government described by Foucault—namely, from the government of territory to the government of populations. This conclusion is further confirmed by the resistance to the new practices of the state. Whereas left-wing parties have constantly (and unsuccessfully) argued for the dismissal of the diaspora policies, attempting to reduce the interference of the Croatian government in domestic affairs abroad and in a way attempting to re-territorialize governmental practices, other organizations (such as the ethnic Serb Croatian citizens who are refugees in Serbia, *Republika Srpska* in Bosnia-Herzegovina or Montenegro) are now claiming that they are the diaspora too. By arguing for their inclusion in the diaspora, these organizations' practices of resistance justify and reinforce the transnationalization of the Croatian political field and legitimize post-territorial practices of power.

Competing rationalities of government

Is this concept of sovereignty and politics specific to Croatia? Can similar rationalizations and practices be found across the world? In this second part of the conclusion, I review heterogeneous rationalizations of the relationship between the government and populations abroad that emerged from the empirical research and draw parallels with other cases across the world. It is important to distinguish here the program of government (the declared policy) versus the diagram of power (technologies and techniques operating in society that governments tap into). Although here I concentrate on the description of at least three sets of coherent rationalizations of the government of populations abroad (programs of government) and the historical predominance of one over the others, I also suggest that they might be tied to particular technologies of power, each functioning within its own logic. As it is outside the scope of this conclusion to establish firm links, I instead argue that the analysis of the Croatian case might illustrate broader trends that could be the object of further research.

Diasporas in the disciplinary state: Aliyah(s), exceptionalism, and cultural policies

In the Yugoslav/Croatian case, the first rationality of government can be called disciplinary, which is characterized by the deployment of three consistent relationships with populations abroad and oriented toward the preservation of a clearly bounded territorial state understood to be essential to security and prosperity.

The first type of relationship bears many similarities to the Zionist Aliyah. It is a nationalist discourse of return. Deployed during the late 1920s and 1930s, and then again in the early 1990s through the Ministry of Return and Development, it offers several equivalents to other historical cases. These government practices are rooted in understandings of diaspora as a pathological form of existence for a nation—a pathology that can only be "cured" by the territorialization of the dispersed populations. This is exemplified in the writings of one of the fathers of Zionism, Leon Pinsker (Pinsker 1947; Marienstras 1985: 219). Moreover, when the population is conceptualized as the main resource of the state, depopulation becomes a cause for concern out of a fear of depleting manpower or the military forces. Such a fear was also found in Italy at the beginning of the twentieth century (Green 2005: 277). In this configuration, the "good" members of the nation (the "good Jew," the "good Albanian," the "good Armenian") are those who return home to build or rebuild their country. Governmental practices under this concept of diaspora include propaganda for return among émigré communities and the funding of returns via financial or tax incentives. Eponymous ministries are usually created to manage the population flow, such as those in Israel. Moreover, the concept of *jus sanguinis* can be used to maintain one's national identity abroad and facilitate one's return (Green 2005: 276).

The second type of relationship, illustrated by the police practices toward the political emigration during communist Yugoslavia, is the one involving a simultaneous policy of banning and exporting the security apparatus abroad. One of the correlates of many return policies is indeed to consider whomever leaves, or stays abroad, as at best suspicious or at worst a traitor. The full actualization of this logic is the creation of the exile enemy category in dictatorial states, in which a section of the population abroad is constructed within a Schmittian friend/foe relationship with the government. Zolberg observed that this phenomenon usually takes place within autarchic logics, "particularly in the case of states that seek to catch up by imposing great sacrifices on the current generation" (Zolberg 1989: 413). In this relationship, categorizations are always polarized; political exiles are branded enemies while separatist groups are branded as terrorists, as in the case of Turkish practices toward émigré Kurdish organizations (Rigoni, 2000). Left- or right-wing political opposition is automatically communist or fascist, respectively, and both of these groups become legitimate categories of the population abroad to be surveilled—and sometimes even executed, as in the famous cases of the Moroccan dissenter Ben Barka (Gallissot and Kergoat 1997), the "Bulgarian umbrella" (Kostov 1988), Russian former agent Litvinenko (Goldfarb and Litvinenko 2008), or the 1979 assassination by Khomeiny's Iran of the shah's exiled nephew (Shain 1990: 160). In a less spectacular manner, many non-democratic states systematically surveil and track their emigrants as a matter of inner security abroad (Cordes 1986). The main governmental techniques for such efforts include the banning (through direct coercion or indirect socio-economic means) and the surveillance of populations abroad through a monopolization of the legitimate means of the circulation of the population (Torpey 1998) and the exportation of the monopoly of legitimate violence through secret security agencies.

A third relationship is the promotion of an official national identity toward domestic populations abroad, constructed as friendly to the state through cultural centers and institutes; such an effort was achieved mainly through *Matica iseljenika Hrvatske*, although, again, many similar historical examples are available. Whereas British Councils and Alliances Françaises were almost exclusively aimed at expanding a colonial culture of *mission civilisatrice*, this was not the case regarding the policies of the newly-founded Germany or Italy. In Germany, for example, the 1889 All-German School Association and post-WWI German Academic Exchange (DAAD, founded in 1925) were both conceived as a way to gather the nation across borders. Similarly, the Dante Alighieri institutes were famously implemented during the 1920s to spread national culture and fascism among the emigrant population (Totaro-Genevois 2005: 30 quoted in Paschalidis). Similar cultural practices of exporting the national culture (or official religion) abroad can be found in many other cases, such as those of Turkey (Rigoni 2000) and Russia (Laruelle 2006). These policies are typically anti-assimilationist in that they "aim to prevent expatriate or same-language communities from being integrated with foreign states, and to maintain them as potential foreign policy instruments, either in relation to territorial claims or to the procurement of economic and political advantage" (Paschalidis 2008: 4). Friendly communities abroad are often constructed in opposition to a set of enemy emigrants. In the case of Yugoslavia, for example, this took the form of differentiated policies between the old migration (*staro iseljeništvo*) and the Yugoslav Enemy Migration (*Jugoslavenska Neprijateljska Emigracija*). Yet such policies were widespread. In 1955, China marked a strong distinction between overseas Chinese citizens (*huaren*) and overseas ethnic Chinese (*huayi*) (Biao 2003: 28). Toward friendly populations, governments deploy(ed) a set of cultural institutions abroad, such as cultural centers, schools, or even religious institutions, thereby exporting the monopoly over the national, official culture. However, such policies are traditionally conceived as temporary and as a means of returning these populations to the homeland—the only other alternative for normalizing the situation being territorial annexation.

Regardless of the particular interests that governments might address by categorizing populations abroad and drafting and implementing specific policies oriented toward them, it appears that these governmental rationalities share the fundamental assumption of the disciplinary form of government—namely, the idea that the optimal condition of the political existence is the nation-state. In a sense, these practices of power could correspond to the circular topology (that is, the "spatialization and temporalization of relations of power"[9]) of bounded units as the foundation for governmental rationalities. Economic models are based on a national space as well as high tariff barriers. All these projects seem destined to reduce mobility, avoiding territorial dispersion and creating and maintaining a clearly bounded and homogeneous inside and outside. Although diasporic connections continue in settings common to dictatorships, protectionist developmental states, or autarchic political ventures, they appear to share the commonality of being judged as negative, suspicious, and forced into the private sphere (Schnapper 2001: 13).

This could be consistent with Michel Foucault's concept of the disciplinary modality of government. According to Foucault, modality takes its roots in the mercantilist political economy born in the sixteenth and seventeenth centuries and has given birth to policies essentially destined to territorialize and homogenize populations (Foucault 2004: 7). The mercantilist political economy is more than a simple economic doctrine; it is a modality of rule of production according to three principles of monetary enrichment of the state, permanent competition with other foreign powers, and strong populationist policies. Mercantilism in this regard is fiercely opposed to emigration (Foucault 2004: 46, 71). Concurrent with mercantilist principles, the disciplinary moment sees a firm affirmation of the division between the inside and outside technologies of power, such as between the police and the army. Similarly, in disciplinary moments, projects of national homogenization emerge. It is not by accident that the traditional institutions of nation-building—schools, factories, and armies—are also the institutions Foucault identified as the paradigmatic institutions where the logic of discipline is concentrated (Noiriel 1996; Foucault 1976; Weber 1976). In sum, the disciplinary modality of government is essentially concerned with territoriality (Foucault 2004: 113).

Liberal governmentality and guest worker programs

The guest worker programs of the 1960s and 1970s correspond to a logic that appears to take root in a different tradition of the political economy of power, which could be defined as part of liberal governmentality. According to Foucault, liberal governmentality originated at the turn of the eighteenth century in the writings of the physiocrats, who promoted a counter-mercantilist understanding of the state with the goal of limiting its coercive power. Population comes to be conceived not as a collective of subjects, but as "a set of processes that have to be managed in their naturality and from their naturality" through calculation, analysis, and reflection on how to influence and take advantage of them (Foucault 2004: 72, 74). However, liberal governmental rationality still functions through a territorial referent: the target of the government is the national population located within a territory. It can be divided into two historical phases.

The early days of liberal governmentality, which is associated with the Industrial Revolution, seem to be concurrent with the emergence of a host of governmental practices characterized as "safety-valve" policies (Hirschman 1978). In liberal rationality, the problem is not with depopulation, but with overpopulation. A line of thought born of Malthusianism asserts that the government's aim is to match the numbers of the population to the resources of the territory; hence, surplus labor forces must be eliminated. Austria-Hungary's policies toward Croatian emigration fall within this context. Yet the practices of "shoveling out" the unwanted, as evident in England's policy toward Irish Catholics in the mid-nineteenth century,[10] Italy's policies toward southerners in the 1910s,[11] Japan's "dumping people" (*Kimin Seisaku*) policies in the first half of the twentieth century (Endoh 2000: 1), and Cuba's more recent policies in 1965–1973 and the 1980s,[12] appear widespread in this logic of solving social and political problems by exporting them (Green 2005: 273; Zolberg 1983: 33). Two elements often come to modify such safety-valve practices over time. First, governments realize and come to encourage the potential benefits of a migration that is not definitive, but rotating between alleviating unemployment and attracting foreign currency. Second, in response to domestic political struggles, governments come to adopt the logic of care developed by a broad range of non-governmental social actors (nationalist and socialist movements, emigrant societies, philanthropists, newspaper editors, and religious organizations such as the Scalabrinians or the Franciscans). The government is forced to adopt a social approach through technologies of social welfare and social insurance (Rose *et al.* 2006: 91).

In this context, guest worker programs first emerged in post-war Europe and in the United States as a way of engineering a rotational migration, thereby tapping into the labor of migratory workers for the purposes of national development, but with the obligation of exporting modalities of long-distance governmental care (Zolberg 1989: 408). To date, guest worker programs have involved very large sections of national populations. The Mexican Bracero Programme (1942–1964) involved four million Mexicans, and guest worker programs in Europe between 1960 and 1975 involved more than 30 million workers from Italy, Greece, Turkey, Yugoslavia, Algeria, Morocco, Spain, and Portugal (Reichert and Massey 1982: 3). Similarly planned programs of labor exportation were later set up in other regions, such as the Philippines in the mid-1970s (Gonzalez 1998: 119) and China in the mid-1980s (Biao 2003: 32). The expected goal for the sending country is always the same; to alleviate unemployment, gain skills from abroad, and produce foreign currency returns. The official categorizations always explicitly denote the functional identity assigned to migrants entering this modality of government as workers who are temporarily abroad.

For example, such workers were called "workers temporarily employed abroad" in Yugoslavia (Baučić 1975) and "*braceros*" in Mexico (Gonzalez 1998: 119). In terms of practices of power—at least for those who came to Europe—these programs govern emigrants not so much through disciplinary practices of policing as through the typical welfare technology of insurance (Ewald 1986). In fact, through a vast array of bilateral agreements, guest workers become caught up in various healthcare, social help, and pension programs that serve as modalities of the "conduct of conducts," the main goal being to keep the populations in circulation, as exemplified by the cases of Turkey and Yugoslavia (Zimmerman 1987; Paine 1974). Recently, Chinese emigration agencies have gone so far as to provide

> information about emigration prospects, helping with passport and visa applications, establishing connections with the destination countries [...]. Some offer settlement services in the destination country such as registering for medical insurance, obtaining driving licenses, opening bank accounts, and providing English language training.
>
> (Biao 2003: 35)

But governmental plans are always prone to fail. For Foucault, the main dichotomy for liberal governmentality falls between the population and the populace. In other words, this dichotomy refers to "those who do not behave rationally according to the calculus planned for the population" (Foucault 2004: 46). In this case, the populace are temporary migrants who cease to circulate and become permanent migrants. This phenomenon was not anticipated by policy makers in either Europe or the United States, but ultimately came to prominence through the sheer number of *braceros* and guest workers who became permanent immigrants.

Therefore, guest worker programs seem possible in the context of precise configurations in the world system and when driven by the short-term interests of governments in harnessing economic gains through the circulation of sections of the population into the international division of labor. However, more importantly, these programs appear to be made possible by a deeper shift in the rationalities of power and particularly the passage from a sovereign rationality of government obsessed with governing a territorialized population to a liberal governmentality in which a derogation of the territorial model is possible, with the condition that it be temporary. Yet the profusion of pejorative folk terms designating labor emigrants in the home countries—"Nuyoricans" (Puerto Rico), "Gastići" (Yugoslavia), American Born Confused Indians or ABCDs (India), "Pochos" (Mexico), "Jook-sing" (China), and "Yordim" (Israel)—highlights that emigration in the liberal governmentality is still considered as suspicious and deviating from the territorialized, domestic existence. Although the practice of power suggests a different topology, the imaginary remains bound to the territorial state.

The neo-liberal movement toward the government of diasporas

The current state of affairs also departs significantly from the liberal or welfare-liberal conditions in which guest worker programs originated. This is not to say that the previous rationalities are not being currently deployed. In the Croatian case, one could argue that the policies of the 1990s are still very much disciplinary modalities of government. Yet the overall decline of the welfare state and the failure of socialist economies have given rise to the progressive diffusion of what is commonly called a neo-liberal or advanced liberal form of governmentality, intended not only as an economic doctrine, but also as a form of government (Barry *et al.* 1993; Rose 1999). Two important changes have occurred with this new political economy of power. First, the economic frame of reference for what it is to be governed is no longer thought of purely in terms of national territories. In other words, competition is no longer predominantly international, but local, regional, and transnational. Hence, policies oriented toward providing welfare are progressively dismantled and become segmented in service to particular professional sectors, geographic locales, or types of activity. Second, the advanced liberal political economy brings about the idea that individuals are no longer to be passively and collectively governed through the impersonal figure of the state (through healthcare, social security, etc.); rather, they should be active in their own government. As a result, forms of allegiance and responsibilities are oriented toward the local, and circles of solidarity are increasingly located in the community. By defining this process as the "death of the social," Rose remarked that "such virtual communities are 'diasporic'; they exist only to the extent that their constituents are linked together through identifications constructed in the non-geographic spaces of activist discourses, cultural products and media images" (Rose 1996: 333).

This is the framework in which practices aimed at governing diasporas or global nations appear to emerge as a displacement of the legitimate object of government from populations within a territory (the social) to populations irrespective of their physical territorial location, according to new criteria of inclusion and exclusion (the diasporic community, "emigrant Croatia," or simply the global nation). Second, these rationalities of government are not concerned with population return or territorial expansion, as in the disciplinary moment, or with circulation, as in the liberal moment; rather, they are primarily concerned with dispersion as a resource and a legitimate modality of political existence. This takes place at several levels.

The first level is that of symbolic politics. Groups abroad previously categorized separately as immigrants, refugees, political exiles, and guest workers are now being re-labeled as diasporas, global nations, or nations abroad; sending states have actively participated in these symbolic politics (Brubaker 2005; Schnapper 2001; Smith 2003a: 728). The terms *diaspora* and *global nation* imply a remapping of the boundaries of belonging and constitute a new dichotomy between the included and the excluded that is independent of territorial considerations. The new official identities, despite being the result of a long

Conclusion: governing diasporas in IR 191

process of nationalization, are exported and repackaged in essentialist terms, as evident in the examples of "italianità" (Italianness), "magyarság" (Hungarianness), and "mexicanidad" (Mexican-ness) (Waterbury 2008: 5; Gonzalez Gutierrez 1999: 546). Previously pejorative terms have become the object of stigma reversals, such as the valorization of the "pochos" by the Programme for Mexican Communities Abroad (Smith 2003a: 728). Heads of states now embrace previously forgotten populations. For example, Zionism was based on a negation of the diasporic existence, but Ariel Sharon recently announced that he understood his mandate as unifying not only Israel but "Jews worldwide" (Shain and Bristman 2002: 77). Furthermore, Mexico's president Vicente Fox announced in 2000 that he would "govern on behalf of 118 million Mexicans"—18 million of which are living in the USA (Varadarajan 2005: 1). Mary Robinson declared that she was the prime minister of Irish everywhere in the world (Gray 2006: 360–361). These symbolic policies take various other forms, such as large conferences and congresses (Østergaard-Nielsen 2003) as well as national diaspora days like the Pravasi Bharatiya Diwas in India (Jaffrelot and Therwath 2007: 293).

Second, diasporas are increasingly becoming a specific state category, which has been translated into administrative modifications of sending states and a multiplication of diaspora ministries and agencies, such as the Ministry of Diaspora in Serbia and Armenia, the Institute for Mexicans Abroad in Mexico, the Irish Abroad Unit in Ireland, the Ministry of Italians Abroad in Italy, the Commission on Filipinos Overseas (Gonzalez 1998: 120), the Overseas Employment Office in China (Biao 2003: 33), and a broad range of diaspora ministries across the Middle East and Africa (Gamlen 2009: 8). Moreover, specific legal statuses and identification documents are often given to expatriates, such as nonresident Indians (NRI) and persons of Indian origin (PIO) in India (Jaffrelot and Therwath 2007) or Matricula Consular in Mexico. Similar types of statuses exist in Argentina, Colombia, Salvador, Honduras, Peru, Morocco, Pakistan, and Turkey (Gamlen 2009; Lomeli-Azoubel 2002).

Third, in addition to long-distance practices of labor management, cultural inculcation, and political policing, sending states are increasingly requiring their populations abroad to act as lobbyists or as a privatization of the state's foreign policy. This has famously been the case for Israel, but it is also now proliferating in other countries, including Mexico, Eritrea, Greece, and Macedonia (Østergaard-Nielsen 2003; Skrbiš 1999; Shain and Bristman 2002: 79–80; Smith 2003b). Similarly, diaspora politics justify what was previously labeled as kin-state politics or proxy-politics, in which ethnic minorities of neighboring states are instrumentalized by their homelands (e.g., Hungary and Romania over Transylvania or Russia toward its minorities abroad) (Ragazzi 2008; Waterbury 2006; Laruelle 2006; King and Melvin 1999). In return—and as a result of political struggles—populations abroad have increasingly obtained dual citizenship, voting rights, and even the right to hold public office; they even have dedicated representation in parliaments (Bauböck 2005; Faist 2001). However, practices of citizenship have often had little to do with populations abroad and have been used as techniques of domestic ethnic engineering to exclude minority groups in the name of including the majority abroad.

As a result, everything happens as if the neo-liberal production of community "as a logic of governing that migrates and is selectively taken up in diverse political contexts" (Ong 2007: 3) created communitarianism in immigration contexts and forms of diasporic governmentality in emigration contexts. But these appear to be two sides of the same coin, indicating a shift in the criteria of belonging from territorial criteria to criteria of race, religion, or ethnicity (Glick Schiller and Fouron 1999; Skrbiš 1999). Recent studies have highlighted transnational nationalism as a new version of the traditional ethnic nationalism (Kastoryano 2006). Drawing on these debates in nationalism studies, it could be argued that diasporic nationalism is a form of nationalism that corresponds to the globalized and transnational neo-liberal modality of government. Twentieth-century projects of national homogenization or even annexation—characteristic of the disciplinary state—have been abandoned as too costly. Instead, the new boundaries of government draw, reinforce, and reinvent previous demarcations—namely, communities. Citizenship and the criteria of belonging have become the new exclusionary criteria. This goes hand in hand with the legitimization of transnational politics. In the two previous moments the nation-state model remained the referent despite transnational governmental practices; in the neo-liberal moment, the diasporic condition is legitimized and normalized. Dispersion is considered an economic and political resource—economically through the constant flow of remittances and politically through the claim of channeling political lobbying. What Didier Bigo outlined for the government of immigration holds true for the government of emigration:

> Topology of security in democracies is no longer the elegant cylinder, but a complicated form, the Klein bottle. The opening of sovereign borders destroys the security construct of a homogeneous society […]. In this case, freedom is limited by a new security device: monitoring of minorities and of diasporas. Identity fences replace territorial fences. While people are allowed to move, their identities must be constructed and controlled. To achieve this Klein bottle process, people need to be reduced to the status of a herd that has only the right to bread and circuses. However this fails to take account of the social practices of resistance and of indifference […]. This transnational program will fail when governments try to enforce it.
> (Bigo 2001: 115)

Further research directions

As Aihwa Ong remarked vis-à-vis the industrializing states in Southeast Asia, "rather than accept claims about the end of sovereignty, we need to explore mutations in the ways in which localized political and social organizations set the terms and are constitutive of a domain of social existence" (Ong 2003: 40). I hope to have shown herein that, although governmental practices toward their

Conclusion: governing diasporas in IR   193

populations abroad can be contradictory and confusing, they can be made more intelligible through an understanding of the broader material, intellectual and political contexts in which they emerge, and particularly the governmental rationality that underpins them. The contemporary proliferation of the diasporic discourse and the social and political struggles associated with it must be understood primarily as political processes that ultimately seek to legitimize a radical shift in the way governments organize the relationships between power and territory. Such a shift deeply questions the traditional Westphalian principle of territoriality. By moving away from juridico-legal conceptions of sovereignty, one can better understand the evolution of the transnationalization processes of governmental practices. Therefore, the discourse of diaspora seems to go hand in hand with the transnationalization of power underpinned by the neo-liberal agenda, described by others as the death of the social and the rise of government through communities (Rose 1996).

Still, the different logics I have outlined here are not intended as historical serializations or as a teleological conception of the evolution of governmentality; instead, they must be understood as a heterogeneous set of rationalizations and practices of power that emerge and become dominant in determinate political and historical contexts. This does not mean that the previous rationalities and practices disappear (Foucault 2004: 109). Indeed, more often than not, governments go back and forth between one form of rationality and the other. Multiple rationalities often coexist and overlap in different bureaucracies, struggling with one another even within the same state. Governmental practices are therefore not the result of a national interest, but rather of the domination of a principle of vision within the bureaucratic and political field.

It seems clear, then, that this conclusion is simply scratching the surface of a phenomenon in need of a good deal of further research. What remains to be explained is how, within domestic bureaucratic struggles, transnational networks of migration and security professionals, and international organizations such as the OECD, the ILO, the UN, the UNDP, the World Bank, and now the EU, we have passed from one rationality to the other. The modalities of change are in fact not mere discursive shifts, but very concrete social and political struggles located in specific institutions. Drawing on the Paris school's approach to the sociology of the professionals of (in)security as well as other scholars who have mapped transnational networks,[13] a thorough analysis of the ideologies of migration and the practical effects they have produced could be a fruitful avenue for future research.

A second possible avenue for research arises from the fact that governmental programs are not diagrams. Practices of power fail to meet their planned objective; they nearly always encounter resistance, bringing new rationalizations and new practices. Comparisons across both history and cases are still needed to map the diagram of these governmental practices to define in which precise locales they are connected to broader principles of the neoliberalization of the state, how persistent the old practices are, which agencies are involved, and what the specific discursive and non-discursive techniques and modalities are through which practices are exported and exerted. Similarly, detailed comparisons are needed to map the newly emerging categorizations and the way in which new functions and responsibilities are attributed to these new categories.

Finally, scholarship needs to take stock of the current counter-conduct emerging in response to the neo-liberal diasporic governmentality. First, one element intentionally left out of the article are the practices of resistance and subjectivities that arise from diasporic organizations and institutions. Diasporic institutions and subjects have been presented here only in light of the practices of power to which they are subjected, yet every analysis of governmental diaspora policies needs to consider the counter-practices enacted by these social actors, which again requires a detailed empirical study as these practices can lead to the development of alternative narratives or instead the appropriation and reinforcement of the governmental practices to which they are subjected. Second, as is often the case, the most effective resistance comes from within the power structures. What are the alternative concepts of belonging and citizenship being articulated in, for example, the Council of Europe as opposed to the European Commission? UNESCO as opposed to the World Bank? Although such research is already in progress to a certain extent, more studies ought to take into account the formulations of belonging that question the deterritorialized exclusionary boundary-making process of diasporic policies and establish other principles that consider the new structures imposed by globalization processes (Bauböck 2005: 685–686; Faist 2000). What forms do they take, in which structural conditions do they evolve, and what resources can be mobilized?

This research promises to revisit the fundamental questions posed by critical scholarship about the untangling of identities, borders, and orders (Albert *et al.* 2001) as well as the territorial trap (Agnew 1994) and formulate alternative topologies to imagine and conceptualize the international, such as the Moebius ribbon proposed by Didier Bigo (Bigo and Walker 2007) from an unexpected angle for IR theory.

Notes

1 Parts of this chapter previously appeared in Ragazzi, F. (2009) "Governing Diasporas," *International Political Sociology*, 3(4), pp. 378–397. Reproduced by permission of Oxford University Press.
2 See India's *High Level Committee Report on the Indian Diaspora* (Singhvi 2002).
3 See the discussion of John Searle with Derrideans and the distinction between brute and institutional facts (Searle 1995).
4 See the heated discussion between Bourdieu and Wacquant (1999) on one hand and Michael Hanchard (2003) on the other.
5 For example, Bourdieu argued that deciding if the relevant division of French society is between rich and poor or between nationals and foreigners implies very different politics (Bourdieu 2000: 60).
6 For a detailed critique of Yossi Shain and mainstream constructivism, see Varadarajan 2005: 31–39.
7 According to Brubaker, "a groupist reading conflates groups with the organizations that claim to speak and act in their name; obscures the generally low, though

fluctuating degree of 'groupness' in this setting; accepts, at least tacitly, the claims of nationalist politicians to speak for the groups they claim to represent; and neglects the everyday contexts in which ethnic and national categories take on meaning and the processes through which ethnicity actually 'works' in everyday life" (Brubaker 2007: 9).

8 As evidence of Adamson's uncomfortable position between constructivism and the realist IR tradition, we can quote her a priori definition of diaspora, which is reminiscent of the categorical brand of definitions:

> A diaspora can be defined as a social collectivity that exists across state borders and that has succeeded over time to (1) sustain a collective national, cultural or religious identity through a sense of internal cohesion and sustained ties with a real or imagined homeland and (2) display an ability to address the collective interests of members of the social collectivity through a developed internal organizational framework and transnational links.
>
> (Adamson and Demetriou 2007: 497)

On the other hand, this definition is footnoted as follows:

> Definitions of "diaspora" have been hotly contested in the literature, making it, like the state, an "essentially contested concept" (Connolly 1993). For examples of definitions of diaspora, see Cohen (1996, 1997); Esman (1986); Safran (1991); Sheffer (1993). We do not attempt to resolve the debate here, but rather survey the existing literature to suggest the contours of what the category of diaspora in IR would include.
>
> (Adamson and Demetriou 2007: 517)

9 See Bigo and Walker (2007: 733).
10 Gray (2006).
11 Cinel, 1991, quoted in Smith (2003a: 738).
12 Camarioca and Mariel cited in Colomer (2000: 435–436).
13 See Dezalay (2001), for example.

References

Adamson, F. and Demetriou, M. (2007) "Remapping the Boundaries of 'State' and 'National Identity': Incorporating Diasporas into IR Theorizing," *European Journal of International Relations*, 13(4), pp. 489–526.

Agnew, J. A. (1994) "The Territorial Trap: The Geographical Assumptions of International Relations Theory," *Review of International Political Economy*, 1(1), pp. 53–80.

Albert, M., Jacobson, D., Lapid, Y., *et al.* (2001) *Identities, Borders, Orders: Rethinking International Relations Theory*, Minneapolis, MN; London: University of Minnesota Press.

Anderson, B. (1998) *The Spectre of Comparisons: Nationalism, Southeast Asia and the World* (p. 374), London: Verso.

Barry, A., Osborne, T., and Rose, N. (1993) "Liberalism, Neo-Liberalism, and Governmentality: Introduction," *Economy and Society*, 22(3), pp. 265–266.

Bauböck, R. (2005) "Expansive Citizenship—Voting beyond Territory and Membership," *PS: Political Science & Politics*, 38(4), p. 5.

Baučić, I. (1975) *The Social Aspects of External Migration of Workers and the Yugoslav Experience in the Social Protection of Migrants*, Zagreb: Center for Migration Studies.

Biao, X. (2003) "Emigration from China: A Sending Country Perspective," *International Migration*, 41(3), pp. 21–48.

Bigo, D. (2001) "The Moebius Ribbon of Internal and External Security(ies)" in Albert, M., Jacobson, D., and Lapid, Y., eds., *Identities, Borders, Orders: Rethinking International Relations Theory* (p. 349), Minneapolis, MN; London: University of Minnesota Press.

Bigo, D. (2008) "Globalized (in)Security, The Field and the Ban-Opticon" in Bigo, D. and Tsoukala, A., eds., *Terror, Insecurity and Liberty: Illiberal Practices of Liberal Regimes after 9/11* (pp. 10–48), London; New York: Routledge.

Bigo, D. and Walker, R. B. J. (2007) "Political Sociology and the Problem of the International," *Millennium*, 35(3), p. 16.

Bourdieu, P. (2000) *Propos sur le champ politique*, Lyon: P.U.L.

Bourdieu, P. and Wacqant, L. (1999) "On the Cunning of Imperialist Reason," *Theory, Culture & Society*, 16(1), p. 18.

Brubaker, R. (2005) "The 'Diaspora' Diaspora," *Ethnic and Racial Studies*, 28(1), pp. 1–19.

Brubaker, R. (2007) *Nationalist Politics and Everyday Ethnicity in a Transylvanian Town*, Princeton, NJ; Woodstock: Princeton University Press.

Colomer, J. (2000) "Exit, Voice and Hostility in Cuba," *The International Migration Review: IMR*, 34(2), pp. 423–442.

Cordes, B. (1986) *Qaddafi: Idealist and Revolutionary Philanthropist*, Santa Monica, CA: Rand Corporation.

Dezalay, Y. and Garth, B. (2001) "The Legal Construction of a Policy of Notables: The Double-Dealing of Patrician Lawyers in India in the Market of Civic Virtue," *Genèses: Sciences Sociales et Histoire*, 45, pp. 69–90.

Dumont, L. (1966) *Homo Hierarchicus, Essai Sur le Système des Castes*, Paris: Gallimard.

Endoh, T. (2000) "Shedding the Unwanted: Japan's Emigration Policy in a Historical Perspective," Columbia University, New York, PhD dissertation.

Ewald, F. (1986) *L'Etat providence*, Paris: B. Grasset.

Faist, T. (2000) "Transnationalization in International Migration: Implications for the Study of Citizenship and Culture," *Ethnic and Racial Studies*, 23(2), pp. 189–222.

Faist, T. (2001) "Dual Citizenship as Overlapping Membership," *Willy Brandt Series of Working Papers in International Migration and Ethnic Relations* 3, Malmö, Sweden: Malmö University School of International Migration and Ethnic Relations.

Foucault, M. (1976) *Surveiller et punir: Naissance de la prison*, Paris: Gallimard.

Foucault, M. (2004) *Sécurité, territoire, population: Cours au Collège de France (1977–1978)*, Paris: Gallimard, Seuil.

Gallissot, R. and Kergoat, J. (1997) *Mehdi Ben Barka: De l'indépendance marocaine à la Tricontinentale*, Paris: Éditions Karthala.

Gamlen, A. (2009) "The Emigration State and the Modern Geopolitical Imagination," *Political Geography*, 27(8), pp. 840–856.

Georgakakis, D. (2002) *Les métiers de l'Europe politique: Acteurs et professionnalisations de l'Union européenne*, Strasbourg: Presses Universitaires de Strasbourg.

Glick Schiller, N. and Fouron, G. (1999) "Terrains of Blood and Nation: Haitian Transnational Social Fields," *Ethnic and Racial Studies*, 22(2), pp. 340–366.

Goldfarb, A. and Litvinenko, M. (2008) *Death of a Dissident: The Poisoning of Alexander Litvinenko and the Return of the KGB*, London: Pocket.

Gonzalez, J. L. (1998) *Philippine Labour Migration: Critical Dimensions of Public Policy*, Singapore: Institute of Southeast Asian Studies.

Gonzalez Gutierrez, C. (1999) "Rethinking History and the Nation-State: Mexico and the United States as a Case Study—Migrants and the Nation-State—Fostering Identities: Mexico's Relations with Its Diaspora," *The Journal of American History*, 86(2), p. 23.

Gray, B. (2006) "Redefining the Nation through Economic Growth and Migration: Changing Rationalities of Governance in the Republic of Ireland?" *Mobilities*, 1(3), p. 19.

Green, N. L. (2005) "The Politics of Exit: Reversing the Immigration Paradigm," *The Journal of Modern History*, 77(2), p. 27.

Hanchard, M. (2003) "Acts of Misrecognition: Transnational Black Politics, Anti-Imperialism and the Ethnocentrisms of Pierre Bourdieu and Loïc Wacquant," *Theory, Culture & Society*, 20(4), pp. 5–29.

Hirschman, A. (1978) "Exit, Voice, and the State," *World Politics*, 31(1), pp. 90–107.

Itzigsohn, J. and Saucedo, S. G. (2002) "Immigrant Incorporation and Sociocultural Transnationalism," *The International Migration Review: IMR*, 36(3), p. 33.

Jaffrelot, C. and Therwath, I. (2007) "The Sangh Parivar and the Hindu Diaspora in the West: What Kind of 'Long-Distance Nationalism'?" *International Political Sociology*, 1(3), pp. 278–295.

Kastoryano, R. (2006) "Vers un nationalisme transnational. Redéfinir la nation, le nationalisme et le territoire," *Revue Française de Science Politique*, 56(4), pp. 533–555.

King, C. and Melvin, N. (1999) *Nations Abroad: Diaspora Politics and International Relations in the Former Soviet Union*, Boulder, CO: Westview Press.

Kostov, V. (1988) *The Bulgarian Umbrella: The Soviet Direction and Operations of the Bulgarian Secret Service in Europe*, Hemel Hempstead, UK; New York: Harvester Press; St Martin's Press.

Laruelle, M. (2006) "La question des Russes du proche-étranger en Russie (1991–2006)," *Les Etudes du CERI*, 126 (May).

Levitt, P. and Schiller, N. G. (2004) "Conceptualizing Simultaneity: A Transnational Social Field Perspective on Society," *International Migration Review*, 38(3), pp. 1002–1039.

Lomeli-Azoubel, R. P. (2002) *La matricula consular y los servicios bancarios*, Los Angeles: Cónsul General de México.

Marienstras, R. (1985) "Sur la notion de diaspora" in Minorités Gpl, ed., *Les Minorités à l'Age de l'Etat Nation*, Paris: Fayard.

Noiriel, G. (1996) *The French Melting Pot: Immigration, Citizenship, and National Identity*, Minneapolis, MN; London: University of Minnesota Press.

Ong, A. (2003) "Zones of Sovereignty in South East Asia" in Perry, R. W. and Maurer, B., eds., *Globalization Under Construction: Governmentality, Law, and Identity* (pp. xxi, 367), Minneapolis, MN: University of Minnesota Press.

Ong, A. (2007) "Boundary Crossings: Neoliberalism as a Mobile Technology," *Transactions of the Institute of British Geographers*, 32(1), pp. 3–8.

Østergaard-Nielsen, E. (2003) *International Migration and Sending Countries: Perceptions, Policies, and Transnational Relations*, Basingstoke, UK; New York: Palgrave Macmillan.

Paine, S. (1974) *Exporting Workers, the Turkish Case*, London: Cambridge University Press.

Paschalidis, G. (2008) "Exporting National Culture: Histories of Cultural Institutes Abroad," 5th International Conference on Cultural Policy Research, Istanbul.

Pinsker, L. (1947) *Auto-Emancipation*, London: Rita Searl.

Portes, A., Guarnizo, L., and Landolt, P. (1999) "The Study of Transnationalism: Pitfalls and Promise of an Emergent Research Field," *Ethnic and Racial Studies*, 22(2), pp. 217–237.

Pries, L. (2001) "The Disruption of Social and Geographic Space: Mexican–US: Migration and the Emergence of Transnational Social Spaces," *International Sociology*, 16(1), pp. 55–74.

Ragazzi, F. (2008) "Annexation Without Territory? Diaspora Politics and Irredentism in Post-Dayton Croatia and Bosnia-Herzegovina," International Studies Association 49th Convention, San Francisco.

Reichert, J. S. and Massey, D. S. (1982) "Guestworker Programs: Evidence from Europe and the United States and Some Implications for US Policy," *Population Research and Policy Review*, 1(1), pp. 1–17.

Rigoni, I. (2000) "Du processus identitaires kurde à l'extrusion de la souveraineté turque," *CEMOTI*, 30, pp. 203–218.

Rose, N. (1996) "The Death of the Social? Re-Figuring the Territory of Government," *Economy and Society*, 25(3), pp. 327–356.

Rose, N. (1999) *Governing the Soul: The Shaping of the Private Self*, London; New York: Free Association Books.

Rose, N., O'Malley, P., and Valverde, M. (2006) "Governmentality," *Annual Review of Law and Social Science*, 2(1), pp. 83–104.

Schnapper, D. (2001) "De l'Etat-nation au monde transnational (Du sens et de l'utilité du concept de diaspora)," *Revue Européenne des Migrations Internationales*, 17(2), pp. 9–36.

Searle, J. R. (1995) *The Construction of Social Reality*, London: Allen Lane.

Shain, Y. (1990) *The Frontier of Loyalty: Political Exiles in the Age of the Nation-State*, Middletown, CT: Wesleyan University Press.

Shain, Y. and Barth, A. (2003) "Diasporas and International Relations Theory," *International Organization*, 57(3), pp. 449–479.

Shain, Y. and Bristman, B. (2002) "Diaspora, Kinship and Loyalty: The Renewal of Jewish National Security," *International Affairs*, 78(1), pp. 69–95.

Singhvi, L. M. (2002) *High Level Committee Report on the Indian Diaspora*, New Delhi: Government of India.

Skrbiš, Z. (1999) *Long-Distance Nationalism: Diasporas, Homelands and Identities*, Brookfield, VT: Ashgate.

Smith, R. C. (2003a) "Diasporic Memberships in Historical Perspective: Comparative Insights from the Mexican, Italian and Polish Cases," *The International Migration Review: IMR*, 37(3), p. 36.

Smith, R. C. (2003b) "Migrant Membership as an Instituted Process: Transnationalization, the State and the Extra-Territorial Conduct of Mexican Politics," *The International Migration Review: IMR*, 37(2), p. 47.

Torpey, J. (1998) "Aller et venir: le monopole étatique des moyens légitimes de circulation," *Cultures et Conflits*, 31–32 (automne/hiver), pp. 63–100.

Totaro-Genevois, M. (2005) *Cultural and Linguistic Policy Abroad: The Italian Experience*, Clevedon, UK: Multilingual Matters Limited.

Varadarajan, L. (2005) *Producing the Domestic Abroad: Diasporas in International Relations*, PhD thesis, University of Minnesota.

Waterbury, M. (2006) "Internal Exclusion, External Inclusion: Diaspora Politics and Party-Building Strategies in Post-Communist Hungary," *East European Politics & Societies*, 20(3), pp. 483–515.

Waterbury, M. A. (2008) "Bridging the Divide: Towards a Comparative Framework for Understanding Kin-State and Migrant Sending-State Diaspora Politics," International Studies Annual Convention, San Francisco.

Weber, E. J. (1976) *Peasants into Frenchmen: The Modernization of Rural France, 1870–1914*, Stanford, CA: Stanford University Press.

Wimmer, A. and Schiller, N. G. (2002) "Methodological Nationalism and Beyond: Nation-State Building, Migration, and the Social Sciences," *Global Networks*, 2(4), pp. 301–334.

Zimmerman, W. (1987) *Open Borders, Nonalignment, and the Political Evolution of Yugoslavia*, Princeton, NJ: Princeton University Press.

Zolberg, A. (1983) "The Formation of New States as a Refugee-Generating Process," *Annals of the American Academy of Political and Social Science*, 467(1).

Zolberg, A. (1989) "The Next Waves: Migration Theory for a Changing World," *The International Migration Review: IMR*, 23(3), pp. 403–430.

Index

11th district of expatriate voters 166–7

Act on Areas of Special State Concern (Croatia 2003) 148
Act on Temporary Take-Over and Administration of Specified Property (Croatia 1995) 148
Act on the Deprivation of Citizenship for Officers, etc. (Yugoslavia 1948) 137
Adamić, Louis 61
African diasporas 9–11
Alexander, King of Yugoslavia 34
All-German School Association 186
AMAC (Almae Matris Alumni Croaticae) 124
American Croatian Relief Project 96
American Slav Congress 61
Anderson, Benedict 14, 76n2
Appadurai, Arjun 12
Aranički, Fedor 35
Argentina, Croatian organizations in 63
Army of Bosnia and Herzegovina (ARBiH) 160, 163, 174n12
Army of the Republika Srpska 162
Assembly of Serbs in Bosnia 161
Austin, John 8–9
Australia, unofficial "Croatian Embassy" 73
Austria, Austro-Hungarian states governed by 29
Austro-Hungarian Empire, emigration under 26–30
autarchy strategy 40

Babić, Ivan 68–9
Badinovac, John 66
Baker, James 102
Bakery, Vladimir 84
banovinas 17n2
Baratta, Mira Radielović 124

Barešić, Miro 69, 74
Bartulica, Milostislav 32
Bashir government of Sudan 9
Baskin, Mark 45
Baučić, Ivo 45
Bauman, Zygmunt 12
Beljo, Ante: attains power in Croatia 112; heads *Matica* 121–2; in nationalist campaign 2; links to Norval center 75; on Israeli model 114–15
belonging, politics of 134–56
Ben Barka, Mehdi 186
Benhabib, Seyla 135–6, 150n1
Benkovac police station attack 95–6
Bigo, Didier 192, 194
Billig, Michael 173
biological survival, diaspora as threat to 113–15
Bishop's Conference for Croatian Migration 42
Bleiburg Massacre 1945 39, 52n46
Boban, Mate 125, 162, 164
Bonifačić, Antun 63
Boric, Gojko 87
Bosna–Herceg *see* Herceg–Bosna
Bosnia–Herzegovina: Croatian component in funded by Zagreb 168–9; Croatia's relations with 16–17, 157–76; Croats in considered citizens of Croatia 138–9; divisive policy in 123–4; Federation of Bosnia and Herzegovina 165; Herceg–Bosna 16, 157, 162, 167
Bosnian–Serb army 164–5
Bosno–Croatian Army 168–9
Bougarel, Xavier 160
Bourdieu, Pierre: and methodological nationalism 179–80; on doxa 79n42; on the practical *epochè* 83–4 on speech acts 9

Index

Bracero Programme 188–9
Brah, Avtar 7
Brezhnev, Leonid 44
Brkić, Križan 73
Brozovich, Franck 126
Bubalo, Steve 91, 100
Buchanan, Pat 103–4
Budiša, Dražen 72, 87
Bulgarian umbrella affair 11
Burrai, Valentina 146
Bušić, Bruno 68–71, 73–4
Bušić, Zvonko 69
Butković, Ivan 62, 77n5
Buzan, Barry 18n10

Campbell, David 164
Canada: Croatian World Congress in 122–3; Croats from return to homeland 112; wealthy Herzogovinians in 87; *see also* Norval group
Carter, Sean 97, 131n40
Cartographies of Diaspora (Brah) 7
categorization of diaspora 25, 111–33
Centre for Migration Studies, Zagreb 42
centre for returnees opened in Zagreb 120
Ćesić Rojs, Ljubo 168
CFU *see* Croatian Fraternal Union
"Cherishing the Irish Diaspora" 11
China: economic importance of remittances to 5; policy on expatriate citizens 186, 189; recognition of non-resident status by 191
Cikoj, Ante 73
circular migration 33–4, 50n15
citizenship: Croatian law 134–56, 151n9, 151n10, 151n14, 152n16; diaspora and 134–56; dual 6; for non-residents 191–2
Clifford, James 7–8
Clinton, Bill 103–4
Cohen, Robin 7–8
Collier, Paul 82–3, 104
colonialism, diaspora in 35–6
Cominform 52n42
Communal Council in Split 29
communism in Croatian political field 60
conflict, diasporas as source of 104
Constitutional Act on National Minorities (Croatia 2000) 144–5, 148
Constitutional Act (Croatia 2010) 143
constructivist approach 182
Čorić, Šimun Šito 122
Council of Emigrants' Organizations 35–6
counter-conducts 59

Croatia *see* Croatia–Slavonia; Kingdom of Serbs, Croats and Slovenes; Republic of Croatia; Socialist Republic of Croatia
Croatian American Association 92–3, 124–7
Croatian Citizenship Act (Croatia 1991) 137–8, 140–2
Croatian Constitution 146
Croatian Constitutional Court 140–1
Croatian Days on the Hill 102
Croatian Declaration of Independence 137–40
Croatian Defence Council (HVO) 162–3, 174n16
Croatian Defence Forces (HOS) 162
Croatian Democratic Union *see* HDZ (*Hrvatska Demokratska Zajednica*)
Croatian Fraternal Union: backs NFCA 123–4; concerns over emigration to US 29; Franjo Tuđman meets with 87; humanitarian aid to Croatia 96–7; internal divisions 61–2; membership numbers 78n25; political stance of 128; relations with *Matica iseljenika Hrvatske* 46; under Badinovac 66
Croatian Heritage Foundation 121–2
"Croatian identity," construction of 94
Croatian Independentist Movement (HDP) 74
Croatian Information Center 117, 122
Croatian language 18n17, 72
Croatian League of Communists 86
Croatian Liberation Movement (HOP) 63, 77n14
Croatian National Council 63, 70, 74
Croatian National Fund 98
Croatian National Resistance 64
Croatian nationalism 2–3, 15–17, 59–81
Croatian Peasant Party 77n10
Croatian Relief Fund 97
Croatian Republic *see* Republic of Croatia; Socialist Republic of Croatia
Croatian Revolutionary Brotherhood 65
Croatian Social and Cultural Center *see* Norval group
Croatian Spring movement 53n56, 65, 86
Croatian War Orphan Fund 97
Croatian World Congress 122–3
Croatian–Canadian Congress of British Columbia 123
Croatia–Slavonia 27–9, 50n4
Culinović, Ferdo 84
Cvetković-Maček Agreement 35, 52n35

Index

Dabčević-Kučar, Savka 65, 86–7
Dalmatia, in Austro-Hungarian Empire 29
D'Amato, Joe 103
Damich, Edward 125–6, 128–9
Dante Alighieri institutes 186
Darfur conflict, effect on Sudanese diaspora 9
Dayton Peace Accords 147, 165; *see also* Bosnia–Herzegovina
"Declaration on the Sovereignty and Autonomy of Croatian Serbs" 95
demonstration by US Croatians 92
Dešpoja, Marijo 73
determinism, doing away with 181–3
Diaspora: A Journal of Transnational Studies 7
diasporas: analysis of 178; as continuation of annexation policies 166–7; Croatian nationalism and 15–17; demographic issues 113–15; election of emigrants to parliament 11; features of listed 17n8; institutions claiming to represent 9; legal recognition of status 191; neo-liberal approach to 190; obtaining and using knowledge of 25; parliamentary representation for 143–4; performativity and 178–81; politics of, defined 3; sense of community and 6–7; sizes by nation 5; spouses of nationals offered citizenship 139
Direct Aid to Democracies Act 1991 (US) 102–3
disciplinary modality of government 187
Djurić, Ivana 72
Đodan, Šime 72
Dole, Bob 93, 102–3
Dora Fund 97, 122
doxa, Bourdieu on 79n42
dual citizenship 6
Dumont, Louis 177
Đureković, Stjepan 73

Eastern Slavonia 143, 147
economic development, diaspora and 115–16
Eden, Julienne 69
Emigrant Fund, establishment of 29
Emigration Act (Hungarian territories 1910) 29
enemy emigration *see* Yugoslav Enemy Migration
epistemic conditions for emigration to arise as issue 25
essentialism, doing away with 181–3

ethnic lobbying by diaspora Croats 116–17
ethnic minorities represented in parliament 145
Europe: Croatian emigration to 31, 40–1; guest worker programs 188–9; pressure to recognize minority rights from 146
exile polity, defined 77n18
extrajudicial executions of Yugoslavs abroad 42

Federal People's Republic of Yugoslavia 136–7; *see also* Yugoslavia
Federation of Bosnia and Herzegovina 165
Foucault, Michel 13, 187
Foundation for Emigrants from Croatia 39
Fox, Vicente 191
France, attitudes to African immigrants 10–11
Frano, Ivan 32
funding for Croatian independence movement 90–4

Gaddafi, Muammar 53n57
Gagnon, Chip 78n41
Galbraith, Peter 128, 165
General Commissioner for Emigration 32
German Academic Exchange 186
Germany 73, 137
Gilroy, Paul 7–8
Global Diasporas (Cohen) 7
Golem, Frane 94, 100
Gotovac, Veselica and Vlado 72, 86–7
governmentality: changing modalities in 36–40; guest worker programs and 187–90; management of diaspora by 12–13, 111–33; rationalizations for 183–92; status of non-residents in 191; treatment of emigrants 24–58
Granić, Mate 98, 118, 130n15, 167
'Great Croatia' movement 72, 86
Grubišić, Ćiro 112, 121
Grubišić, Vlatko 121
guest worker programs, governmentality and 187–90

Hall, Stuart 8
Harff, Jim 100–1, 125
Hatch, Orrin 103
HDP (*Hrvatski Državotvoreni Pokret*) 74
HDZ (*Hrvatska Demokratska Zajednica*): Bosnian branch 16; Croats in Bosnia–Herzegovina and 162–3, 167–8; defines boundaries of Croatian nation 24; electoral success 143–4; ethnic policies

146–8; formation of 88–9, 91; imposes idea of "Emigrant Croatia" 117; influence on overseas organizations 121–3; policy on Bosnia-Herzegovina 163; political positions of 173n7; political project 1–2; takes office in Croatia 16; territorial policies 159–61
Hebrang, Andrija 168
Hefer, Stjepan 63
Herceg–Bosna 16, 157, 162, 167
Hercegovačka Banka 168, 170
Herzegovina 60, 87, 161–3; *see also* Bosnia–Herzegovina
"Herzegovinian Lobby" 143, 165
Hlad, Dragutin 114
HMI (*Hrvatska Matica Iseljenika*) 42–3, 86–7, 121–2
Hockenos, Paul 105n1
Hoeffler, Anke 82–3
Holjevac, Većeslav 34, 51n17, 85
HOP (Croatian Liberation Movement) 63, 77n14
housing issues, for returning Serbs 148–9
HRB group 68
Hrkać, Stipe 112
Hrvatska, Banovina 157, 160
Hrvatska Demokratska Zajednica see HDZ (*Hrvatska Demokratska Zajednica*)
Hrvatska Država 63
Hrvatska Matica Iseljenika (HMI) 42–3, 86–7, 121–2
Hrvatska Revija 63, 67, 78n29
Hrvatska Stranka Prava 131n16
Hrvatski Državotvoreni Pokret (HDP) 74
Hrvatski Oslobodilački Pokret (HOP) 63, 77n14
Hrvatski Svjetski Kongres (HSK) 122–3
Hrvatsko Narodno Vijeće (HNV) 63, 70, 74
Hrvatsko Vijeće Obrane (HVO) 162–3, 174n16
Human Rights Watch report 99
humanitarian aid to Croatia 95–7
Hungary, Austro-Hungarian states governed by 27–9
Huysmans, Jef 135
HVO (*Hrvatsko Vijeće Obrane*) 162–3, 174n16
HVO–ARBiH conflict 163–5

Independent State of Croatia 160
India: attitudes towards emigrants in 11–12; economic importance of remittances to 5; recognition of non-resident status by 191
Institute for the History of the Worker's Movement in Croatia 65, 85
Instruction on the Procedure for Employment Abroad (1963) 42
International Criminal Tribunal for Yugoslavia 148, 157
International Crisis Group report 167–8, 171
International Organization for Migration 4
international relations, diaspora in 4–7
Iraqis in exile groups 4
Ireland: as model for returning diaspora 116, 120–1; attitudes towards emigrants in 11; recognition of non-resident status by 191
Isin, Engin 135
Israel, as a model for returning diaspora 114, 116–18, 120, 185
Istria 29, 51n16
Italy 50n14, 191
Iveković, Stjepan 84
Izetbegović, Alija 161, 165

Jakovčević, Andrija 91
Jambrušić, Slavko 94
Jelavić, Ante 168, 171
Jelić, Branko 63, 67, 77n15, 78n34
Jewish opinion, favours Croatia 101
Joppke, Christian 148

Karađorđevo meeting 44
Karadžić, Radovan 164
Kasapović, Mirjana 143–4, 169
Khuen-Héderváry, Károly 28–9
Kingdom of Serbs, Croats and Slovenes 26, 30–4
Kingdom of Yugoslavia 26, 34–7
Kirshenblatt-Gimbett, Barbara 12
Kljuić, Stjepan 162
"Knin Conclusions" 148
Kolter, Joe 103
Kosor, Jadranka 144, 167
Kosovo Pole, speech at 84
Krajačić, Ivan Stevo 85
Krajina region 141, 143, 147
Krajišnik, Momčilo 161
Križari units 61
Kurds, influence on US Iraq policy 4
Kušan, Jakša 62–3, 67, 87, 121

Lantos, Tom 103
League of Communists of Yugoslavia (LCY) 45, 53n66

Lebanon, economic importance of remittances to 5
Letica, Ilija 92–3, 125–6
Letica, Mara 100, 128
liberal ethos, putting into practice 127
Lipinski, William 103
Litvinenko affair 11
lobbying activities: by Croatian World Congress 122–3; expected of expatriate nationals 6, 191–2; in Australia 116; US organizations set up for 92, 100–3, 125–8
Luburić, Vjekoslav "Maks" 64, 67
Luburićevi group 74
Luketich, Bernard 86–7, 94, 97, 128–9
Lupis-Vukić, F. 29–30, 32

Maglica, Anthony 91
magyarization process 27–9
Majić, Častimir 74
managerial view of emigration 31–2, 36–7
Mandić, Dominik 63, 89
Manolić, Josip 85, 105n1, 106n6
Marjanović, Milan 32, 35–6
Markus, Zlatko 68
Maruna, Boris 69–70, 74, 121
Matica iseljenika Hrvatske (MIH) 66, 116, 121; see also Hrvatska Matica Iseljenika (HMI)
Matica magazine 39
"Matricula Consular" document 11–12
media coverage of emigration issues 29
Memorandum of the Academy of Arts and Sciences in Belgrade 72
Merlino, Jacques 101
Mesić, Stipe 144–5, 167, 170
Meštrović, Mate 70, 74–5, 86
methodological nationalism 3
Mexico: Bracero Programme 188–9; economic importance of remittances to 5; immigrants from in US 10–11; "Matricula Consular" document 11–12; recognition of non-resident status by 191
MIH (*Matica iseljenika Hrvatske*) 66, 116, 121; see also Hrvatska Matica Iseljenika (HMI)
Mihailovic, Draža 37
Mihaljević, Ivan 94
Mikšić, Boris 144
military aid to Croatia 97–8
Milošević, Slobodan: "bureaucratic revolution" 72; ethnic policies in Yugoslavia 84; secret meetings with Tuđman 164; signs Dayton peace agreements 165

ministries catering to the diaspora 118–21
Ministry for Development, Immigration and Reconstruction 119–20
Ministry for Emigration 118–19
Ministry for Return and Immigration 119
Mirth, Karlo 77n8, 77n9, 86
Modern Diasporas in International Politics (Sheffer) 7
Moldova, economic importance of remittances to 5
Mostar, institutions in funded by Croatia 169
Muslims: in Bosnia–Herzegovina 159–60, 164; Muslim–Croat federation 168; position of in Yugoslavia 160

Narodni Glasnik 77n6
Narodni List, coverage of emigration issues 29–30
National Croatian Association (overseas lobby group) 66
National Federation of Croatian Americans 123, 126–7, 132n45
national reconciliation movement (Yugoslavia) 71–2, 89
National Serbian Council (Croatian Serbs) 95
nationalism: in Croatia 2–3, 15–17, 59–81; in Serbia 72, 84; marginalisation of 158; methodological 3, 179–80; see also Croatian nationalism
neo-liberal approach to diaspora politics 190
Nickles–Bentley Amendment (1990) 102
Nikolić, Vinko 63, 70, 86
Nixon, Richard 78n24
Nogalo, Ivan 91
Norval group 74–5, 87–8
Nova Hrvatska journal 62–3, 67
Novak, Pero 91

"old emigration" from Yugoslavia 15, 38–9
Ong, Aihwa 192
Open Letter to the Croatian Communists (Kušan) 62–3
Orešković, Tihomir 74
Organization of Emigrants 32–3
Organization and Finance of Employment Act (Yugoslavia 1966) 42
Otpor Croats arrested in US 73

pan-Slavic movement 30
Paraga, Dobroslav 162

Partizans in BiH 160–1
Pašalić, Ivica 143
Pašić, Nikola 31
Pavelić, Ante 61, 63
Pavlinić, Vladimir 87
Pelivan, Jure 161
Peraica, Anthony 96–8, 100, 125–6
performativity, diasporas and 178–81
Perpich, Rudy 103
Petritsch, Wolfgang 166, 170
Petrović, Marijan 117, 119
Petrušić, Anthony 94
Pinsker, Leon 185
Politeo, Franck 93
"political exiles", groups for 62
political representation in independent Croatia 143–5
pomirba (national reconciliation movement) 71–2, 89
Portes, Alejandro 13
post-territorial citizenship 136–42
postnational citizenship 158–9
Pravasi Bharatiya Diwas celebrations 11
Prce, Miroslav 171
Preaching for Croatians Abroad 42
Primorac, Max 94
"Programme for Return and Housing Care of Expelled Persons, Refugees and Displaced Persons" 147
Proljećari 72
Prpić, George 86
public relations campaign for Croatia 100–1
Puhovski, Žarko 91

Račan, Ivica 144
Radanovich, George 128
Radić, Jure 119
Radić, Stjepan 34
Radica, Bogdan 86
Ramet, Sabrina 51n21, 160, 164
Ranković, Alexander 39, 41
rationalizations for governmentality 183–92
Rađa, Tihomil 87
Redman, Charles 165
Republic of Croatia: citizenship law 134–56, 151n9, 151n10, 151n14, 152n16; electoral laws 152n19, 152n21, 152n22; expectations of diaspora 112–13; handbook for returning migrants 1; nationalism in 2–3, 16–17; political lobbying of US by 98–102; relations with Bosnia–Herzegovina 16–17, 157–76; reluctance of diaspora to return to 120
resource, diaspora as 116–18
Ribičić, Ciril 162
Robinson, Mary 191
Rodna gruda magazine 42
Rohrbacher, Dana 103
Roman Catholic Church: assists emigration and supports emigrants 42; Croatian monks based in Canada 74–5; helps *Ustaše* figures to flee 61; membership of, used as proof of "Croatianness" 138
Rose, Nikolas 181
Rožić, Miroslav 118
Ruder Finn public relations agency 100–1
Rukavina, Steve 126–7

Safran, William 7–8
Šakić, Dinko 67
Salaj, Branko 68, 87
Salimanac, Stjepan 97
Sančević, Zdravko 114, 118
Sarkozy, Nicolas 11
Sayad, Abdelmalek 3
Schiller, Nina Glick 3, 18n16, 179
Schwalgin, Susanne 14
Schwartz, Mladen 68, 74
Scott, James C. 24–5
Serbia: Croatian attitudes to 89–90, 115; Croatian war with 2; proportion of Yugoslavian emigrants from 43; reaction to Tuđman election 95–6; rebels from, occupy Croatian territory 103; rise of nationalism in 72, 84
Serbian Democratic Forum 170
Serbian minority in Croatia: boycott BiH independence resolution 161; claim right to be included in "diaspora" 171; excluded from Croatian citizenship 140–2; representation in Croatian parliament 145; response to Croatian independence 146–7
Serbian Republic of Bosnia and Herzegovina *see* Bosnia–Herzegovina
"seventh republic" of expatriate Yugoslavs 45
Shain, Yossi 7, 94
Sharon, Ariel 191
Sheffer, Gabriel 7–8
Shrader, Charles 164
Simonović, M. 31
Sisak, author's work in 2
Social Democratic Union 141

social fields 13–14, 18n16, 180
Socialist Alliance of the Working People of Yugoslavia (SAWPY) 45, 53n60
Socialist Federal Republic of Yugoslavia *see* Yugoslavia
Socialist Republic of Croatia: citizenship law 136–7; citizenship status extended after independence 140–2; constitution of 173n9; diaspora nationalism 59–81; migrants from 40–1; nationalism in 15–16, 59–81; proportion of Yugoslavian emigrants from 43
Society of Emigrants from Croatia (MIH) 66, 116, 121
Sökefeld, Martin 14
Šola, Domagoj 91
Sopta, Marin 2, 74–5, 119
SORIS, in Kingdom of Yugoslavia 35–6
South Sudan, secession by 9–10
sovereignty 6, 192–3
Soviet Union 44, 84–5
Spain, Croatian organizations in 64
speech acts, diaspora as 8–12, 183
Starčević, Ante 89
state categories, diaspora as 111–33
Stepinac, Alojzije 37
Strossmeyer, Josip 89
Sudanese diaspora 9
Sunić, Mirko and Mirna 54n69
Šušak, Gojko: attains power in Croatia 112; contacts with Tuđman 87–8; death of 170; heads Ministry for Emigration 118; heads Ministry of Defence 168; in "Herzegovinian Lobby" 143; in nationalist campaign 2; influence on Croatian politics 91; links to Norval center 75; role in financing Tuđman campaign 76n2; territorial ambitions 157

Tajikistan, economic importance of remittances to 4–5
Territorial Defense Forces 45, 53n62
territorial nationalism, marginalisation of 158
terrorism, Croatian activists murdered 73
Tito, Josip Broz 44, 46
"Tolić-Oblak" group 68
Tölölyan, Khchachig 7
"Transnational Communities" program 7
transnational exclusion, challenges to 170
transnational political fields 59–81, 178–81
transnational social fields 13–14, 18n16, 180

transnationalism from below 18n15
transnationalization of migration 135
Travel Permits of Yugoslav Citizens Act (Yugoslavia 1965) 42
Treaties of Westphalia, definition of the state 2–3
Tripalo, Miko 65, 86
Trumbić, Ante 31
Turkey, recognizes emigrants with "pink card" 12
Tuđman, Franjo: background of 85–6; backs down on Muslim–Croat federation 165; becomes President of independent Croatia 91–5; claims to unite homeland and diaspora Croats 111; death of 170; on ethnic homogenization 145–6; meetings with Milošević 164; meets organization leaders 106n7; priorities for government 115; rise to power 72, 75, 82–91; statement for returning migrants 1; supports Croatian independence 16; territorial ambitions 157, 159–61; visits Croatian Embassy in US 129; on vulnerability due to diaspora 113–14

Ukrainian Congress Committee of America 18n11
Ukrainian diaspora 10
UNCHR report 151n12
United Croatians of America and Canada 62
United Nations 2, 38, 103
United States: Ambassadors to Croatia 128; Croatian immigrants to 27; Croatian organizations in 61, 92–4, 123–5; diasporas in and chance of conflict 83; guest worker programs 188; Otpor Croats arrested in 73; response to Croatian independence 98–102; second wave of Ukranian disapora 10; treatment of Mexican immigrants 10–12; wealthy Herzogovinians in 87
Ustaša regime: emigrants linked with 60–1, 63; neo-*Ustaša* organizations 65; resurgence of activism 73

Vance–Owen Peace Plan 163–4
Veselica, Marko 72
Vormärz period 50n6
Vujić, Stanko 86
Vukelić, Filip 77n5
Vukojević, Vice 113
Vukovar, fall of 96

Walker, R.B.J 5
Wallerstein, Immanuel 12
war crimes indictments 148
Washington Agreement 165
Westphalian states 2–3
Wimmer, Andreas 3
Winland, Daphne 95
"workers temporarily abroad" from Yugoslavia 15, 40–1, 68
World War II, devastates Yugoslavia 38
world-systems theory 12
Wæver, Ole 40

"Yugoslav Committee" 30–1
Yugoslav Enemy Migration: defining 38–9, 41; discrimination against 45–6, 186; divisions in 62
Yugoslav People's Army 39, 161
Yugoslav Relief Committee 61
Yugoslavia: changing ethnic policies 84; citizenship law 136–7; collective rights in 146; economic policies allegedly favour Serbs 115; emigrants from, by nationality 43; emigration policies 26–7; ethnic affiliations in 17n3; governmental practices 15, 25–6; Kingdom of Yugoslavia 26, 34–7; migration flows by year 41; population figures 52n41

Zadruga farming 50n6
Zagreb, author's research in 15
Zajedničar (journal) 77n9
Zimmerman, William 42–3
Zionist Aliyah movement 185
Zolberg, Aristide 3, 24, 47
Žužul, Miomir: on aid from diaspora Croats 98; on Croatian American voters 104; on inefficient bureaucracy 120; on political stance of diaspora 124–5; on population demographics 114
Zvonimir- Čičak, Ivan 86

Helping you to choose the right eBooks for your Library

Add Routledge titles to your library's digital collection today. Taylor and Francis ebooks contains over 50,000 titles in the Humanities, Social Sciences, Behavioural Sciences, Built Environment and Law.

Choose from a range of subject packages or create your own!

Benefits for you
- » Free MARC records
- » COUNTER-compliant usage statistics
- » Flexible purchase and pricing options
- » All titles DRM-free.

Benefits for your user
- » Off-site, anytime access via Athens or referring URL
- » Print or copy pages or chapters
- » Full content search
- » Bookmark, highlight and annotate text
- » Access to thousands of pages of quality research at the click of a button.

REQUEST YOUR FREE INSTITUTIONAL TRIAL TODAY

Free Trials Available
We offer free trials to qualifying academic, corporate and government customers.

eCollections – Choose from over 30 subject eCollections, including:

Archaeology	Language Learning
Architecture	Law
Asian Studies	Literature
Business & Management	Media & Communication
Classical Studies	Middle East Studies
Construction	Music
Creative & Media Arts	Philosophy
Criminology & Criminal Justice	Planning
Economics	Politics
Education	Psychology & Mental Health
Energy	Religion
Engineering	Security
English Language & Linguistics	Social Work
Environment & Sustainability	Sociology
Geography	Sport
Health Studies	Theatre & Performance
History	Tourism, Hospitality & Events

For more information, pricing enquiries or to order a free trial, please contact your local sales team:
www.tandfebooks.com/page/sales

The home of Routledge books

www.tandfebooks.com